THE MINDUP CURRICULUM

Grades 3–5

Focused Classrooms • Mindful Learning • Resilient Students

SCHOLASTIC

Acknowledgments

With heartfelt appreciation to Goldie Hawn, Founder of The Hawn Foundation, for her vision, commitment, compassion, and dedicated advocacy for children everywhere.

We would like to thank the many scientists, researchers, and educators who contributed to the MindUP curriculum.

Pat Achtyl; Thelma Anselmi; Angie Balius; Lorraine Bayne; Michelle Beaulieu; Peter Canoll, MD, PhD; Beck Collie; Adele Diamond, PhD; Diane Dillon, PhD; Jennifer Erickson; Nancy Etcoff, PhD; Pam Hoeffner; Nicole Iorio; Greg Jabaut; Ann Kelly; Molly Stewart Lawlor; Noreen Maguire; Marc A. Meyer, PhD; Cindy Middendorf; Christine Boardman Moen; Tammy Murphy, PhD; Charlene Myklebust, PhD; Nicole Obadia; Carol B. Olson, PhD; Janice Parry; Lisa Pedrini; Tina Posner; Kimberly Schonert-Reichl, PhD; Patti Vitale; Judy Willis, MD, MEd; Victoria Zelenak

ISBN-10: 0-545-26713-7
ISBN-13: 978-0-545-26713-7

Printed in the U.S.A.

13 14 15 16 17 40 17 16

Table of Contents

Welcome to MINDUP

Imagine ... joyful learning, academic success, and a powerful sense of self and community.

Imagine ... students who are able to engage in a focused, energetic way with one another, with their teachers, and with their learning.

Imagine ... schools that are productive, harmonious centers of successful learning, where all students thrive because they recognize themselves as

- capable, creative learners
- self-aware human beings
- compassionate, responsible citizens

All of this is possible. **MINDUP** can help you achieve it.

MindUP Online Training

At **www.thehawnfoundation.org**, you'll find resources to enrich your MindUP instruction, including

- the entire spectrum of MindUP techniques, addressing social and emotional learning
- classroom demonstrations conducted by experienced MindUP consultants and mentors
- instructional insights, grade-specific teaching strategies, and other resources
- the latest in neuroscience about how the brain works and how it affects learning

Register at **www.thehawnfoundation.org** to access this innovative, interactive training and learning resource, developed in partnership with Columbia University's Center for New Media Teaching and Learning.

Dear Educators,

From Scholastic

For 90 years, Scholastic has been a presence in your classrooms, supporting teaching and learning. The challenges faced by you and your students today are well known and unprecedented. These include the following expectations:

- providing differentiated instruction to students who come with diverse language and experiential backgrounds
- improving academic performance
- addressing new standards geared to career and college preparedness
- helping your students and their families handle economic and social changes

When we met Goldie Hawn and the Hawn Foundation team, we were impressed by their commitment to helping all students achieve their potential socially and academically. Also, we shared their respect for educators who, like all of you, are entrusted with the preparation of the next generation.

We are pleased to introduce MindUP, a collaboration of the Hawn Foundation and Scholastic. MindUP isn't one more program to implement or subject to teach, but a set of strategies that can be integrated with what you are already doing, so that you and your students will become more focused when doing schoolwork and are able to work and play more successfully with others. The essence of what the MindUP program calls for is embodied in the idea of the Optimistic Classroom—a place where all children have the opportunity to achieve their potential.

Thank you for inviting us into your school.

Optimistically yours,

Francie Alexander

Patrick Daly

Francie Alexander
Chief Academic Officer
Scholastic Inc.

Patrick Daley
Senior Vice President, Publisher
Scholastic Inc.

From the Hawn Foundation

Thank you for bringing the MindUP Curriculum into your classrooms.

MindUP has been my focus and my passion for many years. I am so grateful to you, devoted educators who believe in the limitless potential of children and give tirelessly of your time, energy, creativity, and love.

The simple practices at the core of MindUP will help your students to become resilient, focused, and mindful learners. I have seen the MindUP practices at work in classrooms all over the world. I have witnessed its success and have heard from countless teachers in praise of its transformative effect on students' ability to learn.

I know that with your help we can equip our students with the skills they need to live smarter, healthier, and happier lives. Together we will create optimistic classrooms where students successfully cope with the stresses they face in school, at home, and in their communities.

Thank you for accepting the enormous and critically important responsibilities and challenges that accompany your mission as an educator.

From the bottom of my heart, I thank you.

Goldie Hawn

Goldie Hawn
Founder, The Hawn Foundation
and the MindUP Curriculum

What Is MindUP?

MindUP is a comprehensive, classroom-tested, evidence-based curriculum framed around 15 easily implemented lessons that foster social and emotional awareness, enhance psychological well-being, and promote academic success.

The MindUP classroom is an optimistic classroom that promotes and develops mindful attention to oneself and others, tolerance of differences, and the capacity of each member of the community to grow as a human being and a learner. MindUP's expansive dynamic is built to a large extent on routine practices that are inherent to the MindUP Curriculum. Over the course of the MindUP experience, students learn about the brain and how it functions, in the process gaining insight into their own minds and behaviors as well as those of the people around them.

How Does MindUP Work?

The essential work of MindUP is accomplished through the lessons themselves, which include the repetition of the Core Practice—deep belly breathing and attentive listening. The Core Practice makes mindful attention the foundation for learning and interacting; ideally, it is repeated for a few moments of each school day throughout the year. (See Lesson 3, page 42, for a complete overview of the Core Practice.)

> **"Your brain can be like your BFF. It can help you cool down and stop getting frustrated. Then you can learn a lot more and have more friends."**
>
> **—Genieva, fifth grade**

MindUP has the capacity to alter the landscape of your classroom by letting students in on the workings of their own agile minds. Each MindUP lesson begins with background information on the brain, introducing a specific area of concentration with an activity in which students can see concrete examples of how their brain functions. As you and your class become accustomed to learning about the ways in which the brain processes information, your students will become habitually more observant of their own learning process.

MindUP offers teachers and students insights that respond to the natural thoughtfulness of young people and lead to self-regulation of their behavior. MindUP is dedicated to the belief that the child who learns to monitor his or her senses and feelings becomes more aware and better understands how to respond to the world *reflectively* instead of *reflexively*.

Who Needs MindUP?

Everyone. Joyful engagement isn't incidental; it's essential. Yet, young people today are no strangers to stress. From an early age, they experience stress from a range of sources. For some, stress goes hand in hand with the pressure to achieve; for others, it is prompted by economic hardship, poor nutrition, or inadequate health care; for still others, it may be linked to emotional deprivation or limited educational resources. Whatever the particular circumstance, any one of these factors could hamper a student's ability to learn without anxiety. In "communities of turmoil" (Tatum, 2009), children often cope with several problems at once, and suffer from chronic stress—with consequences that can be disastrous for their learning and their lives. MindUP addresses these obstacles to productive learning and living by offering students and teachers simple practices and insights that become tools for self-management and self-possession. At the same time, the MindUP program works to make learning joyful and fun by emphasizing learning modes in which students flourish:

- lively instruction that invites problem solving, discussion, and exploration
- teacher modeling and coaching
- student cross-age mentoring and decision making
- conflict resolution
- inquiry and the arts

Joyful engagement is not incidental; it's essential. MindUP shows you how to put joy into your teaching.

The Research Base

Broadly defined, mindful attention centers on conscious awareness of the present moment: by focusing our attention and controlling our breath, we can learn to reduce stress and optimize the learning capacity of the brain. The use of these practices in MindUP is informed by leading-edge research in the fields of developmental cognitive neuroscience, mindfulness training, social and emotional learning (SEL), and positive psychology. In particular, MindUP pursues objectives roughly parallel to those of the five-point framework of competencies laid out in the work of the Collaborative for Academic, Social, and Emotional Learning (CASEL; www.casel.org), a not-for-profit organization at the forefront in efforts to advance the science- and evidence-based practice of social and emotional learning (SEL). These areas of competency are:

Self-Awareness
Assessing our feelings, interests, values, and strengths; maintaining self-confidence.

Self-Management
Regulating emotions to handle stress, control impulses, and persevere in overcoming obstacles

Social Awareness
Understanding different perspectives and empathizing with others; recognizing and appreciating similarities and differences; using family, school, and community resources effectively

Relationship Skills
Maintaining healthy relationships based on cooperation; resisting inappropriate social pressure; preventing, managing, and resolving interpersonal conflicts; seeking help when needed

Responsible Decision Making
Using a variety of considerations, including ethical, academic, and community-related standards to make choices and decisions

Social and Emotional Learning

It is now well established that social and emotional skills, such as the ability to manage one's emotions and get along with others, play an integral role in academic and life success. Evidence supporting this statement is illustrated in several recent studies. Durlak et al. (2011) conducted a meta-analysis of 213 school-based, universal social and emotional learning (SEL) programs involving 270,034 students from kindergarten through high school and found that, compared to students not exposed to SEL classroom-based programming, students in SEL programs demonstrated significantly improved social and emotional skills, attitudes, behavior, and academic performance that reflected an 11-percentile-point gain in achievement. The importance of SEL in predicting school success has been further demonstrated by Caprara et al. (2000), who found that changes in academic achievement in grade 8 could be better predicted from knowing children's social competence five years earlier than from grade 3 academic competence. As Daniel Goleman, widely recognized as the "founding father" of emotional intelligence (EI), notes, these "remarkable results" make it clear that SEL has "delivered on its promise" (2008).

Adele Diamond, neuroscientist and founder of developmental cognitive neuroscience, found that students who learn SEL techniques such as role-playing consistently score higher on tests requiring use of the brain's executive functions—coordinating and controlling, monitoring and troubleshooting, reasoning and imagining (2007). Similarly, research conducted by social-emotional development expert Kimberly Schonert-Reichl found that "as predicted . . . at posttest teachers in the intervention classrooms described their students as significantly more attentive, emotionally regulated, and socially and emotionally competent than did teachers in the control classrooms" (2010).

As all teachers know, bored children often get into mischief; engaged ones are less likely to act out. Sadly, too often, what students enjoy most is what they get to do the least: discuss, debate, explore the arts, and participate in drama and group research projects. As research demonstrates, "Students experienced a greater level of understanding of concepts and ideas when they talked, explained, and argued about them with their group instead of just passively listening to a lecture or reading a test" (Iidaka et al., 2000). When education is fun, and students are engaged, focused, and inspired to participate, learning flourishes.

SEL programs such as MindUP also significantly impart to students a the sense of hopefulness.

> Hope changes brain chemistry, which influences the decisions we make and the actions we take. Hopefulness must be pervasive and every single student should be able to feel it, see it, and hear it daily (Jensen, 2009; p. 112–113).

Being hopeful mirrors physical activity; both physical activity and hopefulness enhance metabolic states and influence brain-changing gene expression (Jiaxu and Weiyi, 2000). Hope and optimism enable achievement. Hopeful kids are more likely to work diligently and not to give up or drop out—they work harder, persevere longer, and ultimately experience success, which in turn begets more success. It is a simple but profound and life-transforming cycle (Dweck, 2006)—one that is conscientiously cultivated in the MindUP classroom.

The Stressed Brain

The brain's response to stress is linked to the function of the amygdala (uh-MIG-duh-luh), a small, almond-shaped clump of neurons deep in the center of our brain. The amygdala serves as an information filter regulated by our emotional state. When we're calm and peaceful, the filter is wide open and information flows to the prefrontal cortex, where the brain's so-called executive functions take place.

On the other hand, when we are feeling negative and stressed out, these executive functions, which provide cognitive control, are inhibited. Indeed, information stays in the amygdala; it doesn't flow into the prefrontal cortex for executive processing. Instead, it's processed right on the spot as fight, flight, or freeze. In this way, fear and anxiety effectively shut down higher-order thinking. Your impulse to flee a falling branch, or to defend yourself against physical assault, is an example of your body not bothering to "think about" what to do—you react without thinking.

Eric Jensen, veteran educator and brain expert, in *Teaching With Poverty in Mind: What Being Poor Does to Kids' Brains and What Schools Can Do About It* (2009) has this to say about stress and its effect on the brain:

> The biology of stress is simple in some ways and complex in others. On a basic level, every one of the 30–50 trillion cells in your body is experiencing either healthy or unhealthy growth. Cells cannot grow and deteriorate at the same time. Ideally, the body is in homeostatic balance: a state in which the vital measures of human function—heart rate, blood pressure, blood sugar, and so on—are in their optimal ranges. A stressor is anything that threatens to disrupt homeostasis—for example, criticism, neglect, social exclusion, lack of enrichment, malnutrition, drug use, exposure to toxins, abuse, or trauma. When cells aren't growing, they're in a "hunker down" mode that conserves resources for a threatened future. When billions or trillions of cells are under siege in this manner, you get problems (p. 23).

Neurobiological studies of neglected or abused children have revealed alarming alterations in brain development. The "fight, flight, or freeze" stress hormones that our bodies produce in response to physical and emotional adversity "atrophy the areas that control emotional development" (p. 25).

The Happy Brain

To paraphrase Adele Diamond: Happy brains work better (2009).

When we're happy and engaged in activities that we find pleasurable (everything from painting to playing), our brain is flush with dopamine, a neurotransmitter that also helps lubricate our information filter and rev up high-powered thinking in our prefrontal cortex. Dopamine helps get our brains ready for peak performance. Indeed, just the anticipation of pleasurable learning stimulates dopamine flow.

The dopamine pleasure surge is highest when students are fully engaged with their learning and brimming with positive feelings such as optimism, gratitude, hope, and an overall sense of well-being. Classroom activities that give rise to the pleasure surge and prompt the release of dopamine include:

- participating in acts of kindness
- collaborating with peers
- making choices and solving problems
- engaging in physical activities such as sports, dance, and play
- enjoying creative efforts and disciplines such as music, art, drama, reading, and storytelling

Of course, dopamine is also released when people indulge in high-risk activities such as drug or alcohol use, promiscuity, fast driving, and overeating. However, when kids get their pleasure surge from activities that generate positive feelings overall, they are less likely to seek it in high-risk activities that also promote dopamine release (Galvan, et al., 2006; Kann et al., 2006).

The Mindful Brain

MindUP is dedicated to helping students deepen their understanding of their own mental processes; the curriculum begins with an introduction to brain physiology. Once students become familiar with the parts of the brain and with how the parts function and interact, they carry that knowledge forward into their MindUP explorations as well as the rest of their classroom experience. The recommended daily Core Practice and the content of each lesson serve as conduits through which young learners can broaden their awareness of the connections between brain and body, between what goes on "inside" and actual experience. The outcome of this enhanced awareness is a group of resilient students whose awareness of their impulses, thoughts, feelings, and behavior enhances their confidence, pleasure, and sense of agency in their own learning process.

Consider the benefits that MindUP makes possible! Mindful teaching and learning:

- improve student self-control and self-regulation skills
- strengthen students' resiliency and decision making
- bolster students' enthusiasm for learning
- increase students' academic success
- develop students' positive social skills, such as empathy, compassion, patience, and generosity
- infuse your classroom learning with joy and optimism
- reduce peer-to-peer conflict

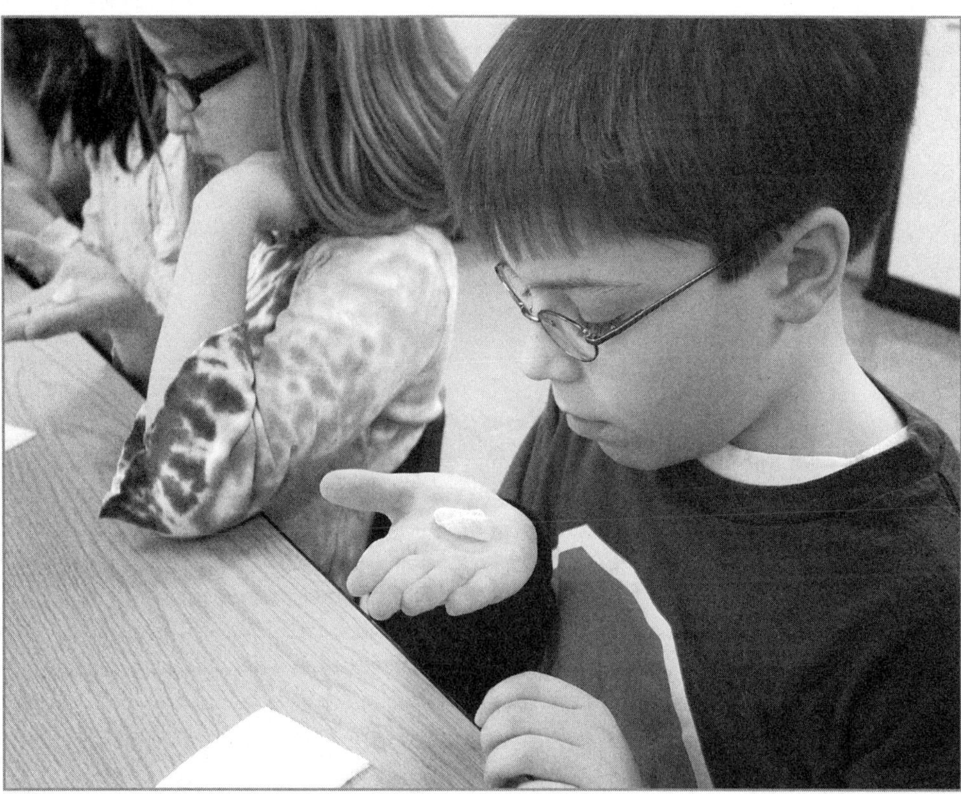

MindUP and the School Day

The MindUP program was developed not only to expand students' social and emotional awareness but also to improve their academic performance. The concepts and vocabulary associated with MindUP will expand the scope of students' thinking in all academic disciplines.

MindUP Core Practice can become a staple routine for the opening and closing of each school day as well as at the moments of transition: settling down after recess, waiting for lunch, moving from one subject to the next. As countless MindUP teachers have discovered, any topic benefits from being approached with focused awareness.

The MindUP lessons themselves can be worked smoothly into a daily routine and require minimal preparation on your part; suggested follow-up activities link each lesson to content-area learning. You'll likely find yourself adopting the MindUP techniques and strategies across subject areas. MindUP may well become a way of life for you and your students!

The Day Begins

The best teachers we know are mindful about the beginning of each school day. They make a point of standing by the school door and greeting with an open heart and welcoming smile every student who passes through their classroom door.

An ideal way to unify the class as they begin their day is to gather and share a few moments of "checking in," followed by the Core Practice of deep breathing and mindful awareness. Once you have established this simple routine, you will find that the day feels more coherent and the group less scattered as this practice brings the group together organically while setting an easygoing tone for engagement with the rest of your daily learning.

Transitions

MindUP Core Practice works beautifully during transition times. With your guidance and thoughtful attention, you can accustom your students to respond to a simple reminder at which they habitually turn to the Core Practices to center themselves and prepare to move easily—even eagerly and joyfully—to the next classroom activity. "Our classroom transition times are some of the most important routines of our day....Our days are full, our curriculum is rich, and we have so much to do together! The tighter our transitions, the more time we will have for instruction" (Allyn, 2010).

The Day Ends

Just as you can help students greet a new day with eagerness and mindful purpose, so can you close the day with a spirit of purpose and celebration—your students will leave the classroom feeling calm yet energized. Eric Jensen, whose "brain-based" teaching has transformed teaching and learning in countless classrooms, explains, "Asking kids to visualize success on an upcoming skill or knowledge set is no 'new Age' strategy. When done well, mental practice is known not only to make physical changes in the brain but also to improve task performance (Pascual-Leone et al., 2005)" (2010). For example, a spirited and energetic clean-up of the room to some upbeat music can be followed by a regrouping for recapping the day's accomplishments, and a brief shared Core Practice before dismissal. The goal is to end the day on a high note.

Breathing First: The Core Practice

From the earliest grades on up, the recommended approach to MindUP is to first establish the habit of deep belly breathing and focused attention—the so-called Core Practice. Well before you teach Lesson 1, you can lay the groundwork for it in your class by introducing the Core Practice in the first days of the school year. Once students have learned the simple techniques of breathing and listening, you will be able to use the Core Practice to unify your classroom community and provide the stability and receptivity needed for days of rich and fruitful learning. (See Lesson 3, page 42, for a full explanation of the practice.)

Literacy expert Pam Allyn has visited and observed hundreds of classrooms around the world. "We have seen many classrooms where there are lots of pieces in place, but one secret, fabulous ingredient is missing. That ingredient is celebration. We see teachers wait to celebrate until the end of the year, until a child does well on a test, until the child actually masters the art of reading. But why wait? Celebration is the ultimate management strategy. . . . It is the core ingredient that infuses the entire life of the classroom with joy, with hope, with faith, and with optimism" (2010, p.107).

Using MindUP in the Classroom

MindUp comprises 15 lessons arranged into four units:

Unit I: Getting Focused (Lessons 1–3)
Introduce brain physiology and the concept of mindful attention; establish daily Core Practice
Lessons: 1. How Our Brains Work, 2. Mindful Awareness, 3. Focused Awareness: The Core Practice

Unit II: Sharpening Your Senses (Lessons 4–9)
Experience the relationship between our senses, our moving bodies, and the way we think
Lessons: 4. Mindful Listening, 5. Mindful Seeing, 6. Mindful Smelling, 7. Mindful Tasting, 8. Mindful Movement I, 9. Mindful Movement II

Unit III: It's All About Attitude (Lessons 10–12)
Understand the role of our mind-set in how we learn and progress
Lessons: 10. Perspective Taking, 11. Choosing Optimism, 12. Appreciating Happy Experiences

Unit IV: Taking Action Mindfully (Lessons 13–15)
Apply mindful behaviors to our interactions with our community and the world
Lessons: 13. Expressing Gratitude, 14. Performing Acts of Kindness, 15. Taking Mindful Action in the World

The framework is designed to strengthen students' sense of social and emotional well-being while creating a cohesive, caring classroom environment. Because the concepts build on one another, you'll find it most productive to teach the lessons in sequential order.

Lesson Structure

Each lesson follows the same format:

Introduction to the Lesson Topic... identifies and explains the subject of the lesson, frames why it's important, and includes testimony from a MindUP teacher.

Linking to Brain Research... explains how each lesson relates to the neuroscience. This section provides background for you, some of which may be appropriate to share with students to help them gain a progressively more sophisticated awareness of how their brains work.

Clarify for the Class... includes guidelines for making brain research concepts accessible to students at various grade levels.

Getting Ready... identifies what the lesson entails as well as learning goals for the lesson. Also listed are materials and resources required for leading the lesson.

MindUP Warm-Up... helps the class prepare for the Engage, Explore, Reflect part of the lesson activity by introducing and discussing subject matter in an easygoing, open-ended way that relates content to students' lives.

Leading the Lesson... offers a step-by-step approach that engages students in the inquiry, helps them explore the topic, and encourages them to reflect upon and discuss their insights and experiences. The lesson layout also establishes concrete links to the learning process and classroom issues at the third to fifth grade levels.

Connecting to the Curriculum... offers specific opportunities for students to bend their minds around language arts, math, social studies, science, health, physical education, the arts, and social-emotional learning. These optional across-the-curriculum learning experiences expand the lesson and offer alternative approaches to content.

Special Features

Creating the Optimistic Classroom... offers classroom management strategies for reaching English language learners, special needs students, and general learners in order to maximize the effectiveness of the lesson.

MindUP in the Real World... connects lesson content to a career or undertaking, expands the discussion beyond the classroom, and grounds ideas in a concrete application.

Once a Day... suggests ways for teachers to apply lesson content to everyday situations involving students or colleagues.

Journal Writing... gives students an opportunity to reflect on motivation, actions, and their consequences, so they can learn to mediate and understand their actions. According to Susan Kaiser Greenland, journaling allows students to use what they've learned to create happier, more successful lives for themselves (2010). We recommend that you provide students with a notebook to create a journal that they can personalize with decorations of their choice, and use this personal record to document responses within Greenland's general framework of

- What I Noticed
- What It Means
- What I Learned

Literature Link... recommends four books that extend the learning.

Lesson Opener

Each MindUP lesson is focused on one aspect or practice of the curriculum.

The targeted curriculum area is defined and placed in context for the teacher.

Experience of MindUP users attests to the effectiveness of the specific practice or lesson.

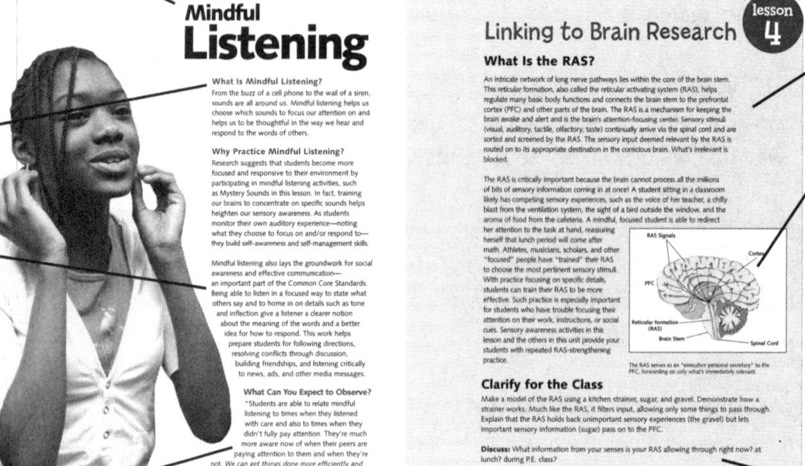

Mindful
Listening

What Is Mindful Listening?
From the buzz of a cell phone to the wail of a siren, sounds are all around us. Mindful listening helps us choose which sounds to focus our attention on and helps us to be thoughtful in the way we hear and respond to the words of others.

Why Practice Mindful Listening?
Research suggests that students become more focused and responsive to their environment by participating in mindful listening activities, such as Mystery Sounds in this lesson. In fact, training our brains to concentrate on specific sounds helps heighten our sensory awareness. As students monitor their own auditory experience—noting what they choose to focus on and/or respond to—they build self-awareness and self-management skills.

Mindful listening also lays the groundwork for social awareness and effective communication—an important part of the Common Core Standards. Being able to listen in a focused way to state what others say and to home in on details such as tone and inflection give a listener a clearer notion about the meaning of the words and a better idea for how to respond. This work helps prepare students for following directions, resolving conflicts through discussion, building friendships, and listening critically to news, ads, and other media messages.

What Can You Expect to Observe?
"Students are able to relate mindful listening to times when they listened with care and also to times when they didn't fully pay attention. They're much more aware now of when their peers are paying attention to them and when they're not. *We can get things done more efficiently and with less resistance and conflict.*"
—Fourth-grade teacher

mindful listening
lesson 4

Linking to Brain Research

What Is the RAS?
An intricate network of long nerve pathways lies within the core of the brain stem. This reticular formation, also called the reticular activating system (RAS), helps regulate many basic body functions and connects the brain stem to the prefrontal cortex (PFC) and other parts of the brain. The RAS is a mechanism for keeping the brain awake and alert and is the brain's attention-focusing center. Sensory stimuli (visual, auditory, tactile, olfactory, taste) continually arrive via the spinal cord and are sorted and screened by the RAS. The sensory input deemed relevant by the RAS is routed on to its appropriate destination in the conscious brain. What's irrelevant is blocked.

The RAS is critically important because the brain cannot process all the millions of bits of sensory information coming in at once! A student sitting in a classroom likely has competing sensory experiences, such as the voice of her teacher, a chilly blast from the ventilation system, the sight of a bird outside the window, and the aroma of food from the cafeteria. A mindful, focused student is able to redirect her attention to the task at hand, reassuring herself that lunch period will come after math. Athletes, musicians, scholars, and other "focused" people have "trained" their RAS to choose the most pertinent sensory stimuli. With practice focusing on specific details, students can train their RAS to be more effective. Such practice is especially important for students who have trouble focusing their attention on their work, instructions, or social cues. Sensory awareness activities in this lesson and the others in this unit provide your students with repeated RAS-strengthening practice.

The RAS serves as an "executive personal secretary" to the PFC, forwarding on only what's immediately relevant.

Clarify for the Class
Make a model of the RAS using a kitchen strainer, sugar, and gravel. Demonstrate how a strainer works. Much like the RAS, it filters input, allowing only some things to pass through. Explain that the RAS holds back unimportant sensory experiences (the gravel) but lets important sensory information (sugar) pass on to the PFC.

Discuss: What information from your senses is your RAS allowing through right now? at lunch? during P.E. class?

Brain research related to lesson exploration is laid out for instructor, along with supporting illustration.

Language and modeling help instructor make the brain research link understandable to students.

Getting Ready

This two-page spread offers an opportunity for preparing and front-loading the main lesson, so that students are most receptive to the language and ideas that follow.

The core lesson ties in with wider self-management and awareness skills. Materials used are basic and usually already available in the classroom or as reproducible pages.

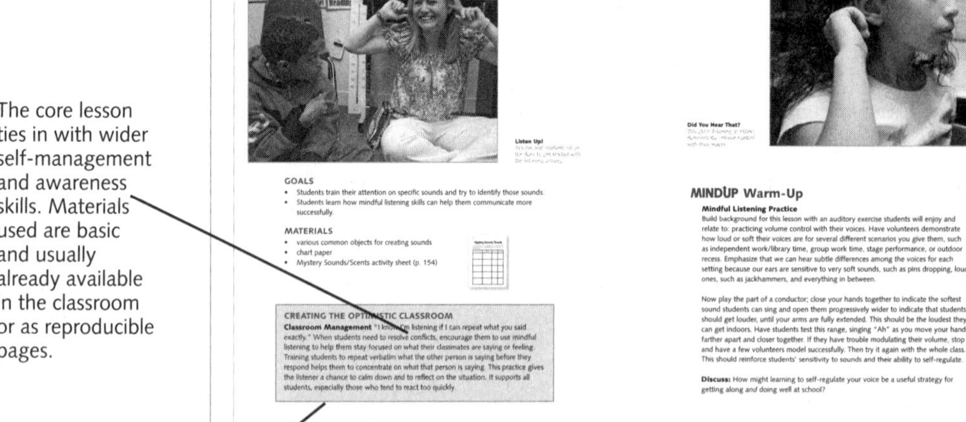

Getting Ready

Listen Up!

GOALS
- Students train their attention on specific sounds and try to identify those sounds.
- Students learn how mindful listening skills can help them communicate more successfully.

MATERIALS
- various common objects for creating sounds
- chart paper
- Mystery Sounds/Scents activity sheet (p. 154)

CREATING THE OPTIMISTIC CLASSROOM
Classroom Management "I know I'm listening if I can repeat what you said exactly." When students need to resolve conflicts, encourage them to use mindful listening to help them stay focused on what their classmates are saying or feeling. Training students to repeat verbatim what the other person is saying before they respond helps them to concentrate on what that person is saying. This practice gives the listener a chance to calm down and to reflect on the situation. It supports all students, especially those who tend to react too quickly.

mindful listening
understand the purpose

Did You Hear That?

MINDUP Warm-Up

Mindful Listening Practice
Build background for this lesson with an auditory exercise students will enjoy and relate to: practicing volume control with their voices. Have volunteers demonstrate how loud or soft their voices are for several different scenarios you give them, such as independent work/library time, group work time, stage performance, or outdoor recess. Emphasize that we can hear subtle differences among the voices for each setting because our ears are sensitive to very soft sounds, such as pins dropping, loud ones, such as jackhammers, and everything in between.

Now play the part of a conductor; close your hands together to indicate the softest sound students can sing and open them progressively wider to indicate that students should get louder, until your arms are fully extended. This should be the loudest they can get indoors. Have students test this range, singing "Ah" as you move your hands farther apart and closer together. If they have trouble modulating their volume, stop and have a few volunteers model successfully. Then try it again with the whole class. This should reinforce students' sensitivity to sounds and their ability to self-regulate.

Discuss: How might learning to self-regulate your voice be a useful strategy for getting along *and* doing well at school?

Before each core lesson, a simple preparatory activity helps both teacher and student know what to expect from the lesson and think in advance about how it may be useful in a broader context of learning.

Suggestions for classroom management, supporting brain-based learning, and helping all language learners address common obstacles to attentiveness and full engagement with learning.

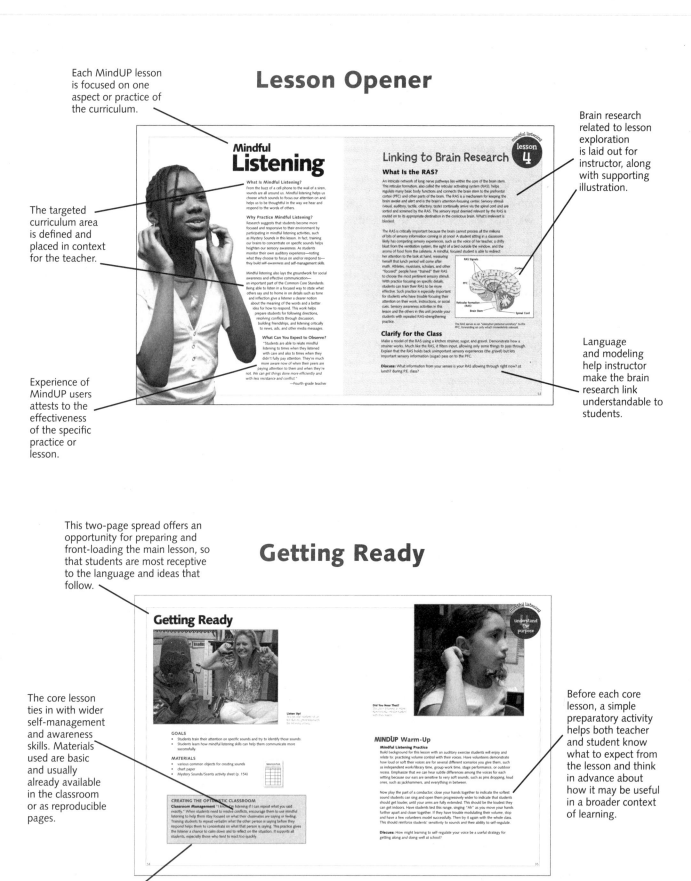

Leading the Lesson

Lessons are supported by findings of educators and researchers on the effectiveness of mindful awareness strategies.

Each lesson routine includes an introduction with scripting to prime students for the exploration and perspective at the core of the teaching.

Core activity of each lesson includes suggested language and procedures to maximize student absorption of the ideas and experience.

Leading the Lesson

From the Research
Novelty, humor, and surprise in lessons expedite students' attention focus, and the use of these strategies results in more successful encoding of data into the memory circuits. (Willis, 2008)

Mystery Sounds

What to Do

Engage

Review mindfulness and the parts of the brain from Unit 1, as needed. Initiate a discussion about listening.

- Let's consider why listening is important—for school, for friendships & family, for pleasure (music) and for safety.
- Do you think listening is a skill or a talent? What might be the difference?
- When there's lots of noise around you, how do you pay attention to just one sound, like a friend's voice in the cafeteria? What are some times when you are able to eliminate distractions and focus on a single important sound?

Explain that together, the class will participate in an inquiry experience that will help students develop mindful listening.

Explore

Ask kids to close their eyes and sit comfortably at their desks while you, or a chosen student, stand out of sight with several objects that can be used to produce recognizable sounds.

- Listen as mindfully as you can to the sound I make—and focus on it. If you think you know what it is, keep it to yourself. Record your answer on the Mystery Sound Activity Sheet.

One at a time, make each sound. Possible actions include:

tap a pencil, shuffle cards, crumple paper, tear newsprint, shake coins in a jar

Give students time to record their answers for each sound, using the Mystery Sound activity sheet. They may include specific descriptions of each sound and/or say what it made them think about.

Finally, reveal the identity of the sound-makers. (Students might enjoy the addition of a drum roll for effect!)

Reflect

Initiate a class discussion. Make sure students understand that they were using brain energy to concentrate on each individual sound as they listened.

- In what ways is this experience different from the way we typically listen to sounds? If you lost your focus on the sounds, explain what you think got in the way.
- How might this kind of listening affect your brain? What areas of your brain did a lot of work during this exercise?

Record student responses on chart paper.

Why It's Important

Engage: There are many sounds surrounding us most of the time. Usually we aren't mindful of every sound, because our brain helps us focus our attention by screening the sounds our ears pick up and bringing to our attention only the ones that are important. That filter in our brain is the Reticular Activating System (RAS). Listening mindfully can help us reinforce the work of the RAS.

Explore: By concentrating on specific sounds, you can train your RAS to listen very carefully. That strengthens the pathways to the prefrontal cortex.

You are more in control of your own thought processes if you are more aware of the constant sensory input that your brain experiences.

Reflect: When you're really listening well, you get the information you need without being distracted. Then you can decide how best to respond.

mindful listening — connect to learning

MindUP In the Real World

Career Connection
Is mindful listening ever a matter of life and death? Sometimes YES! Every day, doctors practice mindful listening on the job. Not only do they need to listen carefully to their patients' bodies—hearts, lungs, and abdomens—but also to the patients themselves. What brings the patient to the doctor? What symptoms is he or she experiencing? Doctors work hard to learn the skill of active listening. Once the patient's medical history is recorded, the doctor can ask informed questions and order the right tests that will lead to the correct diagnosis and effective treatment. In the hospital, mindful listening saves people's lives.

Discuss with students how this and other careers depend on mindful listening. Examples include 911 operators, customer service representatives, and guidance counselors.

Once a Day
Resist the urge to immediately answer a question from a student or colleague. Savor the time to reflect and develop a thoughtful response.

57

Lesson focus is extended into its application in the workplace, encouraging students to link MindUP practices to the world outside the classroom.

At each stage of the lesson, we point out the usefulness of the activity or provide a link to other curriculum areas in which lesson ideas can be implemented.

Suggestions for the teacher to incorporate mindful awareness into his or her everyday interactions with colleagues and students.

Connecting to the Curriculum

The main lesson is linked to other aspects of students' academic experience: content areas, literature, and writing.

Students are given several prompts for writing and/or drawing in response to the lesson and its target exploration.

Lesson is expanded and extended into three curricular areas and social-emotional learning, connections that can be ongoing as subject-area learning goes on over the course of the school year.

Four literature selections that relate to the lesson focus are recommended for extending the learning.

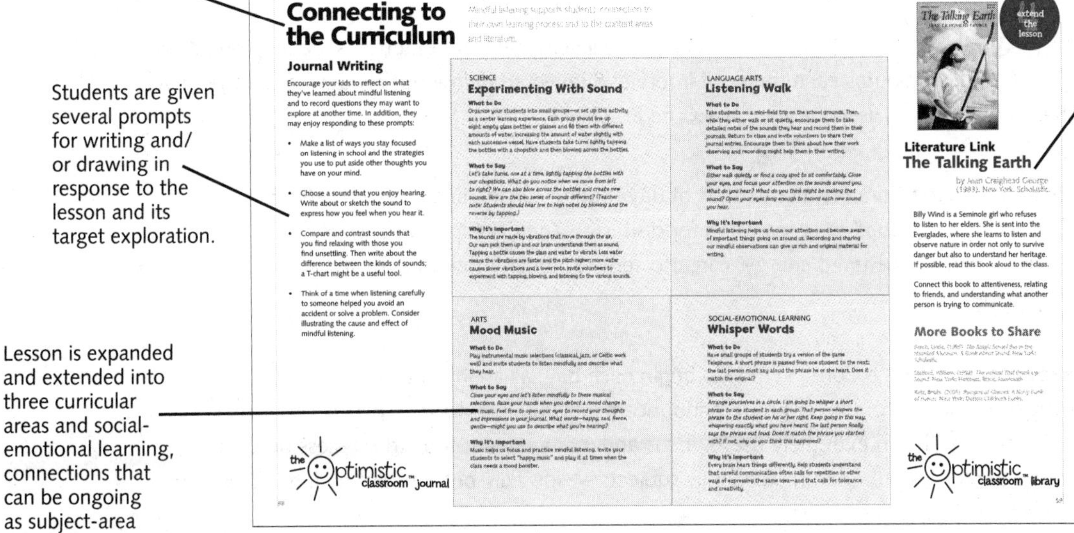

Connecting to the Curriculum

Mindful listening supports students' connection to their own learning process and to the content areas and literature.

Journal Writing

Encourage your kids to reflect on what they've learned about mindful listening and to record questions they may want to explore at another time. In addition, they may enjoy responding to these prompts:

- Make a list of ways you stay focused on listening in school and the strategies you use to put aside other thoughts you have on your mind.
- Choose a sound that you enjoy hearing. Write about or sketch the sound to express how you feel when you hear it.
- Compare and contrast sounds that you find relaxing with those you find unsettling. Then write about the difference between the kinds of sounds; a T-chart might be a useful tool.
- Think of a time when listening carefully to someone helped you avoid an accident or solve a problem. Consider illustrating the cause and effect of mindful listening.

the Optimistic classroom™ journal

SCIENCE
Experimenting With Sound

What to Do
Organize your students into small groups—or set up this activity as a center learning experience. Each group should line up eight empty glass bottles or glasses and fill them with different amounts of water, increasing the amount of water slightly with each successive vessel. Have students take turns lightly tapping the bottles with a chopstick and then blowing across the bottles.

What to Say
Let's take turns, one at a time, lightly tapping the bottles with our chopsticks. What do you notice when we move from left to right? We can also blow across the bottles and create new sounds. How are the two series of sounds different? (Teacher note: Students should hear low to high notes by blowing and the reverse by tapping.)

Why It's Important
The sounds are made by vibrations that move through the air. Our ears pick them up and our brain understands them as sound. Tapping a bottle causes the glass and water to vibrate. Less water means the vibrations are faster and the pitch higher; more water causes slower vibrations and a lower note. Invite volunteers to experiment with tapping, blowing, and listening to the various sounds.

LANGUAGE ARTS
Listening Walk

What to Do
Take students on a mini-field trip on the school grounds. Then, while they either walk or sit quietly, encourage them to take detailed notes of the sounds they hear and record them in their journals. Return to class and invite volunteers to share their journal entries. Encourage them to think about how their work observing and recording might help them in their writing.

What to Say
Either walk quietly or find a cozy spot to sit comfortably. Close your eyes, and focus your attention on the sounds around you. What do you hear? What do you think might be making that sound? Open your eyes long enough to record each new sound you hear.

Why It's Important
Mindful listening helps us focus our attention and become aware of important things going on around us. Recording and sharing our mindful observations can give us rich and original material for writing.

ARTS
Mood Music

What to Do
Play instrumental music selections (classical, jazz, or Celtic work well) and invite students to listen mindfully and describe what they hear.

What to Say
Close your eyes and let's listen mindfully to these musical selections. Raise your hands when you detect a mood change in the music. Feel free to open your eyes to record your thoughts and impressions in your journal. What words—happy, sad, fierce, gentle—might you use to describe what you're hearing?

Why It's Important
Music helps us focus and practice mindful listening. Invite your students to select "happy music" and play it at times when the class needs a mood booster.

SOCIAL-EMOTIONAL LEARNING
Whisper Words

What to Do
Have small groups of students try a version of the game Telephone. A short phrase is passed from one student to the next; the last person must say aloud the phrase he or she hears. Does it match the original?

What to Say
Arrange yourselves in a circle. I am going to whisper a short phrase to one student in each group. That person whispers the phrase to the student on his or her right. Keep going in this way, whispering exactly what you have heard. The last person finally says the phrase out loud. Does it match the phrase you started with? If not, why do you think this happened?

Why It's Important
Every brain hears things differently. Help students understand that careful communication often calls for repetition or other ways of expressing the same idea—and that calls for tolerance and creativity.

mindful listening — extend the lesson

Literature Link
The Talking Earth
by Jean Craighead George (1983). New York: Scholastic.

Billy Wind is a Seminole girl who refuses to listen to her elders. She is sent into the Everglades, where she learns to listen and observe nature in order not only to survive danger but also to understand her heritage. If possible, read this book aloud to the class.

Connect this book to attentiveness, relating to friends, and understanding what another person is trying to communicate.

More Books to Share

the Optimistic classroom™ library

MindUP Implementation

In order to ensure successful implementation of the MindUP program, consider these points:

- MindUP is not a set of strategies to teach in isolation: the curriculum is meant to be an integral part of a complete classroom life. In deciding when to introduce MindUP lessons, consider how to link MindUP to inquiries you are already engaged in from diverse content areas.
- MindUP lessons depend on both whole-group and small-group discussion. Think about how you can best use the floor space for gathering or arrange desks so that students can see one another.
- MindUP lessons draw on students' life experiences and invite students to look closely at their behaviors—for example, their interactions with peers and family. Bear in mind that some students may prefer not to share, for whatever reasons; give students the option to consider their responses privately, or record them in their journals. Additionally, recalling personal experiences, especially for students with challenging lives outside of school, may bring up unsettling emotions. Creating the Optimistic Classroom, featured in each lesson, has classroom management suggestions that address this and other possibly sensitive situations.

Recommended Implementation Scenarios

MindUP pilot-site teachers have discovered several effective routes to establishing MindUP teaching and practices in their classrooms across the school day and school year. Some of these scenarios are summarized here, followed by an implementation chart to be used for quick reference as you adjust the program to the specific demands of your educational setting, day, and year.

Starting With the Core Practice: At all grade levels, the Core Practice is ideally done three times a day (for a few minutes each time), at intervals suggested below but always adjustable to your needs. (See Lesson 3 for a description of the Core Practice.)

- **Pre-K–2:** Use the Core Practice at start of day (during Circle Time), after recess or lunch, and to "regroup" in preparation for dismissal. The Core Practice, which effectively reins in scattered energy, can also serve as an antidote to end-of-day disruptiveness.

- **Grades 3–5:** Use the Core Practice to begin each day, as an introduction to any daily sharing routine or group announcements you may have in place. This simple routine can also be an extremely useful focus and management tool after recess or lunch, in order to redirect attention to academic subjects—especially before splitting into small groups for collaborative projects.

Because the Core Practice is aimed in part at making the mind more receptive to learning for understanding, it is an ideal tool before embarking on a new area of study or in preparation for tests that are likely to demand that students "keep their cool" while being asked to summon up stored information.

The Core Practice can be built into your routine summing-up of the day especially as a means for reunifying the class prior to dismissal. The Core Practice by its nature precludes conflict; it is especially effective as a self-regulating skill for upper-elementary students, who are about to experience dramatic physical and emotional changes they may not be well prepared to deal with.

- **Grades 6–8:** By middle school, students are capable of engaging in the Core Practice on their own. As a homeroom, advisory, or content-area instructor, you may wish to build the Core Practice into your class meeting to establish important stability in preparation for the "gear shifting" required as students move among multiple subjects, rooms, and teachers.

  Because the Core Practice prepares the ground for learning, make a point to remind students that they can use it for their own self-regulation and focus when they feel it necessary. This sense of agency is critical for students at this age, as they learn to take responsibility for their own learning and social interactions. In addition, when implementing MindUP at the middle grades, it is extremely helpful to coordinate with other teachers a grade-wide or school-wide plan for incorporating MindUP Core Practice into classroom routines in various contexts across the curriculum and throughout the year.

- **Alternative and Pullout Settings:** The Core Practice is a natural way to begin and end sessions in after-school, English-language learning, or special needs settings. It brings calm, unity, and focus to individuals and groups, and sets the stage for introducing almost any area of study or collaborative activity.

MindUP Lessons

The 15 MindUP lessons can be presented at regular intervals and in diverse forms throughout the typical 32-week school year.

In the first few weeks of the year, as explained earlier, "Breathe first!" can be your motto. This is the time for students to become acquainted with the Core Practice and habituated to the daily experience of mindful listening and focused attention to their own breathing and thought processes. By the third week of school, classroom routines and schedules are in place and students have adjusted to the new academic year. You can then launch your MindUP curriculum in earnest, working through the program in sequence beginning with Unit I.

Implementation Scenarios: The following recommendations are based on the experience of MindUP pilot teachers at all grade levels. "Chunking" the lessons is entirely adaptable to your classroom needs; below is an approximation of how to approach incorporating MindUP into the generally busy days all teachers face.

Review thoroughly the information in Linking to Brain Research on the second page of the lesson. Plan at least one 15-minute chunk of time to familiarize students with this material, which always deals with some aspect of how the brain works; a second 15-minute session may be advisable in order to solidify that learning.

Getting Ready, on pages 3 and 4 of the lesson, can also be treated as a learning chunk to be repeated or extended as necessary in advance of the core lesson, outlined on the following two pages. The MindUP warm-up is an opportunity to refer back to the Brain Research segment, and to reinforce students' Core Practice competencies as they prepare for the lesson.

Leading the Lesson may take place over a few days, depending on how much time you are able to devote to it. You may wish to treat Engage and Explore as one chunk, then move on to Reflect and MindUP in the Real World in a separate meeting. If you have the time to rewind a bit and incorporate previous discoveries, students will gain from the recap and reinforcement.

The final two pages of the lesson are the most open-ended in terms of time chunking. The adaptability of lesson content to other curriculum areas and the extension of the lesson into reading and writing activities are important assets of MindUP. These extensions can be carried out in several chunks, feasibly encompassing parts of several days or weeks, depending on the organization of your academic curriculum.

Unit I In most classrooms, teachers have found that the Unit I lessons are best introduced in concentrated doses over the course of approximately two weeks each, spending time to become familiar with the brain basics. The self-regulatory routine of the Core Practice will serve as a backdrop for students' discoveries about what is going on inside as they learn and interact. Because the material here is concrete "science information," it may be best to set aside 30 minutes at a time, in order to be able to discuss and review as needed.

Units II and III These lessons, numbered 4 through 12, can be covered in 15-minute chunks, extending over approximately two weeks. You may wish to occasionally use a 30- to 45-minute period to go into depth on lesson segments. However, since a fundamental purpose of MindUP is to apply mindful awareness in other areas of the curriculum and parts of the school day, there is a benefit to working MindUP knowledge into other discussions and practices.The final two pages of each lesson offer specific applications of the lesson to other parts of students' academic experience.

Unit IV The final three lessons are geared toward reaching beyond the immediate context of a lesson, applying MindUP insights to behaviors and actions in the larger community or the world. For these lessons, the time frame can be more open-ended, with classroom discussions serving as an anchor for independent work and reflection on how students' skills at self-regulation, self-discipline, and self-examination have affected their confidence and competence.

At each grade level, there are key factors to consider when implementing MindUP.

- **Pre-K–2:** At the earliest grades, a predominant focus of the program will be on the development of children's skills at self-regulation. Children are usually eager to become skilled practitioners of the Core Practice at these early grades. Once the Core Practice have been established, children become more receptive to and engaged in learning in all areas, and more successful at integrating the academic and social considerations of school life. Keeping MindUP an adventurous exploration rooted in self-awareness is key to helping children enjoy and apply the exciting knowledge they will acquire.

- **Grades 3–5:** Students' broadening self-awareness during this period dovetails well with MindUP's introduction of brain science to broaden the base of students' core knowledge. Learning about their own thinking and gaining some control over their thought processes are useful not only for taking in new information but also for responding, as on standardized testing, to somewhat stressful demands that they "show what they know."

- **Grades 6–8:** At middle school, students will increasingly be able to use MindUP as a tool to prepare themselves to learn. As they acquire agency over their own learning and determine with greater independence how to direct their energies, use their time, organize their lives, and interact with their peers, students in grades 6–8 can look to MindUP for both knowledge and practical skills over the course of a school day and school year.

Alternative Settings: MindUP can be implemented in after-school programs as well as in pullout programs for special needs students or English language learners. The focus in these settings can be on developing the Core Practice; by doing this, you can establish a setting that is receptive to learning—for each student as well as for the group as a whole. The Core Practice can become the beginning and end practice each time you meet; you can reinforce the concepts and principles of MindUP by reminding students of the self-regulation tools at their disposal, as well as the mindful attention they can make habitual in every learning situation.

For all students, paying attention to their own thinking process and behaviors consistently enhances receptivity to learning in other academic and social-emotional areas.

Implementation Charts

Sample MindUP Lesson Chunking for Grades Pre-K–2 and 3–5

Time	Chunk/Content	Lesson page
10–15 min	Linking to Brain Research & Clarify for the Class	2
10–15 min	Getting Ready, MindUP Warm-Up & Discuss	3–4
10–15 min	Leading the Lesson: Engage & Explore	5
10–15 min	Leading the Lesson: Reflect & MindUP in the Real World	6
(variable)	Extend: Journal Writing*	7
10–15 min	Extend: Connecting to Curriculum*	7–8
10–15 min	Extend: Connecting to Curriculum*	7–8
(variable)	Extend: Literature Link (Independent Reading)*	8

* It is highly recommended that you take advantage of extension links, in order to apply MindUP principles to support and facilitate all kinds of learning.

Sample MindUP Lesson Chunking for Grades 6–8

Time	Chunk/Content	Lesson page
10–15 min	Linking to Brain Research & Clarify for the Class	2
10–15 min	Getting Ready, MindUP Warm-Up & Discuss	3–4
10–15 min	Leading the Lesson: Engage & Explore	5
10–15 min	Leading the Lesson: Reflect & MindUP in the Real World	6
(variable)	Extend: Journal Writing*	7
10–15 min	Extend: Connecting to Curriculum*	7–8
10–15 min	Extend: Connecting to Curriculum*	7–8
(variable)	Extend: Literature Link (Independent Reading)*	8

* It is highly recommended that you take advantage of extension links, in order to apply MindUP principles to support and facilitate all kinds of learning. (Curriculum links may be handled by content area instructors.)

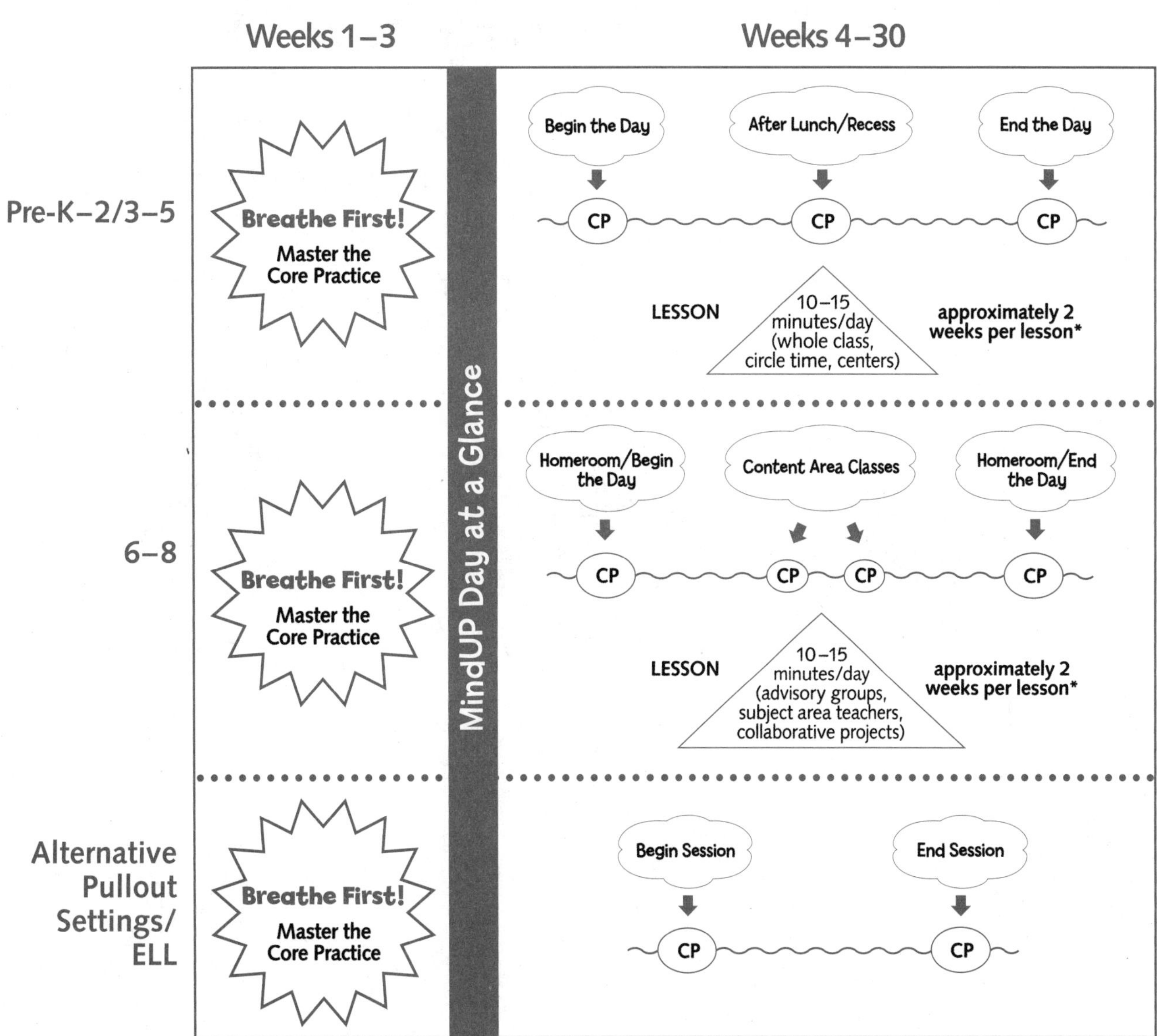

* NOTE: Lessons 14 and 15 require student time spent outside of the classroom; schedule and duration of these lessons should be adjusted accordingly.

CP=Core Practice

Getting Focused

By learning how their brains respond to stress and by practicing strategies for quieting their minds, students become better at self-regulating, increase their capacity for absorbing information, and improve their relationship skills.

unit I

Do you ever wonder why high-pressure situations make us "lose our cool"? An accelerated heartbeat and butterflies in the stomach seem to happen no matter how well prepared we are.

The human brain is wired to respond to stress as if something were immediately threatening, often placing us at the mercy of our physical and emotional responses. Yet, we can actually train our brains to respond reflectively. This realization is empowering for students, who deal with many stresses in and out of the classroom—from bullying to homework.

The focus of this unit is on the interplay of three key parts of the brain—the amygdala (reactive center), the prefrontal cortex (reflective center), and the hippocampus (memory and information storage and processing center). Students will learn practical strategies, including listening and breathing exercises, to prime their brains for learning and behaving mindfully.

How Our Brains Work

What's So Important About the Brain?

Our brain can serve as a map for showing us how we learn and why we behave the way we do. Neuroscience provides a wealth of information that can help us and our students become better thinkers and healthier people.

Why Introduce Students to Brain Research?

Students are fascinated by facts about their brains. Sharing scientific information about how the brain processes information and is wired to react under stress is a great way to introduce a challenge to your students: How can we learn to react differently, helping our brain make wise choices about our words and actions?

As students become more familiar with three key parts of the brain involved in thinking and learning, they'll begin to understand how their feelings arise—and that they have the ability to change what they do in response. This understanding lays the groundwork for them to monitor and regulate their behavior by calming themselves in the face of anxiety, focusing their attention, and taking control of their learning.

What Can You Expect to Observe?

"Students enjoy learning and sharing facts about their brains. They easily pick up the scientific names and functions of the three parts of the brain and that gives us a common language to start talking about the choices they make in learning and in interacting with peers."

—Third-grade teacher

Linking to Brain Research

Meet Some Key Players in the Brain

The limbic system controls emotions and motivations from deep inside the brain. A key player of the limbic system is the amygdala. The amygdala is a pair of almond-shaped structures that reacts to fear, danger, and threat. The amygdala regulates our emotional state by acting as the brain's "security guard," protecting us from threats. When a student is in a positive emotional state, the amygdala sends incoming information on to the conscious, thinking, reasoning brain. When a student is in a negative emotional state (stressed or fearful, for example) the amygdala prevents the input from passing along, effectively blocking higher-level thinking and reasoned judgment. The incoming stimuli and signals are left for the amygdala itself to process as an automatic reflexive response of "fight, flight, or freeze."

The hippocampus is another limbic system structure. These twin crescent-shaped bodies reside in the central brain area, one behind each ear, in the temporal lobes. The hippocampus assists in managing our response to fear and threats, and is a storage vault of memory and learning.

Information from the limbic system is fed to the prefrontal cortex—the learning, reasoning, and thinking center of the brain. This highly evolved area of the brain controls our decision making, focuses our attention, and allows us to learn to read, write, compute, analyze, predict, comprehend, and interpret.

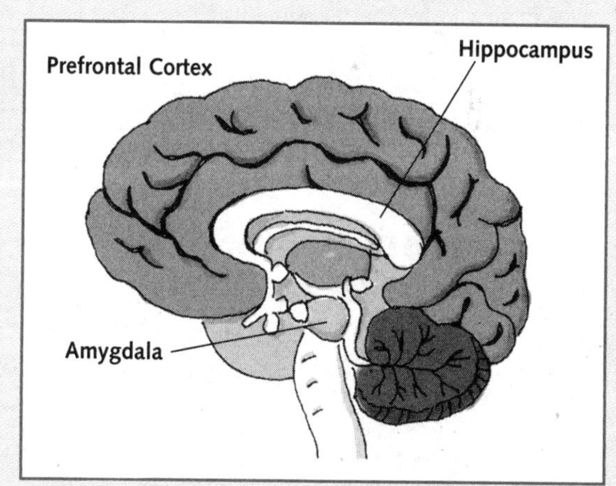

Learning about these key players helps students understand how their brains respond to stress and prepares them for creating a calm mind-set for thoughtful decision making, led by the prefrontal cortex.

Clarify for the Class

Make a model to show how the brain processes information under stress. Fill a clear plastic bottle with water, an inch of sand, some glitter, and metallic mini-confetti. To demonstrate the way the amygdala on alert scatters information, shake the bottle and mix up the solution. The settling solution represents the calming mind—eventually the bits of information flow in a clear direction, some of them to the PFC for thoughtful decision making.

Discuss: Name a time when you felt so worried or anxious your mind was working like the shaken bottle. What helped you think more clearly?

Getting Ready

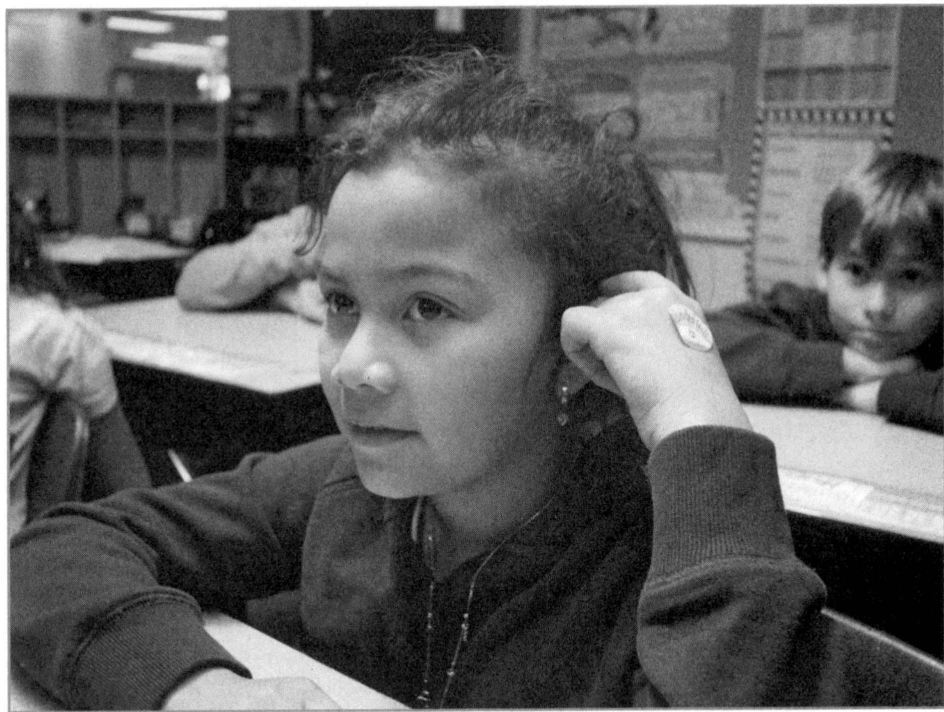

Where is it?
A student points to the location of the amygdala, deep inside the brain.

GOALS

- Students identify the amygdala, the hippocampus, and the prefrontal cortex (PFC) on a diagram of the brain.
- Students will give a simple definition of these three parts of the brain.

MATERIALS

- chart paper
- MindUP poster "Getting to Know and Love Your Brain"
- Brain Power! activity sheet (p.152)

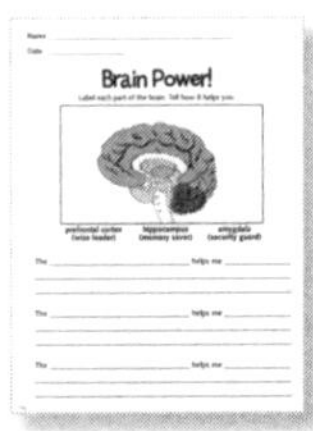

CREATING THE OPTIMISTIC CLASSROOM

Classroom Management Nurture students' sense of independence and control by doing the following:

- Teach students where in the room to look or go for supplies or resources before asking for help.
- Encourage discussion in partners or small groups.
- Allow students to generate questions before lessons and reflect on learning afterward.
- Encourage self-assessment and self-monitoring.
- Provide choices, whenever possible, in tools and avenues for learning.
- Celebrate times when students have worked hard to learn something new or succeeded in honing their skills.

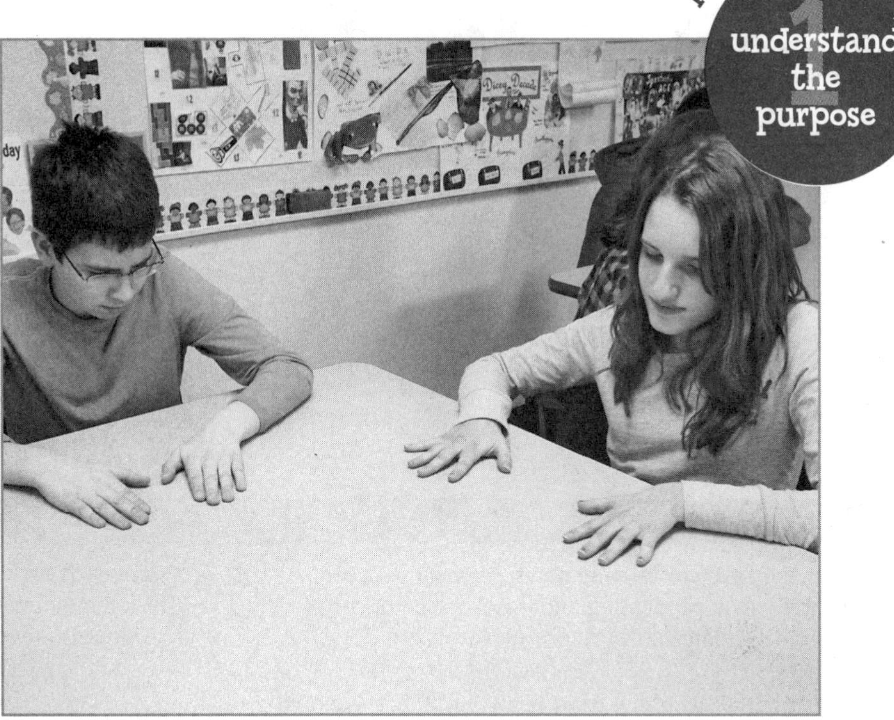

How did my brain do that?
Students build background about their brains, learning how their brain activates muscle responses in their fingers.

MINDUP Warm-Up

Brain Exercise Discussion

Display photos of a few famous athletes and ask students to name others. Invite students to brainstorm what these athletes have in common. List on chart paper their responses, such as working hard, eating well, and committing to regular practice.

Point out that in order for athletes to succeed, they need to exercise their minds as well as their bodies. Successful athletes learn to focus their attention, manage distractions, and continuously improve their skills in their sport. Have students reflect on Olympic events or other sporting events they've watched and how they've seen top athletes focus (e.g., baseball players may study a pitcher and time their swings before they go to bat, runners may visualize their course before they begin a race, and so on).

Explain that by participating in MindUP lessons, students are going to learn ways to exercise their brain—the more they exercise it, the stronger, smarter, and more confident it becomes!

Discuss: The word "brainstorm" means to allow ideas to tumble out of your brain—it's one kind of activity for strengthening your thinking skills. What types of activities do you already do on a regular basis (such as crossword puzzles, concentration, or number games) to exercise your mind?

Leading the Lesson

The Brain in Action

Engage

What to Do

Review the brainstorming notes, reminding students of the power of focusing and training their brains the way top athletes do.

Using handouts of the Brain Power! activity sheet and the "Getting to Know and Love Your Brain" poster for reference, introduce the three key parts of the brain involved in thinking and acting: the prefrontal cortex, the amygdala, and the hippocampus.

- The brain operates like an orchestra with thousands of instruments, each playing its own tune but all working together to create a beautiful piece of music. Today we're going to learn about three parts of the brain that are important in thinking, in dealing with our feelings, and in learning new things.

Have students pronounce the terms with you and discuss the role and location of each part. Let them point to their own head as a model (PFC—right behind the forehead; amygdala—deep inside, behind each ear; hippocampus—just behind the amygdala on both sides.)

Why It's Important

Using analogies like the orchestra and visual models to establish the locations of the brain parts captures students' interest, reinforces concepts in several different ways, and helps them build a foundation of background knowledge for future lessons.

Explore

What to Do

Give each part of the brain you've discussed a role or nickname that is related to its function and is easy for students to remember.

- Imagine the prefrontal cortex is an orchestra leader who directs the different instruments to produce a harmonious, unified musical sound.
- Imagine the amygdala is the musicians themselves, whose playing expresses their feelings in response to music but who must also collaborate and follow the directions of the conductor.
- Imagine the hippocampus is the sheet music, which the musicians can refer to in order to help them remember the notes they must play.

Invite students to give examples of times when their amygdala alerted them to real danger (e.g., reacting to a ball flying toward you, the sound of screeching tires, or the smell of smoke) and when it made them nervous or worried about something stressful, but not dangerous (e.g., performing a piece of music for the first time).

- How did your reaction affect your ability to think and plan?

Why It's Important

- Reactions to stress and to danger are both controlled by the amygdala. It's important to understand that while the amygdala can help keep us safe, sometimes it signals danger when there is none—and that shuts down our ability to think clearly by blocking information to the PFC.

From the Research

Students are more likely to remember and really understand what they learn if they find it compelling or have some part in figuring it out or discovering some part of it for themselves. (Willis, 2006)

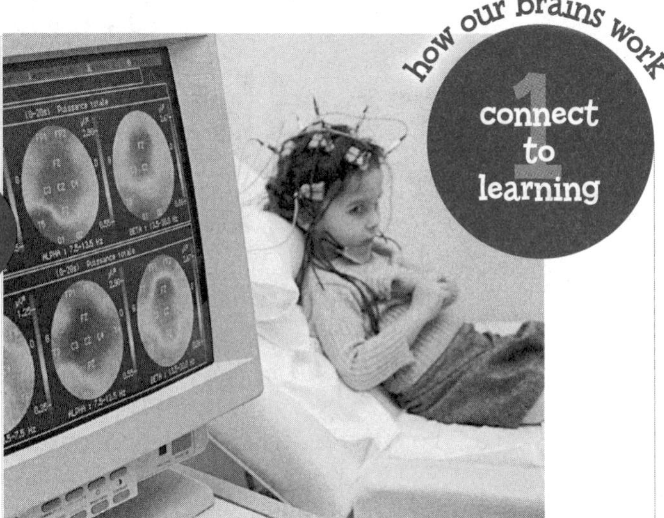

how our brains work

1 connect to learning

Reflect

To review, have students pair up and retell in their own words the function of each brain part. Then have them fill in the name of each part on the activity sheet and explain its function. Encourage students to add notes and words that help them remember what each part does.

Share a few scenarios to ensure that students can identify the brain parts and their functions.

- Try to imagine this situation: You are walking to school and suddenly you see a small squirrel run out in front of a car. How does your body react? What are you thinking? How does your body feel?
- Was it your brain's wise leader (the prefrontal cortex), your brain's security guard (the amygdala), or your brain's memory saver (the hippocampus) that came into play?

Conclude this lesson by sharing with students that future MindUP lessons will help them calm their amygdala when there's no danger, strengthen their ability to focus by getting information to the PFC efficiently, and store important ideas in their hippocampus.

Providing real-life scenarios about different types of reactions to everyday situations gives students useful examples to attach meaning to. This review lays the groundwork for the next lesson, which connects mindful and unmindful behaviors to the roles of the amygdala and PFC.

MINDUP In the Real World

Career Connection

If you're fascinated by the brain and how it works, you might consider a career as a neuroscientist. A neuroscientist is anyone who studies the brain and central nervous system. Within the wide-ranging field of neuroscience, there are many specialized jobs; for example, a *neuroanatomist* studies the structure of the nervous system, while a *neurochemist* investigates how neurotransmitters work. If operating on the brain sounds exciting, consider the work of a *neurosurgeon*, or, if you're concerned about diseases that affect the brain, become a *neuropathologist*. A *neuropsychologist* explores brain-behavior relationships.

Discuss: What type of "brain work" most appeals to you? What would you enjoy learning about the brain?

Once a Day

Take a break to self-assess: Do your responses reveal the dominance of your amygdala (reaction) or your PFC (reflection)? If your amygdala is being activated, what is triggering its response? What would you like to change about your style of reaction?

Connecting to the Curriculum

Learning about the brain supports students' connection to their own learning process and to the content areas and literature.

Journal Writing

Encourage students to reflect on what they've learned about how their brains think and learn and to record questions they may wish to explore at another time. They may also enjoy responding to these prompts:

- Draw a picture of yourself when your amygdala was activated. Below your picture, describe the situation in words. Explain whether your amygdala reacted to real danger or alerted you to a situation that wasn't an actual threat.
- Draw a picture of yourself when you are feeling calm and thinking clearly. Below your picture, describe the situation in words. Tell how your PFC was working.
- Make a comic strip with your amygdala talking to your PFC. What would one character say to the other?
- Which do you think helps your hippocampus work better to remember information and ideas—the amygdala or PFC? Tell why you think so.

SCIENCE

Did You Know...? Brain Facts!

What to Do

Invite volunteers to read fascinating facts about the brain on the "Getting to Know and Love Your Brain" poster. Encourage students to become "brain experts" by having them research new facts about the brain on the Internet or in books. Have students write their facts on large sticky notes and post the facts around the poster's perimeter (or you may want to have them connect the facts to specific points on a brain illustration with lengths of yarn and sticky tack).

What to Say

Did you know that your brain never stops thinking, even when you're asleep? Or even that you can solve problems when you dream? Can you share some amazing things you know about the brain and how it works?... Now let's see if this poster tells us any new information—Then we'll go on a brain-fact hunt to add even more facts that we find to this poster.

Why It's Important

Inviting students to become experts about the brain puts them in the driver's seat of their own learning. That self-motivated learning will build background for future lessons and keep their engagement high.

PHYSICAL EDUCATION

Amygdala on the Move

What to Do

Have students line up on one side of the gym and explain that they are little bits of information trying to get to the other side of the gym where the prefrontal cortex can use them to make better decisions. Then choose two students to be in the center of the gym as the amygdala, assigned to determine whether the bits of information scatter, freeze, or move calmly to the prefrontal cortex.

What to Say

I'm going to shout out the words "flight," "freeze," or "MindUP" in a random order. The amygdala will either run around wildly (taking flight), freeze rigidly, or calmly direct the bits of information toward the prefrontal cortex.

Why It's Important

Acting out the role of the amygdala and showing how information gets processed when it's calm and when it's on alert give students a powerful kinesthetic way to review concepts from the lesson.

LANGUAGE ARTS

Brain Tunes

What to Do
Challenge students to write a song or rap about one or more parts of the brain. Have them work with a partner or small group to review what they've learned about three main parts of the brain and then think about how they can create a rhyming message about the topic. Give students time to write and then practice singing or chanting it. Invite students to perform their songs for their peers and teach them the lyrics.

What to Say
One of the best ways to teach yourself or someone else about the brain (or any other topic) is through a song. Let's think of the roles each of the three brain parts plays—that ever-ready amygdala, the thoughtful prefrontal cortex, and the memory-collecting hippocampus. You may want to write about one or all of them and the work they do to help us think, learn, and act.

Why It's Important
Making a mnemonic connection to the parts of the brain through song increases students' investment in their learning.

SOCIAL-EMOTIONAL LEARNING

Quick Stress Release

What to Do
Show students two options for getting rid of worries and clearing their minds: Laugh for 15 seconds before taking a test or starting a challenging task. (Invite students to make funny faces, or twist their bodies into silly shapes.) Invite students to stand and "shake" like a wet dog. After shaking a few times, have them take three deep, slow breaths.

What to Say
Let's start building a toolbox of things to do if you get worried and your thoughts get jumbled or your brain freezes. We'll try two quick activities we can do anytime we are likely to get nervous or worried—before we take a test or when trying to solve a conflict with someone or just having something on our minds.

Why It's Important
Everyone needs tools for dealing with stress—the simpler and more enjoyable your mind-clearing tips and tactics are, the more readily students will use them. As you move through the lessons, ask students to share effective strategies they've discovered on their own.

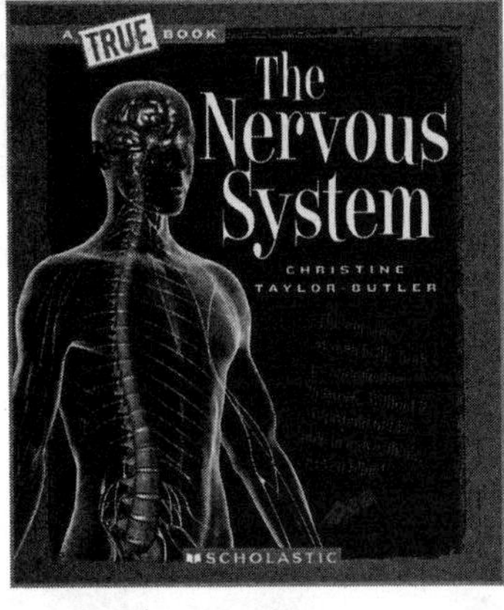

Literature Link
The Nervous System: A True Book

by Taylor-Butler, Christine (2008). Danbury: Children's Press.

How do nerve impulses travel throughout the body? How to they affect our actions and emotions? This colorful book is packed with facts and appealing visuals that reveal how the nervous system shuttles messages back and forth between the brain and the body.

As you explore this book with students challenge them to link new ideas to what they already know about the brain.

More Books to Share

Lichtenheld, Tom. (2003). *What Are You So Grumpy About?* Boston, MA: Little, Brown, and Company.

Simon, Seymour (2010). *The Brain*. New York: Scholastic .

Weierbach, Jane and Elizabeth Phillips-Hershey. (2008). *Mind Over Basketball*. Washington, DC: Magination Press.

Mindful Awareness

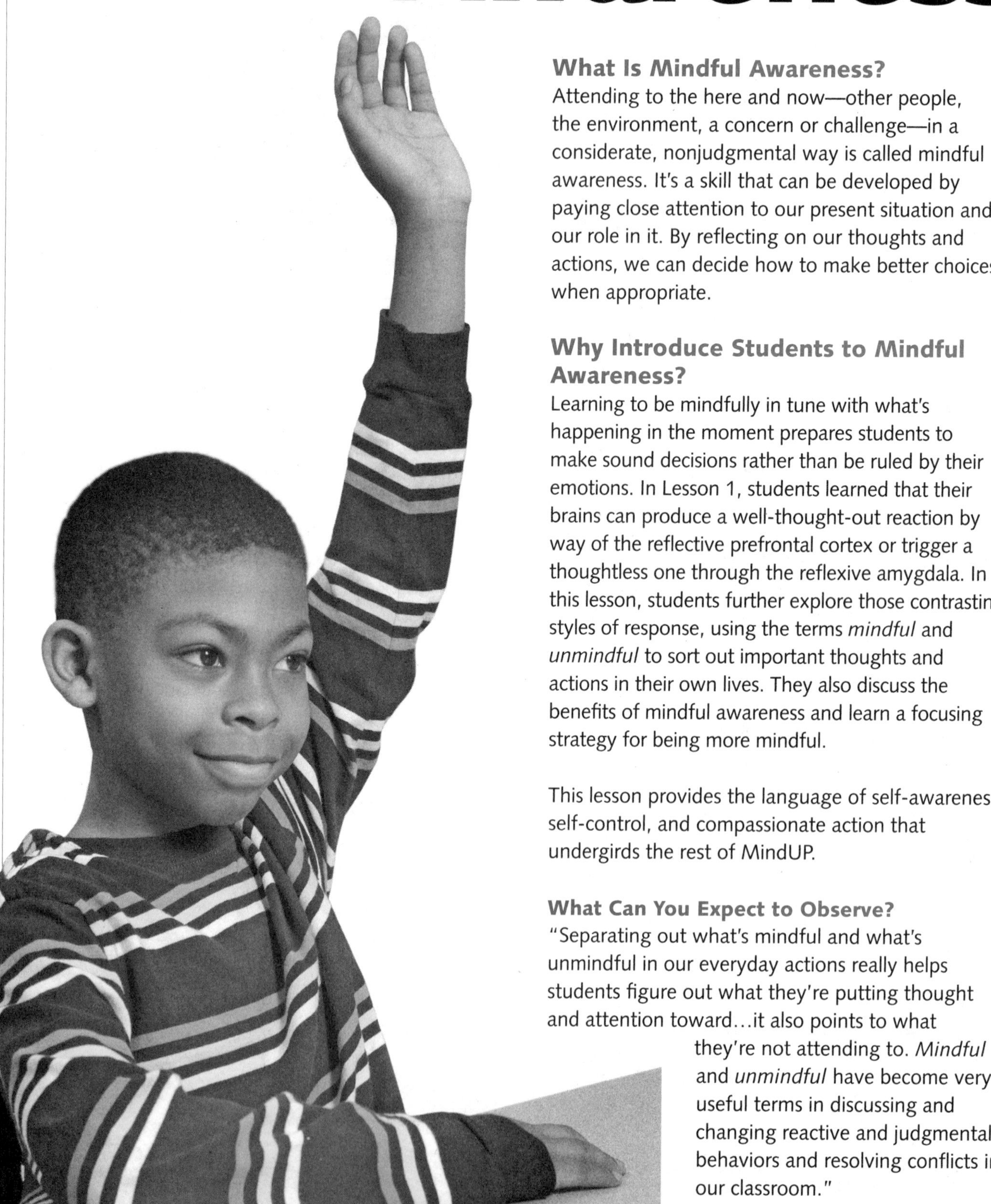

What Is Mindful Awareness?

Attending to the here and now—other people, the environment, a concern or challenge—in a considerate, nonjudgmental way is called mindful awareness. It's a skill that can be developed by paying close attention to our present situation and our role in it. By reflecting on our thoughts and actions, we can decide how to make better choices when appropriate.

Why Introduce Students to Mindful Awareness?

Learning to be mindfully in tune with what's happening in the moment prepares students to make sound decisions rather than be ruled by their emotions. In Lesson 1, students learned that their brains can produce a well-thought-out reaction by way of the reflective prefrontal cortex or trigger a thoughtless one through the reflexive amygdala. In this lesson, students further explore those contrasting styles of response, using the terms *mindful* and *unmindful* to sort out important thoughts and actions in their own lives. They also discuss the benefits of mindful awareness and learn a focusing strategy for being more mindful.

This lesson provides the language of self-awareness, self-control, and compassionate action that undergirds the rest of MindUP.

What Can You Expect to Observe?

"Separating out what's mindful and what's unmindful in our everyday actions really helps students figure out what they're putting thought and attention toward…it also points to what they're not attending to. *Mindful* and *unmindful* have become very useful terms in discussing and changing reactive and judgmental behaviors and resolving conflicts in our classroom."

—Fifth-grade teacher

Linking to Brain Research

The Amygdala and Mindful Awareness

The amygdala determines emotional responses by classifying incoming sights, sounds, smells, and movements as either potentially threatening or pleasurable. Input deemed pleasurable goes on to the prefrontal cortex where it is analyzed before it is responded to. Input perceived as threatening is blocked by the amygdala and instead prompts an immediate reflexive reaction—fight, flight, or freeze.

The amygdala does not make a distinction between perceived threats and actual dangers. It can trigger "false alarm" reactive behavior that is unwarranted and potentially problematic. For instance, we sometimes freeze in stressful situations, such as taking a test. This is an example of unmindful behavior. A reaction happens *before* the mind thinks about it. Conversely, when we consciously process sensory input, we create a time buffer between the input and the response. This gives the prefrontal cortex time to analyze, interpret, and prioritize information, allowing us to choose the best course of action. We call this mindful behavior. A response happens *after* our mind thinks about it.

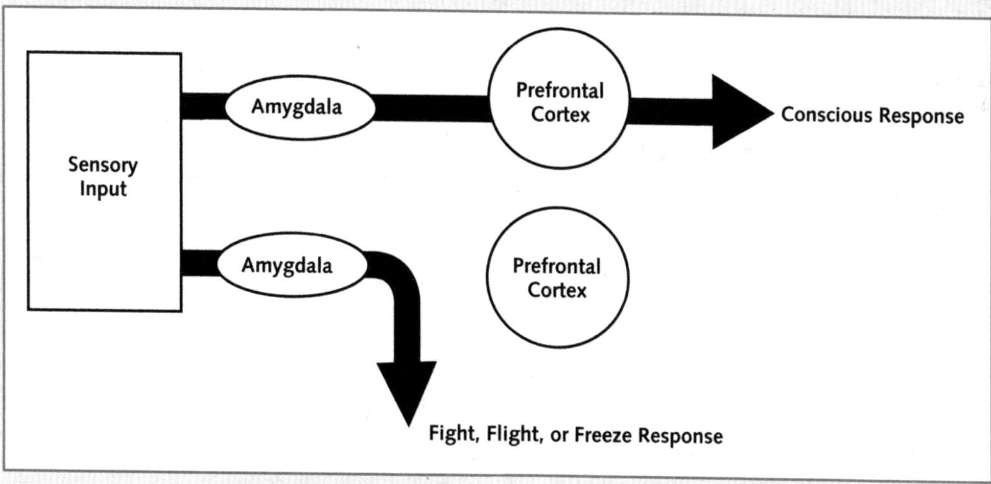

Unmindful thoughts and actions occur when the gate-keeper amygdala blocks the flow of sensory input to the prefrontal cortex and unconsciously reacts.

Clarify for the Class

Explain that giving your brain time to process something you hear, see, taste, smell, or feel before responding produces mindful thinking. An example is "counting to ten" when you're frustrated or angry. Counting allows the brain time to play catch-up and think more clearly—and mindfully.

Discuss: Has anyone ever been asked to count to ten when angry? Did it help? Why? What do you think the amygdala was doing at "1" and later at "10"?

Getting Ready

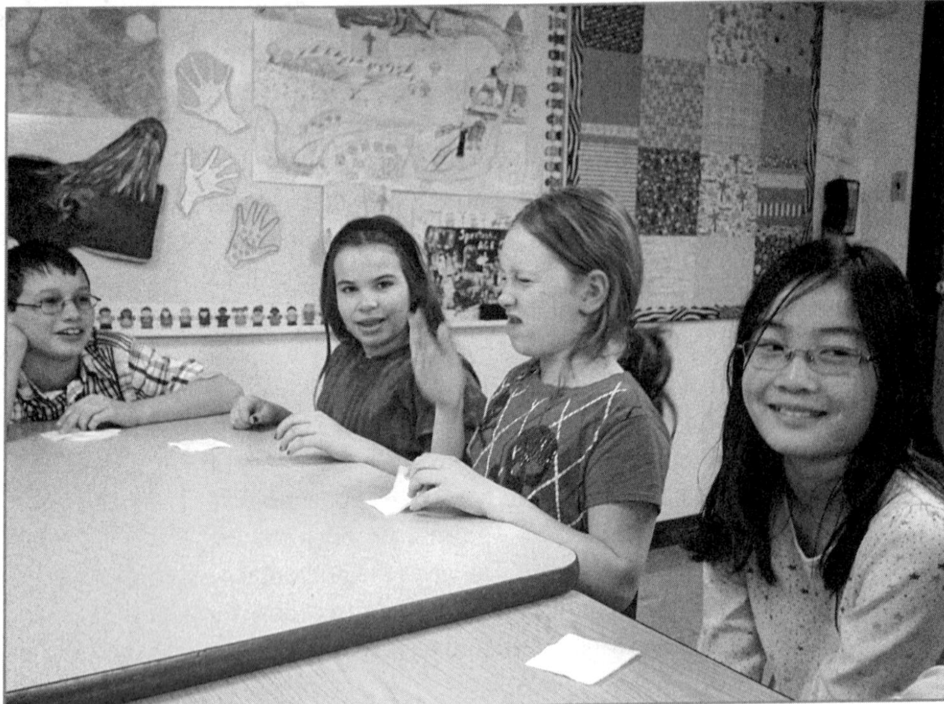

Mindful Reactions?
A student demonstrates an unmindful way to respond to trying a new food.

GOALS

- Students define and describe the difference between mindful and unmindful thoughts and actions.
- Students apply the concept of mindful awareness to their own lives.

MATERIALS

- chart paper
- index cards or scratch paper
- Mindful or Unmindful? activity sheet (p. 153)

Mindful or Unmindful?

CREATING THE OPTIMISTIC CLASSROOM

Classroom Management At the end of the lesson, record on chart paper students' mindful behavior reminders. Post these reminders on the wall or feature them on a bulletin board so that the class can refer to them during discussions and conflict resolutions. Statements might include:

- I think before I act or speak.
- I pay attention to things around me.
- I focus when I listen.
- I always do my best to be "in the moment."

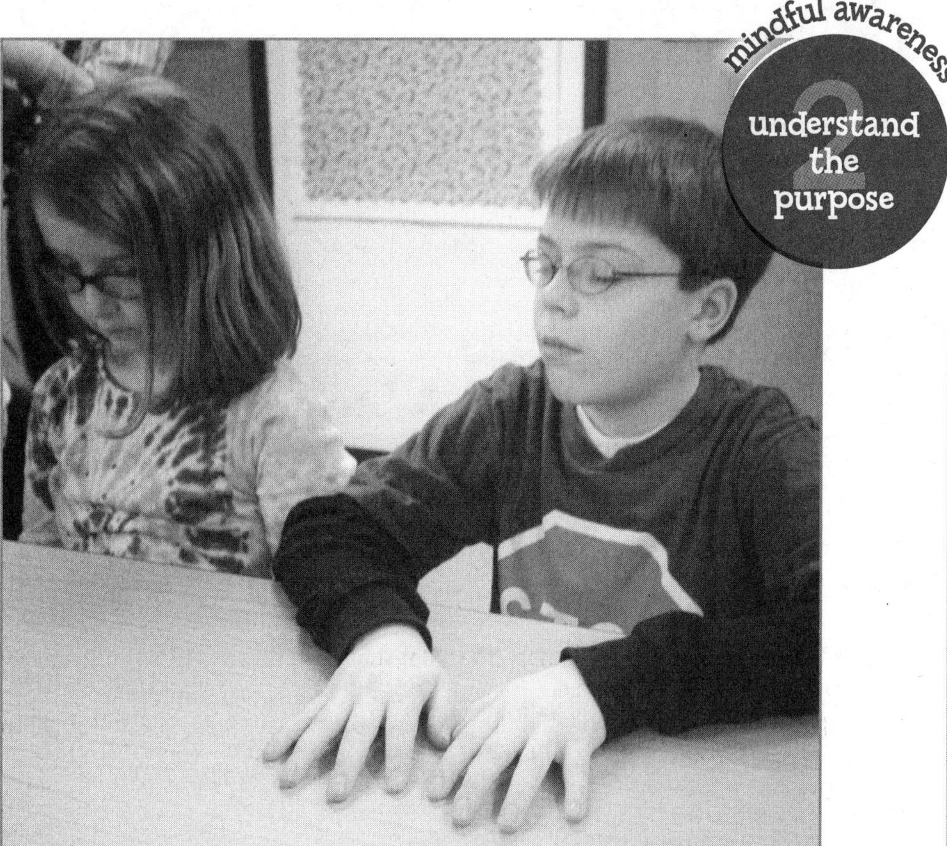

Sounds Around Us
Students focus their attention on ambient sounds.

MINDUP Warm-Up

Practice Focusing on Sounds

Give students a context for understanding mindful awareness through an auditory focusing exercise.

Provide each student with an index card or scratch paper. Ask students to sit comfortably and close or cover their eyes, then listen very carefully for all the sounds they can hear around them in the classroom, the hallway, outside, and in the school. After 30 seconds, ask students to open their eyes and list everything they heard on the index card or scratch paper. Let them share their lists in pairs and then record a class list on chart paper.

Challenge them to try the exercise again and see if there were any sounds they didn't hear the first time. Invite them to add the new sounds to their lists.

Discuss: When we are busy in our classroom, we don't hear many of the sounds we've listed because our attention is not focused on those sounds. This exercise is one way to help our mind settle down and focus our attention. What are worrisome or stressful times at which you might benefit from an exercise like this one, focusing your attention on listening to all the sounds around you?

Leading the Lesson

Minds Full of Mindful Awareness

What to Do

Engage

Reflect on the warm-up. Connect it to what students have learned about the brain.

- Wasn't it surprising how many sounds we heard when we were really focused on just listening? We kept our amygdala calm and that allowed lots of sound information through to our PFC, which passed it on to our memory saver, the hippocampus.

Explain that focusing our attention on what's happening here and now is part of being mindful, or paying close attention. The second part of being mindful is being nonjudgmental—waiting to form an opinion until you have considered a situation more carefully. Invite students to explore the term *nonjudgmental*.

- Not forming an opinion too quickly is one way to be nonjudgmental. I bet you've heard people use the expression "Don't judge a book by its cover." ... Can you think of a situation where it would be a good idea not to pass judgment on someone or something based only on a part of the whole picture, such as judging a person based on hair color or shoe size?

Explore

Help students differentiate between mindful behavior and its opposite, unmindful behavior. Share an example to contrast the two.

- A mindful approach to making friends would be getting to know someone before deciding whether to be friends. An unmindful approach would be deciding not to be friends because you dislike the person's taste in clothes.

- How do you think each approach would make you and the other person feel?

Read each example from the Mindful or Unmindful? sheet and have students vote thumbs up or thumbs down to indicate mindful or unmindful behavior. Let them explain their reasoning to a partner.

- Consider which examples show paying attention and thinking and acting in a nonjudgmental way.

As you review these examples, encourage students not to take a critical stance against unmindful behavior, but rather to see that recognizing our behavior as lacking in awareness is one way to initiate a change.

Why It's Important

Engage

Mindful awareness can be described as "focusing without judgment." Because this definition can get abstract, it's important to break down the meaning for students. Talking about mindful awareness in two parts (focusing attention and withholding judgment) is especially helpful for upper-elementary students who can handle the concepts but may need to absorb them in separate chunks.

Explore

Having students evaluate decisions they can relate to like the ones described on the activity sheet (e.g., helping someone with special needs or trying a new food for the first time) helps them begin to make connections with their own thoughts and behaviors.

From the Research

.Many of our core mental processes, such as awareness and attention and emotion regulation . . . should best be conceptualized as trainable skills.
(Lutz, Dunne, and Davidson, 2007)

Reflect

Invite students to think of a time when they really thought through a decision and made a mindful choice. Have a few volunteers share their decisions with the class.

Reassure students that all of us are occasionally unmindful, and that through practice—really thinking about what we're about to say or do—we can more often make mindful choices that will help ourselves and the people around us.

- We're going to do our best to be mindful, always thinking before we speak or act, but we're all learning this together and it will take some practice.

- When we notice unmindful behavior, we can gently and politely remind one another and ourselves to "use your PFC, please!"

Conclude this lesson by creating a class set of "I am mindful" statements to post to serve as a reminder of the mindful approach the class wants to take (see Creating the Optimistic Classroom box, page 36).

Encouraging students to evaluate memorable actions in their lives as mindful or unmindful behavior gives them useful examples to attach meaning to. Remind them that being unmindful does not mean we are bad people—but it probably means our amygdala is more in charge than our PFC. Reflecting on unmindful decisions simply gives us an opportunity to make ourselves and the people around us safer, healthier, and happier.

MINDUP In the Real World

Career Connection

At the first wail of an ambulance siren, an Emergency Medical Technician (EMT), often the first to arrive at the scene of an accident, is trained to remain calm and focus on what has happened and what immediate action is required. EMTs are typically dispatched to an emergency scene by a 911 operator and often work with police or fire departments. All EMTs must know how to assess an emergency, control bleeding, apply splints, assist with childbirth, administer oxygen, and perform CPR and other basic life-support skills. Mindfulness that enables quick, decisive thinking is the EMT's most essential skill.

Discuss: We always want to control our emotions and focus our attention while we're at work, but some jobs would not even be possible if not for our laser-like attention. What kind of transportation jobs might require mindful focused attention?

Once a Day

Share with students an observation about a mindful decision you or a student made in a demanding situation. Reflect on how your PFC may have guided the wise choice.

Connecting to the Curriculum

Learning about mindful behavior supports students' connection to their own learning process and to the content areas and literature.

Journal Writing

Encourage your students to reflect on what they've learned about being mindful and to record questions they may wish to explore at another time. In addition, they may enjoy responding to these prompts:

- Copy and illustrate one of the following statements about mindfulness:

  Being mindful is paying attention the best way I can.

  When I am being unmindful and not paying attention, I can make mistakes.

- Draw a cartoon or write about a specific time when you were mindful.
- Think of a time when you acted unmindfully. How could you have acted more mindfully? Draw a box and divide it in half. On one side, draw or write about the time when you were unmindful and on the other side, show how you could have changed the way you acted.
- Tell your family about our class discussion. Then ask an adult to share a time when they were mindful or unmindful. Record their story in words and pictures.

the Optimistic classroom™ journal

LANGUAGE ARTS

Vocabulary Demo

What to Do
A number of terms introduced in this lesson are useful academic words that students will hear repeatedly throughout the MindUP lessons: *mindful, unmindful, focus, attention,* and *reaction* are a few. Help students acquire these rich words by demonstrating them or having students act them out or draw them. For example, if students are unfamiliar with the term *focus,* you might use the focusing function on a projector to show an image both in and out of focus. Finally, you can help children create and decorate a MindUP word wall for the key terms associated with the program.

What to Say
The best way to get to know a word is to see it or act it out in a way that you can always remember. Now that you know what it means to be focused and unfocused, can you think of a way to show or draw those words so that we really get the difference?

Why It's Important
Keys to reinforcing vocabulary acquisition are to provide strong visual memories and to use the target word repeatedly in different contexts.

SOCIAL STUDIES

Mindful Role Models

What to Do
Demonstrate how to create a web-style graphic organizer with "Mindful People" in the center circle and several blank circles radiating from it. Have students brainstorm role models to add to these circles. Encourage them to choose people they know, as well as historical figures or current leaders who act in mindful ways. Then have them add to the web specific ways in which each person acts mindfully.

What to Say
Who are the people in your life, in the news, and from history who have made very mindful decisions? Perhaps they have provided food or medical assistance during an emergency, helped pass an important law, worked to protect wildlife, or simply been a great friend.

Why It's Important
Establishing role models for mindful behavior encourages students to strive to do their personal best.

SCIENCE/ART

Being Mindful for Our Earth

What to Do

Brainstorm with students things people do without thinking that harm the earth, air, and water (e.g., leaving the water running; holding the refrigerator door open; littering). Encourage students to find photographs in newspapers or on the Internet that show mindful activities that preserve and protect the environment (e.g., people planting trees; people putting trash and recyclable items in the appropriate containers in a park). They can then make collages with incorporated text or captions that convey a message about mindful behaviors.

What to Say

You are all able to list unmindful actions people take that hurt the environment. Let's be on the lookout for photographs of people doing mindful actions to conserve or improve the air, earth, and water, which are essential for our well-being. Use these images and your own words to create collages that create a message about mindful awareness of the world around us.

Why It's Important

Like the Mindful Role Models activity, this search for ways to put mindfulness in action for the greater good helps students place in a larger context the concepts they're learning.

SOCIAL-EMOTIONAL LEARNING

A Class Act

What to Do

Ask students to think of an activity they do at school that involves focusing with deep attention and helps them or others. Have students draw pictures of themselves doing their chosen task and write a caption on an index card. Post pictures and captions on a bulletin board.

What to Say

We can show what we're learning about mindful awareness by drawing a picture of an activity that calls for mindful thought and action. Let's brainstorm activities that we do alone or with others that take a lot of concentration and are helpful. Select an idea from our list or one of your own, illustrate it, and write a caption describing how that activity is mindful.

Why It's Important

Having students represent and share mindful actions helps them reflect on mindfulness in their own actions and in those of peers. Posting their drawings builds a sense of community effort toward mindful awareness.

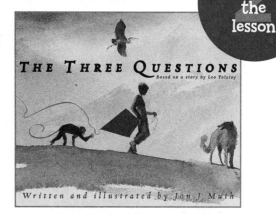

Literature Link
The Three Questions

by Jon J. Muth
(2002). New York: Scholastic.

Nikolai goes on a quest to find a way to be the best person he can be. By acting mindfully, he discovers his answer. Underscoring what he has learned, a wise old turtle advises him to pay close attention to the moment, his environment, and the needs of others.

Connect this subtle but powerful read-aloud to the work of the prefrontal cortex and amygdala, mindful awareness, and compassionate behavior.

More Books to Share

Mora, Pat. (1998). *This Big Sky.* New York: Scholastic.

Reynolds, Peter H. (2005). *So Few of Me.* Cambridge, MA: Candlewick Press.

Williams, Mary. (1996). *Cool Cats, Calm Kids.* San Luis Obispo, CA: Impact Publishers.

Focused Awareness: The Core Practice

What Is the Core Practice?

Pause. Listen. Breathe. It can take less than a minute to cue our minds to relax and focus. A short listening and breathing exercise introduced in this lesson—the Core Practice—helps students quiet their minds and get ready to learn

Why Practice Focused Awareness?

Designed to be used several times a day—especially during transitions when students need help settling down to work or shifting their attention between subjects or tasks—the MindUP Core Practice is the signature daily routine of the MindUP program. The Core Practice puts students in control of their mental and physical energy. By concentrating on the sensations of a resonant sound and then of their breathing, students calm their minds and get ready to focus on the next part of their day. For the individual student, the Core Practice supports self-regulation and mindful action. For the class community, the Core Practice becomes a time for setting the tone and getting everyone—teacher and students—to achieve a state of mind in which they can all participate purposefully and thoughtfully.

What Can You Expect to Observe?

"As my students practice concentrating on listening and breathing with the Core Practice, they notice that they are starting to learn how to pay attention better and calm themselves down when they feel stressed out. One of our class reminders is 'I can take control of myself.'"

—Fifth-grade teacher

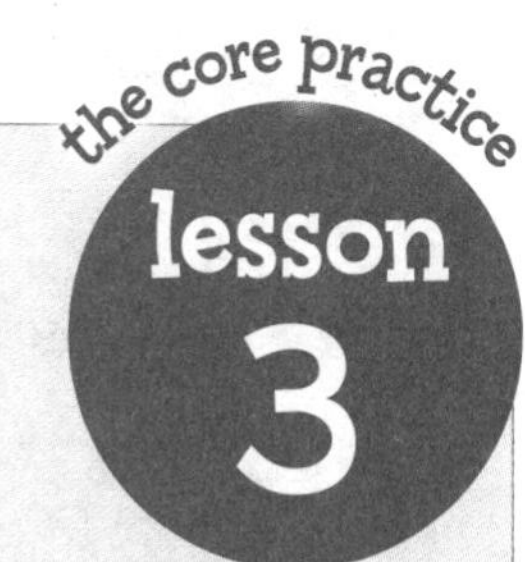

Linking to Brain Research

Controlling Our Breathing

Focusing on breathing helps calm the body by slowing heart rate, lowering blood pressure, and sharpening focus. Paying attention to breathing also supports strong functioning in the higher brain. Controlled breathing lessens anxiety by overriding the "fight, flight, or freeze" response set off by the amygdala and gives control to conscious thought, which takes place in the prefrontal cortex. When breathing is deliberately regulated, the brain is primed to think first and then plan a response, enabling mindful behavior.

Teaching students to focus on and control their breathing can help them become less reactive and more reflective when feeling anxious or stressed. The short daily activity of listening and breathing (Core Practice) introduced in this lesson capitalizes on neuroplasticity, the brain process that creates and strengthens nerve cell (neuron) connections through practice or repeated experience. One example of this growth occurs on the receiving end of the neurons involved in repeated thoughts and actions: Branch-like receptors called dendrites increase in number and size, enabling a more efficient passage of information along frequently used neural pathways. This is one of many ways in which the structure of the brain is flexible and ready to grow.

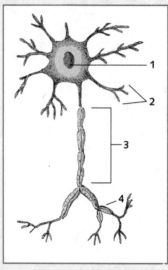

As students practice controlled breathing, their brains develop and reinforce the "habit" of responding to anxiety by focusing on breathing. This leads to reflective rather than reactive responses. The more controlled breathing is practiced, the more self-managed and mindful students can become.

Nerve cells, or neurons, carry messages through electrochemical impulses or signals. The cell body (soma) [1] houses the neuron's control center (nucleus). Dendrites [2] receive information from other neurons. The axon [3] relays the signal from the dendrites to [4] the nerve endings, which transmit the information to other neurons.

Clarify for the Class

Have students use their hand and forearm to show the parts of a neuron: The palm is the nucleus, the fingers are dendrites, the forearm is the axon, and several sticky flags attached at the elbow are the nerve endings. Show how the information moves from the dendrites through the axon and gets sent along to another neuron's dendrites (students can link up fingers to elbows to create an information path).

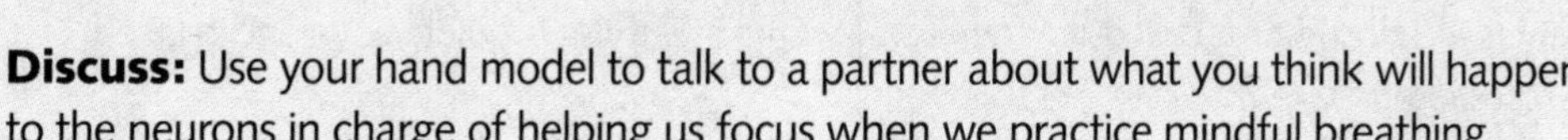

Discuss: Use your hand model to talk to a partner about what you think will happen to the neurons in charge of helping us focus when we practice mindful breathing.

Getting Ready

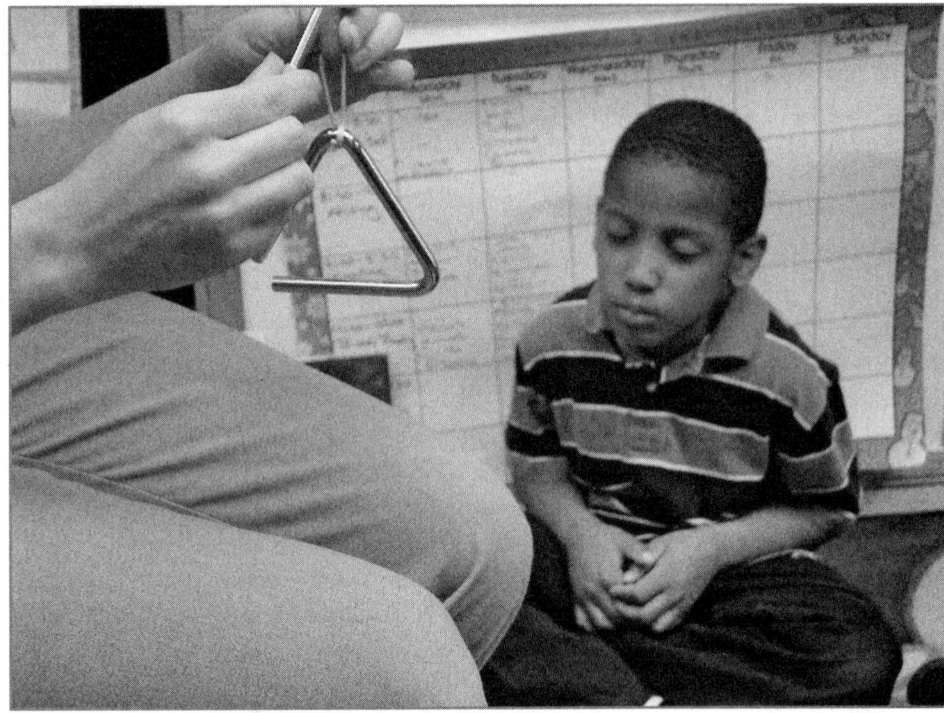

Resonant Sound!
Gently striking a resonant instrument creates the opening and closing note of the Core Practice.

GOALS

- Students learn an exercise that combines listening and breathing to calm and focus their minds.
- Students discover the importance of practicing focusing exercises regularly.

MATERIALS

- chart paper
- instrument that resonates with a clear, distinctive tone for 10–20 seconds (e.g., triangle, xylophone, chimes, piano, bell, violin)

CREATING THE OPTIMISTIC CLASSROOM

Classroom Management Set norms for mindful practices. Discuss what the Core Practice and other mindfulness exercises look and sound like when the class is doing them effectively. Elicit students' help in creating a simple T-chart like this one:

What Mindfulness Looks Like	What Mindfulness Sounds Like
We look comfortable.	Our voices are silent.
Our bodies are as still as they can be.	There are no loud noises in the room.
Our eyes are closed or focused downward.	Our breathing is quiet, slow, and relaxed.
Our faces look relaxed.	

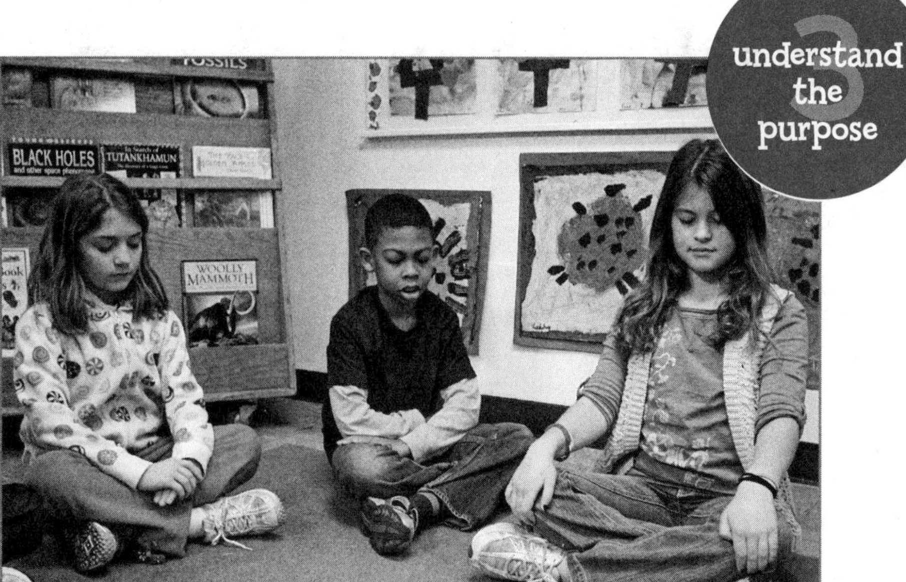

A One-Minute Investment
Students learn to center themselves during the Core Practice.

MINDUP Warm-Up

Remind students of the mindful exercise they practiced in Lesson 2, listening for all the sounds around them. Tell them that this time, they'll try to monitor their breathing in a way that helps their brain think more clearly. Using the following script, guide students through a simple breathing exercise:

- *Sit in a comfortable position. Close your eyes or look down.*
- *Pay close attention to your breathing. Feel air come in through your nose, then fill your chest and your belly. Calmly and slowly, let the breath leave your belly, then your chest, and finally your nose.*
- *Keep your shoulders dropped and relaxed. Think about the air coming into your body and the air going out.*
- *Bring your attention back to your breath, if your mind tries to think about other things.*
- *Notice your stomach rising and falling. Let your belly be soft and relaxed.*
- *Open your eyes slowly and take a slow, deep breath.*

Discuss: How did it feel to control your breathing? What did you notice? How did you keep your mind focused on breathing?

Leading the Lesson

Explore the Core Practice

Engage

What to Do

Play a note from the instrument you will be using for the Core Practice. Invite students to comment on the sound and encourage them to notice its resonance and duration. If time permits, allow each student to strike a note.

- This is a sound you'll become very familiar with—it will begin and end a daily exercise we'll be doing as a class. Let's practice listening to it closely for as long as it lasts.

Ask students to prepare themselves by

- sitting upright and comfortably at their desks, feet flat on the floor (or sitting in a circle on the floor, cross-legged)
- resting their hands comfortably in their laps.
- closing their eyes or looking down at their hands.

Ring the instrument. When the sound fades, have students open their eyes. Invite initial reactions. Repeat once or twice. Ask students to be conscious of their body (e.g., alert to any movements or tension) while they are listening.

Why It's Important

Once students have practiced with the same resonant sound several times, their brains will begin to connect that sound with quieting and concentrating their attention for a length of time. This resonant sound will become a signal for beginning and ending the Core Practice, so it is essential that you **use the same resonant instrument consistently.**

Explore

What to Do

Prepare students for combining mindful listening with mindful breathing to begin the Core Practice

- Now we will try both mindful listening and breathing together, and help our brains learn that this is the signal for our prefrontal cortex to take charge!

Explain the exercise.

- We start our Core Practice by sitting comfortably and closing our eyes or looking into our hands.
- When you hear the instrument, listen as long as you can.
- When the sound has faded, begin to focus on every breath as you take it in and let it out.
- When you hear the sound the second time, listen as long and as carefully as you can, still breathing calmly.
- When you can't hear the sound any longer, slowly open your eyes, but remain still and quiet.

Check that students understand the directions. Then play a note. Pause for at least 10 seconds after the sound has stopped, for mindful breathing. Play the note a second time, and observe as students open their eyes.

Why It's Important

Physical preparation supports mental focus. You may want students to sit in chairs with their feet flat on the ground or sit cross-legged on the floor with head "floating" above shoulders. Both positions encourage good posture, breathing, and circulation, and support visual distractions, especially making eye contact, during the exercise.

From the Research

Neuroimaging studies...have revealed that students' comfort level has critical impact on information transmission and storage in the brain. (Ashby, 1999)

Reflect

Guide students to share their experiences. Relate the Core Practice to the key parts of the brain.

- What do you think is happening right now in your brain?

Help students understand that although the activity may feel awkward at first, as they continue to practice, their brain will get better at it.

You might point out some challenges you have had while practicing, such as keeping your attention focused on your breathing without thinking of other things, focusing your listening on only the sound of the instrument, and/or staying still.

Announce to the class the scheduled times during the day that students will be encouraged to practice their new skill. Invite them to try controlled breathing on their own, as well.

- From now on, we'll do this Core Practice as a class three times a day every day. What are some other times when you might want to practice focusing on your breath to stay calm and make good decisions?

When students do the exercise in a mindful, focused way, they establish a precedent that they can follow—with practice, their bodies and minds will become comfortable and familiar with it.

For this reason, it is critical to keep a consistent schedule for leading the Core Practice and make sure that students are fully seated and silent before you begin.

MINDUP In the Real World

Career Connection

Listen, aim, focus, breathe, shoot. We can see that the core practice helps us every day no matter what we're doing. One profession that really depends on mindful breathing and listening is that of the wildlife photographer. We owe our most spectacular wildlife photography to the mindful steps the photographer follows before each shot. Sometimes enduring months in remote, challenging environments stalking an elusive animal like the snow leopard, the photographer must listen intently to know when the animal is near and breathe mindfully to assure a steady hand and an in-focus photograph snapped at exactly the right moment.

Discuss: Let's list at least three jobs that demand stillness and complete focused attention to be done well. What is about these jobs that requires this kind of work?

Once a Day

Do one minute of mindful breathing or listen to a piece of calming music just prior to a task or part of your day that demands your full concentration and focus.

Connecting to the Curriculum

Learning about focused awareness supports students' connection to their own learning process and to the content areas and literature.

Journal Writing

Encourage your students to reflect on what they've learned about the Core Practices and to record questions they may wish to explore at another time. In addition, they may enjoy responding to these prompts:

- Draw a before-and-after cartoon showing how you might look before and after mindful breathing.
- Choose a quiet place at home to breathe mindfully. Describe where that place is and what makes it a good place to practice.
- When might be the most helpful time for you to practice mindful breathing in school? Why?
- Make a schedule for mindful breathing during your day.

MATH & PHYSICAL EDUCATION

Taking Your Time Counts

What to Do

Have students perform a task that requires focus and balance or coordination, can be done in teams relay-race style, and can be timed at a very rushed pace and then at a slower pace. (For example, players might carry water by spoonfuls to fill their team's container a distance away. Each team is timed filling the container—or spilling—in a rushed round and then in a round that allows them to fill it at a slower pace.) Have students compare their times.

What to Say

What is your prediction about how well your team will do at this task going first as fast as you possibly can and then at a slower pace that helps you stay focused? Now that you've compared times, think about some things that you would rather not do in a rush.

Why It's Important

Nothing serves better as a healthy reminder to slow down and pay attention than a funny incident in which students are able to act out and contrast a mindful and an unmindful approach to the same task. Connect this learning back to the kind of effort needed for effectively practicing something students want to do well, like the Core Practices.

HEALTH & SCIENCE

The Facts About Healthy Lungs

What to Do

Encourage students to learn about lung function and about how to keep their lungs healthy. Organize four groups to research and report on parts of the respiratory system, how lungs work, breathing-related terms, and lung disease and its prevention. Gather articles and books, and bookmark online sources, that have high-interest, age-appropriate information about the respiratory system and lung health.

What to Say

Did you know that your lungs are more like air sponges than like balloons? You're going to work in groups to learn about how breathing, or respiration, works and how to keep your lungs healthy. When your group has some information to share, you'll discuss how to show what you've learned and share it with the class so we can all benefit.

Why It's Important

Encouraging students to research in groups allows them to better understand the information they gather or generate questions about it. It also allows you to group students of mixed levels or provide appropriately leveled materials for different groups.

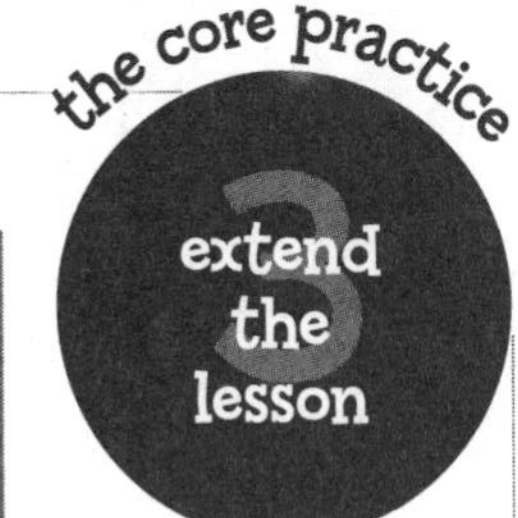

SCIENCE

Networking Neurons

What to Do
Review the key parts of a neuron (see page 43). Give each student a set of three or four different-colored craft (chenille) stems. As a class, assign each part of the neuron a different color and determine how to shape the stem and connect it to the other parts (e.g., fold one stem in half to represent the axon and thread it through a rolled-up stem representing the cell body). When the class has finished, ask groups to model how the neurons form a network, from one cell's nerve endings to the dendrites of another.

What to Say
In order for our brains to follow a repeated set of actions and behaviors, such as our Core Practice, nerve cells must connect and fire a series of signals, sending information in a web. Let's create a giant model of what a neural network might look like. First, let's use these colored stems to make a neuron with all its parts—cell body, dendrites, axon, nerve endings. How can we connect our models to create a neural network?

Why It's Important
Although a neural network is composed of millions of neurons, this model, which can be displayed on a wall, will serve as a helpful visual reference for students.

SOCIAL-EMOTIONAL LEARNING

Deep Belly Breathing

What to Do
Give each student a small object, such as a domino. Invite them to lie down on their backs and place the object on their belly. Guide them through mindful breathing by drawing attention to the object as it rises and falls with each breath they take.

What to Say
One great way to relax our bodies and minds is to lie on our backs and breathe deeply. Put your domino on your belly and focus on filling your belly with air. Watch your domino rise and fall as you inhale and exhale. See if you can make it ride the wave of your breath evenly, rising up for five slow counts and down for five slow counts. breathe through your nose if you can.

Why It's Important
This breathing exercise is a great tool for settling down after high-energy activities such as physical education or recess. It requires tremendous concentration to keep the domino moving at an even pace.

Literature Link
Ellie McDoodle: New Kid in School

by Ruth McNally Barshaw (2008). New York: Scholastic.

Ellie's lively sense of humor and her feelings about the challenges of being the new kid in school come across in this book told in notebook form. Handwritten text, line drawings, comic frames, and dialogue balloons together express Ellie's challenges and triumphs as she attempts to make new friends.

Encourage a discussion about patience and steady effort and see if students can make a connection between the character's thoughts and actions and the two control centers they've learned about. Ask: *When is Ellie more likely driven by her amygdala? by her PFC?*

More Books to Share

Schroeder, Alan. (1995). *Carolina Shout*. New York: Dial Books for Young Readers.

Stille, Darlene R. (1998). *Respiratory System*. New York: Scholastic.

Tolan, Stephanie S. (2006). *Listen!* Waterville, ME: Thorndike Press.

Sharpening Your Senses

By mindfully observing their senses, students will become adept at sharpening their attention and using sensory experiences to enhance memory, problem solving, relationships, creativity, and physical performance.

Expanding on Lessons 2 and 3, students practice honing their skills in focused listening by participating in an auditory awareness activity.

This lesson demonstrates and emphasizes the importance of paying close attention to detail, using visual memory.

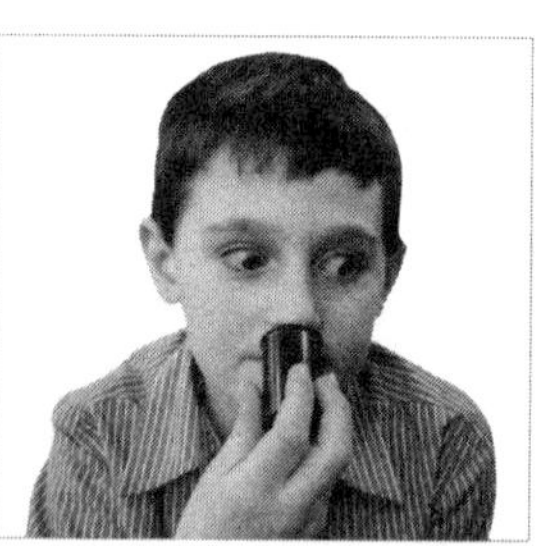

Students use their sense of smell to help focus their attention and gain access to key memories and feelings.

Slowing down to focus on the taste of food can completely change a routine activity and make it a mindful, healthy experience.

Comparing and contrasting excited and calm states of the body helps students make important connections between physical sensations and stress levels.

Students learn two balancing postures that foster awareness of how healthy movement practice can improve physical, emotional, and social well-being.

If you can detect a scent of basil as you walk by a restaurant or spot a contact lens that's dropped on a tile floor, your brain is well trained to zero in on important sensory details.

That same ability to notice important details and differentiate among all the scents, sounds, visual images, and other sensory details your brain receives can also help you respond more mindfully to people and events around you.

We know that each time students deliberately focus their attention, as they do in this unit's lessons, they activate their sensory data filter, the reticular activating system, and its pathways to the prefrontal cortex. This repeated stimulation makes the neural circuits stronger.

The practice of focused, mindful awareness enhances the ability of all young learners to direct their attention where it is needed.

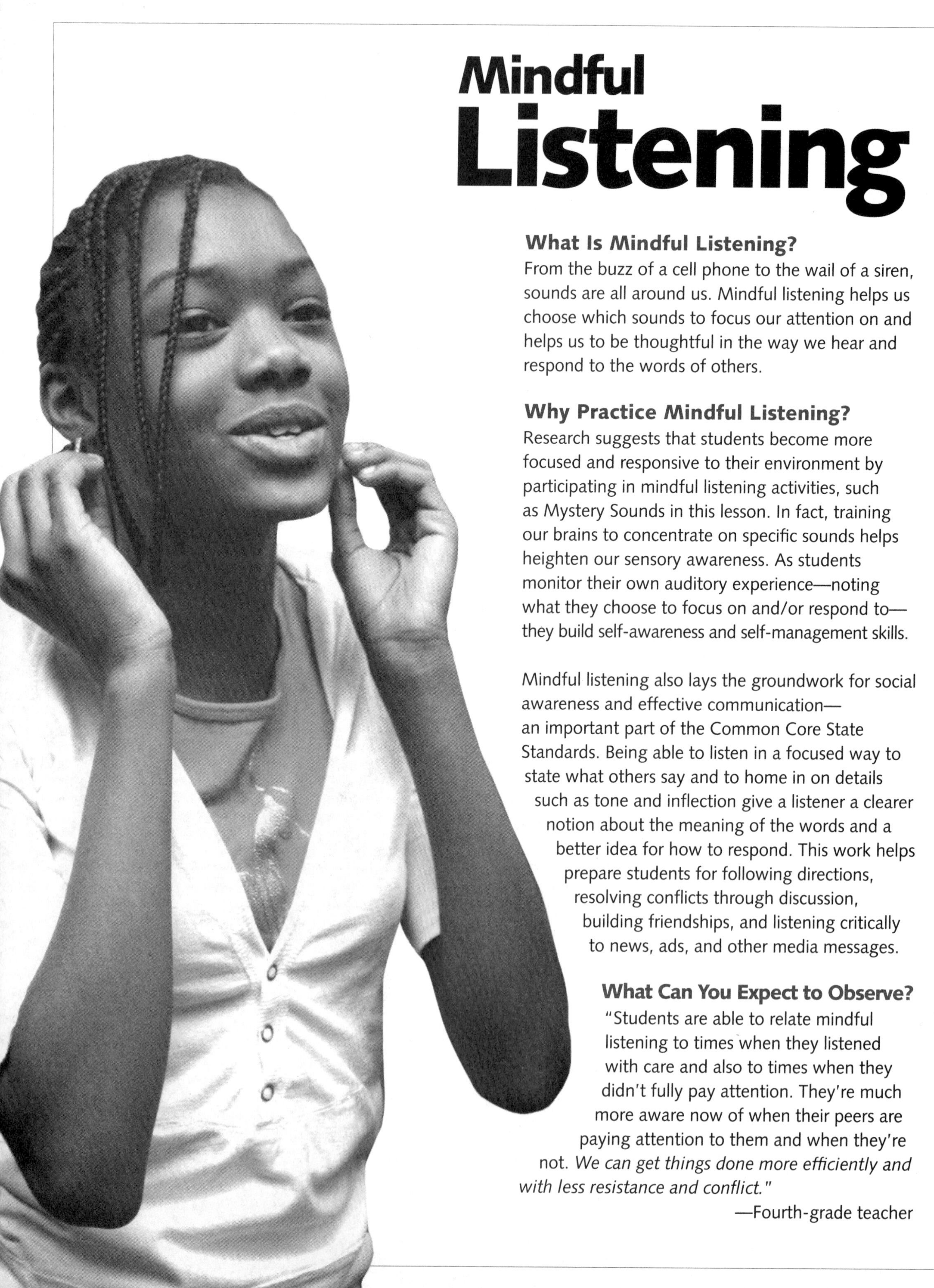

Mindful Listening

What Is Mindful Listening?

From the buzz of a cell phone to the wail of a siren, sounds are all around us. Mindful listening helps us choose which sounds to focus our attention on and helps us to be thoughtful in the way we hear and respond to the words of others.

Why Practice Mindful Listening?

Research suggests that students become more focused and responsive to their environment by participating in mindful listening activities, such as Mystery Sounds in this lesson. In fact, training our brains to concentrate on specific sounds helps heighten our sensory awareness. As students monitor their own auditory experience—noting what they choose to focus on and/or respond to—they build self-awareness and self-management skills.

Mindful listening also lays the groundwork for social awareness and effective communication—an important part of the Common Core State Standards. Being able to listen in a focused way to state what others say and to home in on details such as tone and inflection give a listener a clearer notion about the meaning of the words and a better idea for how to respond. This work helps prepare students for following directions, resolving conflicts through discussion, building friendships, and listening critically to news, ads, and other media messages.

What Can You Expect to Observe?

"Students are able to relate mindful listening to times when they listened with care and also to times when they didn't fully pay attention. They're much more aware now of when their peers are paying attention to them and when they're not. *We can get things done more efficiently and with less resistance and conflict.*"

—Fourth-grade teacher

Linking to Brain Research

What Is the RAS?

An intricate network of long nerve pathways lies within the core of the brain stem. This reticular formation, also called the reticular activating system (RAS), helps regulate many basic body functions and connects the brain stem to the prefrontal cortex (PFC) and other parts of the brain. The RAS is a mechanism for keeping the brain awake and alert and is the brain's attention-focusing center. Sensory stimuli (visual, auditory, tactile, olfactory, taste) continually arrive via the spinal cord and are sorted and screened by the RAS. The sensory input deemed relevant by the RAS is routed on to its appropriate destination in the conscious brain. What's irrelevant is blocked.

The RAS is critically important because the brain cannot process all the millions of bits of sensory information coming in at once! A student sitting in a classroom likely has competing sensory experiences, such as the voice of her teacher, a chilly blast from the ventilation system, the sight of a bird outside the window, and the aroma of food from the cafeteria. A mindful, focused student is able to redirect her attention to the task at hand, reassuring herself that lunch period will come after math.

Athletes, musicians, scholars, and other "focused" people have "trained" their RAS to choose the most pertinent sensory stimuli. With practice focusing on specific details, students can train their RAS to be more effective. Such practice is especially important for students who have trouble focusing their attention on their work, instructions, or social cues. Sensory awareness activities in this lesson and the others in this unit provide your students with repeated RAS-strengthening practice.

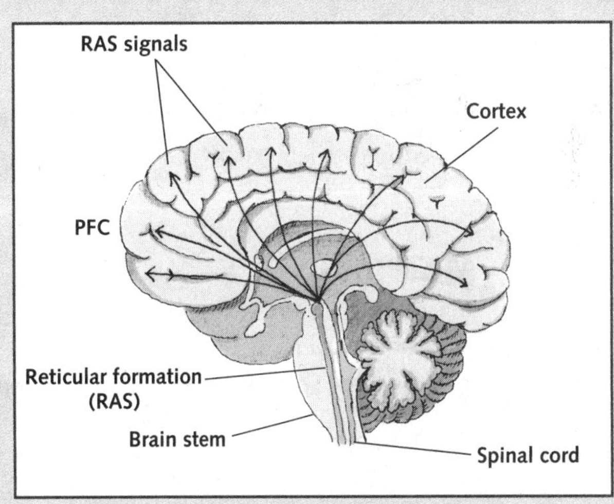

The RAS serves as an "executive personal secretary" to the PFC, forwarding on only what's immediately relevant.

Clarify for the Class

Make a model of the RAS using a kitchen strainer, sugar, and gravel. Demonstrate how a strainer works. Much like the RAS, it filters input, allowing only some things to pass through. Explain that the RAS holds back unimportant sensory experiences (the gravel) but lets important sensory information (sugar) pass on to the PFC.

Discuss: What information from your senses is your RAS allowing through right now? at lunch? during P.E. class?

Getting Ready

Listen Up!
Teacher and students sit on the floor to get started with the listening activity.

GOALS

- Students train their attention on specific sounds and try to identify those sounds.
- Students learn how mindful listening skills can help them communicate more successfully.

MATERIALS

- various common objects for creating sounds
- chart paper
- Mystery Sounds/Scents activity sheet (p. 154)

Mystery Sounds/Scents

CREATING THE OPTIMISTIC CLASSROOM

Classroom Management "I know I'm listening if I can repeat what you said exactly." When students need to resolve conflicts, encourage them to use mindful listening to help them stay focused on what their classmates are saying or feeling. Training students to repeat verbatim what the other person is saying before they respond helps them to concentrate on what that person is saying. This practice gives the listener a chance to calm down and to reflect on the situation. It supports all students, especially those who tend to react too quickly.

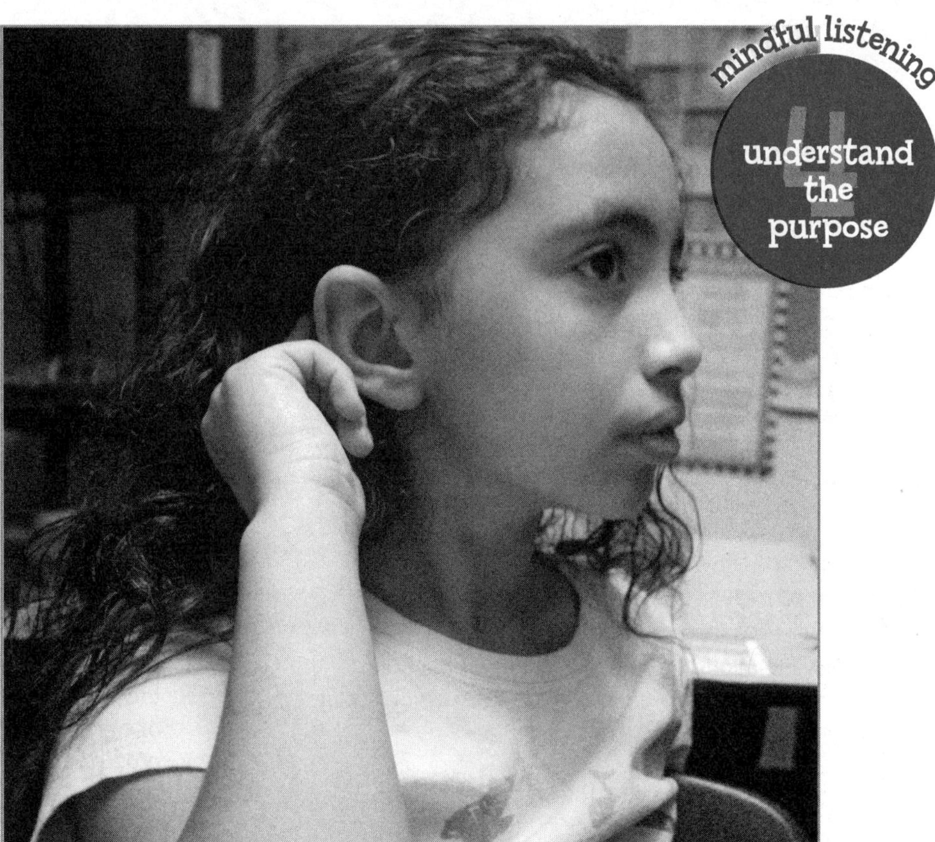

Did You Hear That?
This girl is listening as others demonstrate volume control with their voices.

MINDUP Warm-Up

Mindful Listening Practice

Build background for this lesson with an auditory exercise students will enjoy and relate to: practicing volume control with their voices. Have volunteers demonstrate how loud or soft their voices are for several different scenarios you give them, such as independent work/library time, group work time, stage performance, or outdoor recess. Emphasize that we can hear subtle differences among the voices for each setting because our ears are sensitive to very soft sounds, such as pins dropping, loud ones, such as jackhammers, and everything in between.

Now play the part of a conductor; close your hands together to indicate the softest sound students can sing and open them progressively wider to indicate that students should get louder, until your arms are fully extended. This should be the loudest they can get indoors. Have students test this range, singing "Ah" as you move your hands farther apart and closer together. If they have trouble modulating their volume, stop and have a few volunteers model successfully. Then try it again with the whole class. This should reinforce students' sensitivity to sounds and their ability to self-regulate.

Discuss: How might learning to self-regulate your voice be a useful strategy for getting along *and* doing well at school?

Leading the Lesson

Mystery Sounds

Engage

What to Do

Review mindfulness and the parts of the brain from Unit 1, as needed. Initiate a discussion about listening.

- Let's consider why listening is important—for school, for friendships & family, for pleasure (music) and for safety.
- Do you think listening is a skill or a talent? What might be the difference?
- When there's lots of noise around you, how do you pay attention to just one sound, like a friend's voice in the cafeteria? What are some times when you are able to eliminate distractions and focus on a single important sound?

Explain that together, the class will participate in an inquiry experience that will help students develop mindful listening.

Why It's Important

There are many sounds surrounding us most of the time. Usually we aren't mindful of every sound, because our brain helps us focus our attention by screening the sounds our ears pick up and bringing to our attention only the ones that are important. That filter in our brain is the Reticular Activating System (RAS). Listening mindfully can help us reinforce the work of the RAS.

Explore

What to Do

Ask kids to close their eyes and sit comfortably at their desks while you, or a chosen student, stand out of sight with several objects that can be used to produce recognizable sounds.

- Listen as mindfully as you can to the sound I make—and focus on it. If you think you know what it is, keep it to yourself. Record your answer on the Mystery Sound Activity Sheet.

One at a time, make each sound. Possible actions include:

tap a pencil
crumple paper
shake coins in a jar
shuffle cards
tear newsprint

Give students time to record their answers for each sound, using the Mystery Sound activity sheet. They may include specific descriptions of each sound and/or say what it made them think about.

Finally, reveal the identity of the sound-makers. (Students might enjoy the addition of a drum roll for effect!)

Why It's Important

By concentrating on specific sounds, you can train your RAS to listen very carefully. That strengthens the pathways to the prefrontal cortex.

You are more in control of your own thought processes if you are more aware of the constant sensory input that your brain experiences.

From the Research

Novelty, humor, and surprise in lessons expedite students' attention focus, and the use of these strategies results in more successful encoding of data into the memory circuits. (Willis, 2008)

Reflect

Initiate a class discussion. Make sure students understand that they were using brain energy to concentrate on each individual sound as they listened.

- In what ways is this experience different from the way we typically listen to sounds? If you lost your focus on the sounds, explain what you think got in the way.
- How might this kind of listening affect your brain? What areas of your brain did a lot of work during this exercise?

Record student responses on chart paper.

When you're really listening well, you get the information you need without being distracted. Then you can decide how best to respond.

mindful listening

4 connect to learning

MINDUP In the Real World

Career Connection

Is mindful listening ever a matter of life and death? Sometimes YES! Every day, doctors practice mindful listening on the job. Not only do they need to listen carefully to their patients' bodies—hearts, lungs, and abdomens—but also to the patients themselves. What brings the patient to the doctor? What symptoms is he or she experiencing? Doctors work hard to learn the skill of active listening. Once the patient's medical history is recorded, the doctor can ask informed questions and order the right tests that will lead to the correct diagnosis and effective treatment. In the hospital, mindful listening saves people's lives.

Discuss with students how this and other careers depend on mindful listening. Examples include 911 operators, customer service representatives, and guidance counselors.

Once a Day

Resist the urge to immediately answer a question from a student or colleague. Savor the time to reflect and develop a thoughtful response.

Connecting to the Curriculum

Mindful listening supports students' connection to their own learning process and to the content areas and literature.

Journal Writing

Encourage your kids to reflect on what they've learned about mindful listening and to record questions they may want to explore at another time. In addition, they may enjoy responding to these prompts:

- Make a list of ways you stay focused on listening in school and the strategies you use to put aside other thoughts you have on your mind.
- Choose a sound that you enjoy hearing. Write about or sketch the sound to express how you feel when you hear it.
- Compare and contrast sounds that you find relaxing with those you find unsettling. Then write about the difference between the kinds of sounds; a T-chart might be a useful tool.
- Think of a time when listening carefully to someone helped you avoid an accident or solve a problem. Consider illustrating the cause and effect of mindful listening.

SCIENCE

Experimenting With Sound

What to Do
Organize your students into small groups—or set up this activity as a center learning experience. Each group should line up eight empty glass bottles or glasses and fill them with different amounts of water, increasing the amount of water slightly with each successive vessel. Have students take turns lightly tapping the bottles with a chopstick and then blowing across the bottles.

What to Say
Let's take turns, one at a time, lightly tapping the bottles with our chopsticks. What do you notice when we move from left to right? We can also blow across the bottles and create new sounds. How are the two series of sounds different? (Teacher note: Students should hear low to high notes by blowing and the reverse by tapping.)

Why It's Important
The sounds are made by vibrations that move through the air. Our ears pick them up and our brain understands them as sound. Tapping a bottle causes the glass and water to vibrate. Less water means the vibrations are faster and the pitch higher; more water causes slower vibrations and a lower note. Invite volunteers to experiment with tapping, blowing, and listening to the various sounds.

ARTS

Mood Music

What to Do
Play instrumental music selections (classical, jazz, or Celtic work well) and invite students to listen mindfully and describe what they hear.

What to Say
Close your eyes and let's listen mindfully to these musical selections. Raise your hands when you detect a mood change in the music. Feel free to open your eyes to record your thoughts and impressions in your journal. What words—happy, sad, fierce, gentle—might you use to describe what you're hearing?

Why It's Important
Music helps us focus and practice mindful listening. Invite your students to select "happy music" and play it at times when the class needs a mood booster.

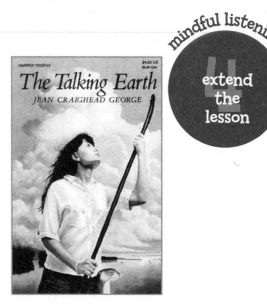

LANGUAGE ARTS
Listening Walk

What to Do
Take students on a mini-field trip on the school grounds. Then, while they either walk or sit quietly, encourage them to take detailed notes of the sounds they hear and record them in their journals. Return to class and invite volunteers to share their journal entries. Encourage them to think about how their work observing and recording might help them in their writing.

What to Say
Either walk quietly or find a cozy spot to sit comfortably. Close your eyes, and focus your attention on the sounds around you. What do you hear? What do you think might be making that sound? Open your eyes long enough to record each new sound you hear.

Why It's Important
Mindful listening helps us focus our attention and become aware of important things going on around us. Recording and sharing our mindful observations can give us rich and original material for writing.

SOCIAL-EMOTIONAL LEARNING
Whisper Words

What to Do
Have small groups of students try a version of the game Telephone. A short phrase is passed from one student to the next; the last person must say aloud the phrase he or she hears. Does it match the original?

What to Say
Arrange yourselves in a circle. I am going to whisper a short phrase to one student in each group. That person whispers the phrase to the student on his or her right. Keep going in this way, whispering exactly what you have heard. The last person finally says the phrase out loud. Does it match the phrase you started with? If not, why do you think this happened?

Why It's Important
Every brain hears things differently. Help students understand that careful communication often calls for repetition or other ways of expressing the same idea—and that calls for tolerance and creativity.

Literature Link
The Talking Earth

by Jean Craighead George (1983). New York: Scholastic.

Billy Wind is a Seminole girl who refuses to listen to her elders. She is sent into the Everglades, where she learns to listen and observe nature in order not only to survive danger but also to understand her heritage. If possible, read this book aloud to the class.

Connect this book to attentiveness, relating to friends, and understanding what another person is trying to communicate.

More Books to Share

Beech, Linda. (1995). *The Magic School Bus in the Haunted Museum: A Book About Sound.* New York: Scholastic.

Stafford, William. (1992). *The Animal That Drank Up Sound.* New York: Harcourt, Brace, Jovanovich.

Katz, Bobbi. (2001). *Rumpus of Rhymes: A Noisy Book of Poems.* New York: Dutton Children's Books.

Mindful Seeing

What Is Mindful Seeing?

Crimson or ruby? Ovoid or oblong? Smile or smirk? Our ability to visually distinguish details has given rise to a rich and precise descriptive vocabulary. Mindful seeing enables us to better observe ourselves, other people, and our surroundings to more fully enjoy and learn from them.

Why Practice Mindful Seeing?

As with mindful listening, mindful seeing helps students sharpen their focus by calling on one sense to very purposefully observe an object. This lesson takes advantage of students' natural visual curiosity about people and things in their environment—and their desire to share their observations.

As students practice mindful seeing exercises, they become increasingly attuned to observing details by slowing down and focusing their attention. We can build on these skills of observation by encouraging students to apply their curiosity and perceptiveness to their academic work. In fact, sharpening visual discrimination skills can help improve skills critical in almost any subject area, whether students are recognizing nuances in word structure or identifying relationships between numbers in a sequence. And in the area of social-emotional learning, these skills can be tied to reading social cues and acting perceptively in response to the facial expressions and body language of others.

What Can You Expect to Observe?

"Mindful seeing activities make students look more closely. Students are always surprised by the details they didn't notice at first glance—or details only they have noticed. That puts them in the role of 'mindful detective.' They like that term so much, I use it whenever academic work calls for visual discrimination skills."

—Third-grade teacher

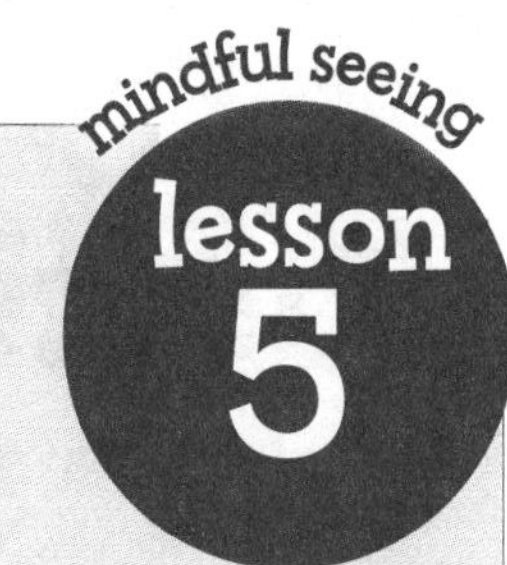

Linking to Brain Research

Emotions Shape Behavior and Learning

The amygdala, that reactive watchdog of the brain, elicits the same fear response for perceived danger as for genuine danger. The behavior of a child who feels unsafe, threatened, inadequate, judged, or vulnerable to ridicule is driven by his or her brain's reaction to threat. Children who feel continually "on alert" are unable to engage in mindful behavior because their amygdala blocks incoming stimuli from reaching the rational prefrontal cortex.

The brain gives priority to emotions because they matter. Emotions are associated with the places and people in children's lives. Children who learn to associate school with a feeling of safety become confident enough to move out of their comfort zone. They feel safe expressing their ideas, working together, asking questions, and trying new things—even if it means making mistakes. You might say they train their amygdala to remain calm, keeping the information pathways to their higher brain open. And the more a child feels safe at school, the stronger those neural pathways become. The chains of neurons that result in a feeling of safety become more efficient, passing the message along faster.

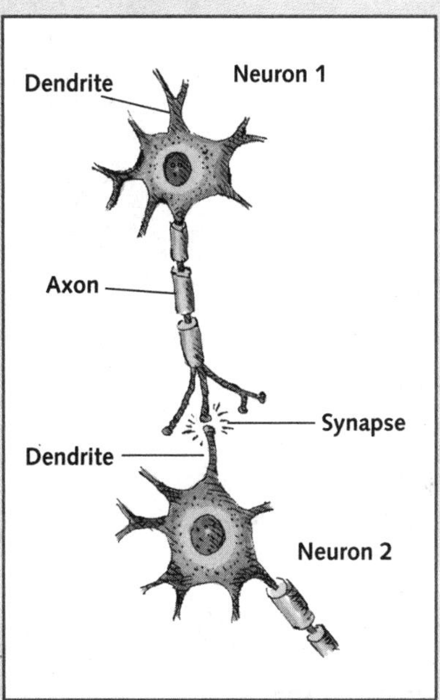

Neurons connect axon to dendrite, passing messages along via gap-jumping electrochemical exchanges called synapses.

Clarify for the Class

Use a relay race to model how neural pathways get faster and stronger with use and repetition. Review the parts of a nerve cell (see page 43) as you explain how everyone is going to represent a neuron: left hands are dendrites and receive messages; torsos are the cell bodies; right arms are message-shuttling axons; right hands are the nerve endings and transfer messages to the dendrites of the next neuron (left hand). Create two teams and choose a "message" for each to pass, such as a coin, eraser, bottle cap, or similar small item. At "GO," the first in each lined-up chain of "neurons" passes the message from its nerve endings (right hand) to the dendrites (left hand) of the adjacent "neuron," who passes it along to its nerve endings (right hand) and so o until the message reaches the final neuron.

Discuss: Which message traveled faster? Would the messages move more quickly with practice? How is that like what happens in the brain?

Getting Ready

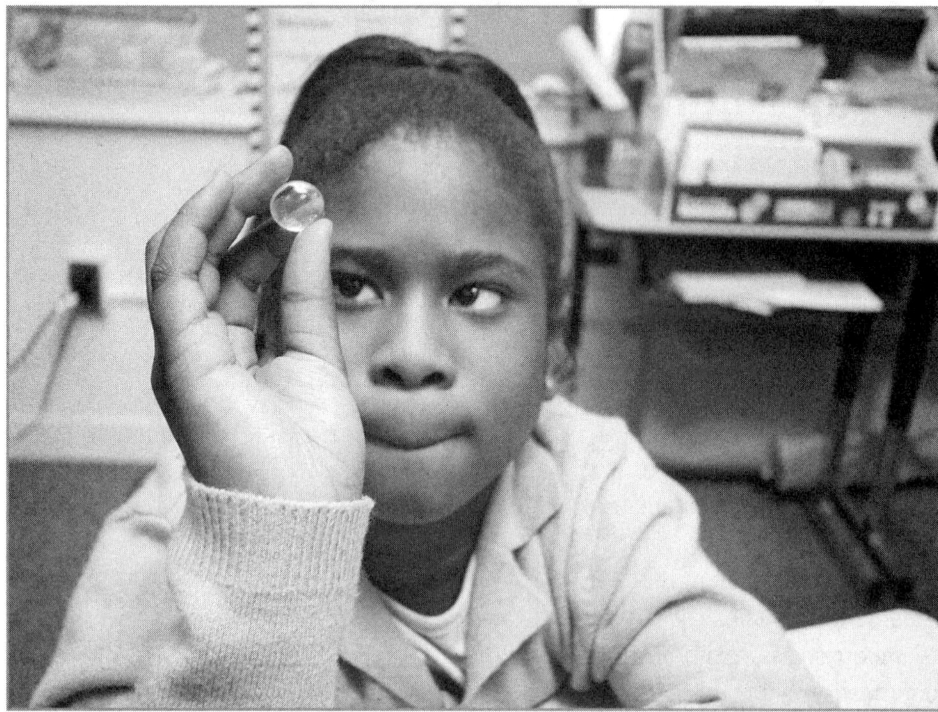

Looking Closely
A student examines her glass bead specimen, taking notes.

GOALS

- Students practice focusing their attention on an object and describe the visual details they observe.
- Students strengthen their visual vocabulary and memory through mindful seeing.

MATERIALS

- a class set of the same object for students to examine (coins, unsharpened pencils, glass beads, or any other objects that have the same general features but that, upon close inspection, have noticeable distinguishing details)
- (optional) Sensory Web activity sheet (p. 155)

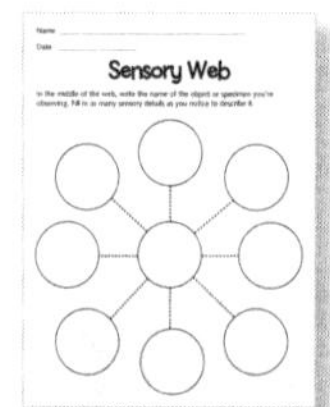

CREATING THE OPTIMISTIC CLASSROOM

Supporting English Language Learners Making second-language learners feel welcome and safe to participate among fluent English speakers is critical to helping them prime their brains for learning. One effective tool is a Word Experts bulletin board where students can post words they are curious about. After a student posts a new word, invite the class to post the same word in other languages. Sometimes students may be able to discover similarities in word structure between the English word and words from other languages, particularly from Romance and Germanic languages. Make online language dictionaries available and show students how to use them to translate to and from English.

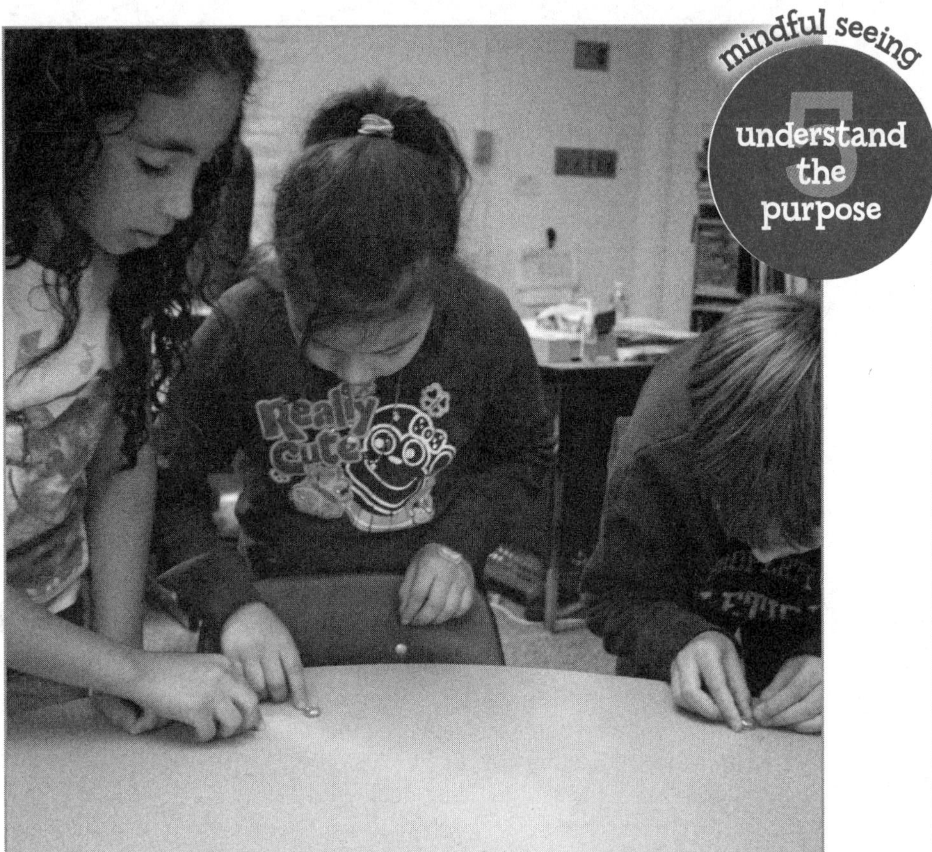

This Might Be the One!
A group compares their specimens, working to locate their original object.

MINDUP Warm-Up

Describing What We See

Help students expand their vocabulary to describe the things they notice accurately and precisely. Find art posters or display images from online sites that use color, line, texture, shape, and other key visual elements very differently (e.g., prints of a portrait by van Gogh and a dancing figure by Keith Haring).

Ask students how each artist described his or her subject. Guide them to compare different uses of color (bright or dark, bold or soft, primary or secondary, most noticeable colors), line quality (solid, fragmented, straight, thick, thin, curvy, angular), shapes (soft- or hard-edged, distinct or blurry, two- or three-dimensional), and sizes of objects. Record on chart paper the descriptive words students have generated, then post them. Add to the list new words students generate while working with other mindful seeing exercises.

Discuss: When we describe things we've looked at closely, like these paintings, we want to be able to use just the right words to explain details we think are important. These two painters painted people, but they did it in very different ways. What are some words could we use to show some of these differences in a very clear way?

Leading the Lesson

Specimen Sort

Engage

What to Do

Review the three parts of the brain students learned about in Unit I. Then remind students of the terms generated from their warm-up exercise and connect accurate description to mindful seeing. Introduce the concept of a specimen and set the lesson goal.

- We won't use descriptive terms like these just when we're talking about art; we'll use them anytime we look at something very mindfully—for recording our observations in science, for example.
- The objects that scientists study—such as ancient bones for archaeologists and unusual leaves for botanists—are called *specimens*. Who remembers a time when you've looked very closely at something, like a scientist who is determined to find something he or she has never seen before?
- Today you're going to examine some specimens so closely that each of you will be able to pick out the one you've studied from a group of specimens that look almost exactly the same.

Why It's Important

The quest to discover something new is a great way to motivate students and establish a curiousity-based mind-set. Setting students in the role of scientist helps to provide them with a real-world context for mindful seeing. This also builds a foundational skill in science and can be repeated or recalled any time you plan to teach a lesson or plan an experiment that requires visual observation.

Explore

What to Do

Organize students in groups of five or six. (The more students in the group, the more challenging the activity is.) Distribute the specimens.

- When you get your specimen, be very quiet and focus all of your attention on it. Let your RAS gather all the images it can and let your PFC note every little detail.

Ask students to hold the specimen in the palm of their hand and look at it from all sides. Prompt them to notice color, shape, and size, and to notice any imperfections or unique details. Make sure they have at least a minute of complete silence with their specimen. (Depending on the sophistication of your students, you may also want them to take notes or use the Sensory Web activity sheet to describe the visual features they notice.)

For each group, gather the specimens in a box, mix them up, hand the box back to the group and invite students to find their original specimen by comparing and contrasting those in the set.

Why It's Important

Using prompts can guide students to notice important details they may not have registered otherwise. This is a useful activity to repeat, especially if students don't notice many details the first time—as with other mindful awareness activities, building visual observation skills takes practice.

From the Research

The human brain never stops adapting to its environment in a quest to formulate what the mind perceives based on what the eyes see. (Vanderbilt University, 2010)

Reflect

Have groups share features that helped them sort their specimens. Discuss their focused attention and how that helped them notice those details.

- What were the important details that helped you decide which specimen belonged to you and which ones were definitely not yours?
- How was this kind of seeing different from the way we usually see things?

Compare this to the mindful listening activity.

- How was mindful seeing with your specimens similar to mindful listening to the mystery sounds? Which was easier for you?

Have students consider how mindful seeing helps them (or could help them) in different situations.

- Think about how mindful seeing might help you in an emergency, such as a fire. How could mindful seeing help you enjoy hobbies or sports more?

Suggest to students that they consider how they can benefit from mindful seeing in daily life. You may need to help them generate ideas, including using examples from your experience (e.g., finding the correct position of a puzzle piece in a jigsaw puzzle or creating a crossword pattern by organizing a set of spelling words to intersect at common letters).

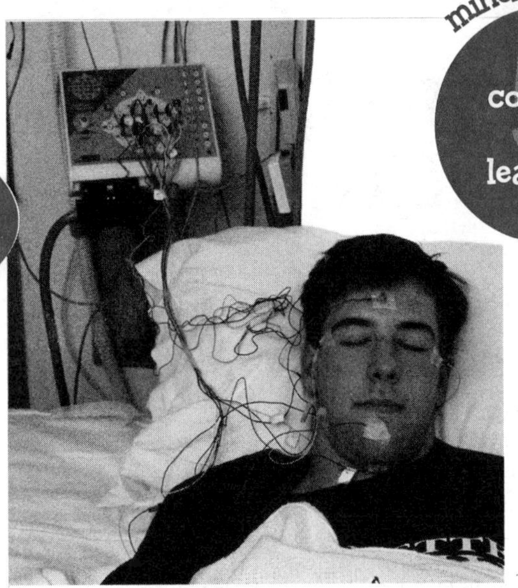

MINDUP In the Real World

Career Connection

What do waves have to do with sleep? If you're a sleep technologist—everything! By monitoring instruments that measure a sleeping patient's brain, eye movements, muscle activity, and heart rhythm, the technologist charts sleep stages and identifies problems that may affect a person's sleep. Technologists receive input from 12 different channels and 22 wire attachments to the patient. While keeping an eye on the patients to make sure they are safe, technologists must also continuously monitor an array of electronic equipment. Only an experienced technologist can read and interpret the wave patterns that flow across the computer screen.

Discuss: What other professions depend on sharply focused visual attention? Think about jobs that require having to watch people, events, or things very closely.

Once a Day

Choose two similar assignments to scrutinize, such as writing samples done several days apart. Use mindful seeing to observe areas of growth. Review with students what you've noticed so they can build on these improvements.

Connecting to the Curriculum

Mindful seeing supports students' connection to th[e]ir own learning process and to the content areas and literature.

Journal Writing

Encourage your students to reflect on what they've learned about mindful seeing and to record questions they may want to explore at another time. In addition, they may enjoy responding to these prompts:

- Find a welcoming spot in your classroom, school, or home. Take one minute to quietly and mindfully look at the space. For the next minute, list as many details as you can about your chosen spot.
- Think about a favorite article of clothing. Draw a picture of it, labeling each detail that makes it visually appealing to you.
- Choose a favorite classroom item. Study it and describe every aspect of the way it looks. Also note its color, size, shape, and location.
- Make a T-chart labeled "Morning" and "Afternoon." Mindfully observe the scene from a window in your classroom or the hallway: In the morning, observe the space for several minutes and note in the first column what went on there and how it looked. In the afternoon, observe again and put a check in column two alongside details that stayed the same. For details that changed, note the differences you see.

SCIENCE

To See a Leaf

What to Do

Gather a collection of leaves and distribute one to each student. Provide magnifying glasses if possible. Guide children to look mindfully at their leaf from every direction and then draw the leaf, including as many details as they can. In pairs, have students take turns describing their leaf clearly from memory. Then let them reveal their leaf to their partner, find the details each partner mentioned, and add any new details to their drawing. Encourage students to also find out what kind of tree the leaf is from.

What to Say

Compare your leaf to your partner's leaf. Note the details that are alike and those that are different. Did you notice more details of your own leaf when you compared it with your partner's? Go back to your drawing and include any new details you hadn't observed the first time.

Why It's Important

Making the process of mindful seeing one that invites repeated attempts at observation teaches students that careful study can be improved by collaboration (sharing with peers new ways of seeing), by looking closely more than once, and by revising the notes and drawings they've recorded. This exercise also ties in with the careful observation used in scientific investigations and research.

MATH

"Squareflake" Symmetry

What to Do

Provide directions for folding a square piece of paper into triangles (fold on the diagonal, then twice more) and cutting to make positive and negative spaces. Have students open their "squareflakes" and with a partner, observe the lines of symmetry and the symmetrical patterns. Display the squareflakes and discuss similarities and differences among them.

What to Say

As you observe your squareflakes, first notice the shapes you created by cutting along the line of symmetry. You may want to refold and open the paper to observe the mirror images along the fold lines. Count the number of lines of symmetry. How many more can you create if you fold the flake again to make new shapes?

Why It's Important

Creating a model that can be compared and contrasted with other models, then changed to test out a prediction, is an exciting way to learn. Discoveries are absorbed quickly, processed by the PFC, and stored by the hippocampus.

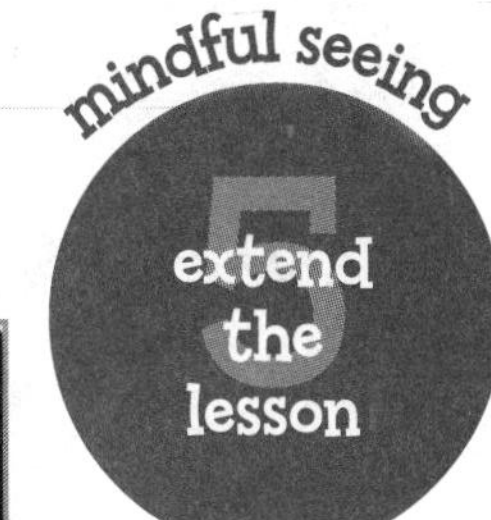

LANGUAGE ARTS

Simile Poems

What to Do
Introduce (or review) the term *simile*. Have students compose a haiku or free-verse poem that describes their object by comparing it to other things with similar qualities. To help students gather ideas, suggest that they pick two or three aspects of the object to describe using similes. Model how to get started by generating ideas for your own object in a think-aloud.

What to Say
Here are some of the similes I've been thinking of that will help paint a picture in my reader's mind about the shell I've mindfully observed: my shell is as small as a baby's fist, its black stripes look like braids, its inside peeks out like pink satin slippers, and its pointy tip twirls like a winding staircase. With your help, I'm going to write those out, choose an order for the lines, and add a title. Now, let's reread it and see if we want to revise anything.

Why It's Important
Modeling what you want helps students experience the task or skill through example. That reassures the amygdala that no nerve-racking event is about to unfold and activates special nerve cells called mirror neurons that help us replicate the actions of others—so we are primed to learn by example.

SOCIAL-EMOTIONAL LEARNING

Fingerprint Findings

What to Do
Show students how to gather fingerprints by rubbing their fingertips over a pencil tip, then lifting the print with transparent tape. (Have them tape their print to a blank index card and write their initials on the back.) Discuss the patterns students observe. Have groups of five or six sort their prints into several common patterns, then find the uniqueness of each print.

What to Say
Though each of us has a unique fingerprint, our prints also contain patterns—such as loops, swirls, and arches. As you examine your prints together, look within your group for prints that share a pattern. Now take a second careful look at the pattern group to find the unique features of each.

Why It's Important
Understanding that we can uncover both similarities and unique qualities when we look closely at ourselves and at one another goes more than skin deep. Use this exercise as a reference point for both discovering commonalities and celebrating individual qualities.

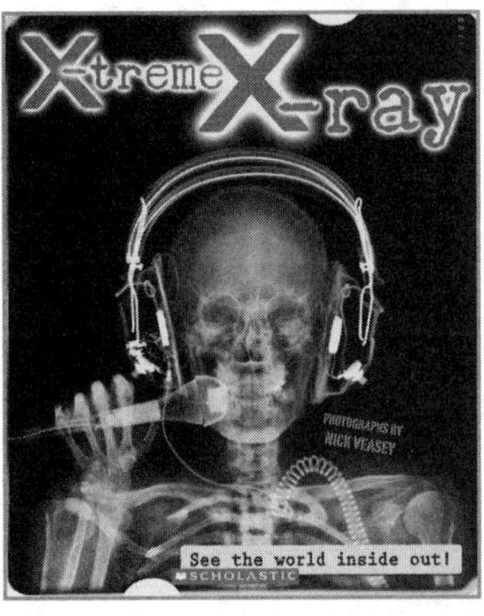

Literature Link
X-treme X-ray: See the World Inside Out!

by Nick Veasey
(2010). New York: Scholastic.

Take students on a visual tour…behind walls, inside objects, and even through skin! Each page features an X-ray photo of a person or object in nature, sports, or technology with engaging descriptions and facts about the images, and a brief explanation of how X-rays work.

Connect this book to a science lesson on X-ray imaging or to seeing "beneath the surface"—mindfully examining other people around us to get a bigger, fuller picture of who they are.

More Books to Share

Baumbusch, Brigitte. (1999). *Animals observed.* New York: Stewart, Tabori & Chang.

Chic, Suzy and Monique Touvay. (2007). *Watching.* Tunbridge Wells, UK: Winged Chariot.

Weiss, Ellen (2009). *The Sense of Sight.* New York: Scholastic

Mindful Smelling

What Is Mindful Smelling?

Just by catching a whiff of a familiar scent, our brain can call to mind the people, places, or things we associate with it. Mindful smelling—using our sense of smell to be more aware of our environment—can help us to keenly observe our world and sharpen our memory.

Why Practice Mindful Smelling?

Practicing focused awareness with a new sense, smell, continues to broaden students' ability to observe and enjoy their experiences. As they slow down to study and take notes on several distinct aromas during this lesson, students practice taking in new information without jumping too quickly to judgment—deciding, for example, that a smell is "gross" without further consideration.

By prompting them to stay with their observations, we give students an opportunity to be fully engaged in what they're doing and to reflect on their experiences, which bolsters their sense of self-awareness and self-control. In this lesson, students also discover how memories and important information can be attached to and triggered by smells, because the smell and memory centers in the brain are close to each other, providing another tool for learning new material as well as recognizing and regulating emotional responses that may be triggered by a sense memory.

What Can You Expect to Observe?

"Figuring out how our brains link memories of our experiences through our senses really intrigues students. We've actually begun to work together to use more sensory details in our writing and even create sensory tools for remembering important information for tests."

—Fifth-grade teacher

Linking to Brain Research

Dopamine: The Chemistry of Pleasure and Reward

Our brains have more than four dozen types of neurotransmitters, chemicals that allow signals to pass between neurons. One of these neurotransmitters, dopamine, plays a role in producing and regulating positive feelings such as pleasure, hopefulness, optimism, and keen interest. When we have sufficient levels of this "feel-good" neurotransmitter in our brain, we are more able to maintain motivation, delay gratification, and feel rewarded and content. As levels of dopamine in the brain change, so does our outlook on life.

Dopamine release is triggered during pleasure-inducing experiences including smelling and eating a favorite food, seeing friends, enjoying sports, solving a puzzle, and accomplishing a task. Studies show that students who learn at a young age to connect the "feel-good" times with positive behaviors are better able to access the self-soothing, internal reward system that comes as standard equipment in every human brain. As those students mature, they are less likely to seek the dopamine surges that come with high-risk behaviors like drugs, alcohol, promiscuity, reckless driving, and overeating. In fact, young people who consistently feel pleasure and reward during sports, music, theater, dance, art, social interaction, and positive classroom experiences are not as likely to be involved in risky behaviors.

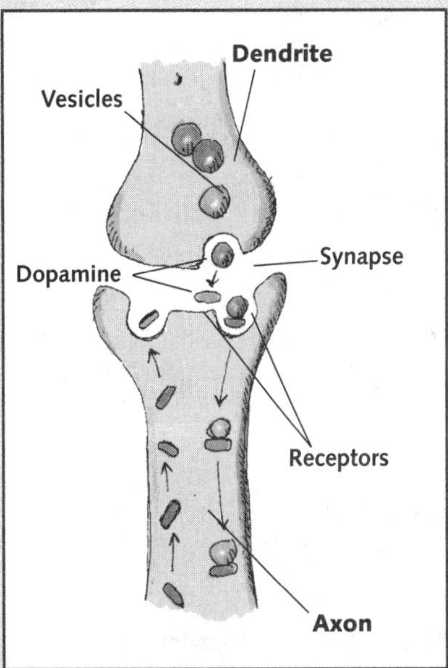

When a dopamine release is triggered, vesicles in the dendrites empty their dopamine and receptors in the axon of the receiving cell are activated to pass the message forward, across the synapse.

Clarify for the Class

Learning is much harder when we feel unmotivated, negative, and hopeless. Explain that the chemical messenger dopamine affects the brain's ability to create the positive feelings necessary to concentrate, pay attention, remember, and keep trying. We can help our brains release dopamine and create positive feelings with activities that give us pleasure and a feeling of accomplishment. Some examples are going for a walk, painting a picture, or playing a game. Sports, music, art, talking to friends, and participating in class are all good ways to feel your best.

Discuss: What are some activities you find both enjoyable and rewarding? Can you give an example of a time when you felt better after doing one of these activities? What do you think was going on in your brain before and after?

Getting Ready

Olfactory Observations
These film canisters with holes punched in their lids provide an easy way to observe scent specimens and to avoid spills.

GOALS

- Students focus their attention through their sense of smell and describe observations.
- Students identify thoughts and feelings triggered by various scents.

MATERIALS

- chart paper
- four sets of small opaque containers with lids (e.g., film canisters)
- at least four familiar scents (e.g., coffee beans, vinegar, lemon juice, vanilla, cinnamon, baby powder, dried bacon bits, peppermint) (NOTE: Check first for food allergies!)
- scratch paper or Mystery Sounds/Scents activity sheet (p. 154)

PREPARATION TIP

- Place the scent samples in containers (for liquid scents, use saturated cotton balls). Label each container on the bottom. Create a reference key.

CREATING THE OPTIMISTIC CLASSROOM

Brain-Inspired Instruction Consider how your daily routines and lesson support students in developing the ability to delay immediate gratification. Plan activities that are intrinsically rewarding and extend learning over a period of time, such as

- chart results of a science project over time (e.g., plant growth)
- build a class mural or other project over several class periods
- pose problems that require at least two periods to work through.

Each time they work on a challenging task or project, have students reflect on how it feels to persevere and work in a focused way to achieve their goals.

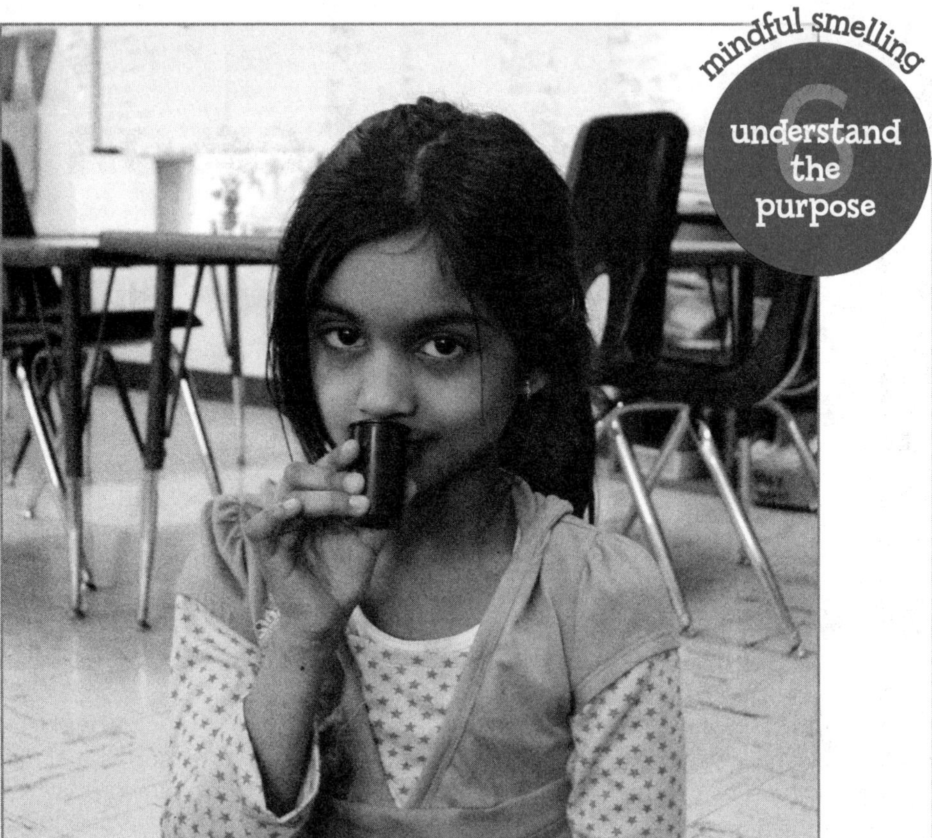

Curious Scents
Students pass the scent canister, mindfully observing what they sense.

MINDUP Warm-Up

Scent Associations Practice

Help students understand that their brain uses the sense of smell to tag experiences. Invite students to sketch pictures or print free images from the Internet that show places they go regularly, such as a laundromat, a fast-food restaurant, a gas station, the school cafeteria, or a park. Choose several popular examples to let the group consider. For each, ask, "What scents come to mind when you think of this place?"

As with mindful seeing exercises, encourage students to use descriptions that give a clear sense of the place, not just an opinion (e.g., "disgusting" or "amazing"). To help them precisely describe specific smells, ask them to connect smells with food or other objects found in the place (e.g., cocoa powder, freshly cut grass, frying onions) and make a list on chart paper of descriptive terms they volunteer (or you introduce), such as *sweet, strong, fresh, mild, pungent, aromatic, rotten, minty, fruity, spicy, sour, flowery, fishy,* and *moldy.*

Discuss: Think of your favorite special meal. How does your brain use what you smell to help make a meal memorable? Can you think of a way our sense of smell could help us remember information we need to know in class?

Leading the Lesson

Common Scents

Engage

What to Do

Build background for the lesson by making connections to previous mindful sensing exercises.

Point out how much sensory information is available for students to focus on through their sense of smell alone. Have them take a moment to close their eyes and smell the area around their desk. Note that even the most commonplace objects, such as sharpened pencils and hand soap, give off scents that are part of our environment. You may want to refer to the scent descriptions chart from the warm-up activity as students describe the scents or add to the chart as they offer new descriptions.

- Let's get our minds alert to all the scents around us before we focus in on single scent specimens.
- Freshly sharpened pencils are one scent I often notice in our room. What are some other things around you that have noticeable scents?

Why It's Important

As with mindful listening and seeing exercises, concentrating on using a single sense to identify details helps students prime their RAS to gather lots of information from their environments that they might not otherwise have noticed. Taking an account of the smells around them gets them focused on taking cues from their nose—signals they may not be used to noticing.

Explore

What to Do

Organize the class into four groups and explain the procedure: You will give the same scent to each group. Students will pass the container around, allowing each group member at least ten seconds to smell it (you may want to give a signal when it's time to pass the container). Set expectations that while this should be an enjoyable experience, it should also be a silent, focused one.

When everyone has had a chance to smell the first scent, use these prompts to help students take notes on scratch paper or record their ideas on the Mystery Sound/Scent activity sheet.

- What person, place, or thing does this scent make you think about?
- What words best describe this scent?
- What do you think the scent is?

As students take notes, prepare the second set of scent containers.

Follow the same procedure for each set of scents.

Why It's Important

Setting clear expectations for behavior helps students handle the novelty of smelling unnamed scents in a way that sustains their concentration. Be specific in your request that the smelling exercise be done without words or sounds, inappropriate gestures, or exaggerated facial expressions, and that students keep their responses "secret" until the discussion.

From the Research
Any pleasurable activity used even as a brief break can give the amygdala a chance to "cool down" and the neurotransmitters time to rebuild as the students are refreshed.
(Kato & McEwen, 2003)

Reflect

Circulate each scent sample again as you invite students to share the notes they took about the scent. Have them compare this mindful smelling exercise to the way they associated scents with a picture of a familiar place in the warm-up to this activity.

- In the warm-up activity, you described scents that you connect with a place you know well. How was this exercise different? Which activity was more challenging? Why do you think that is?
- Which part of the brain stores our scent memories? Can you think of how animals and humans might use scent memories to live in their surroundings?

Help students see mindful smelling as a focusing tool.

- Sometimes our amygdala is on alert and thoughts in our brain may be racing, even though we're not in danger. What are some times during the day when you might pause, close your eyes, and take a moment to smell mindfully to calm and focus yourselves?

Most students will find it more challenging to identify scent and then link it to a memory than to start with a place and naming a scent they associate with it. Remind students that the scent specimens were not necessarily significant for them and also that we have to build our vocabulary to put words to some of the scents we can smell.

MINDUP In the Real World

Career Connection

Do you have a nose for rocks? If you have a keen sense of smell, your nose may lead you to a career in geology. Geologists identify rocks and minerals by relying on a range of sensory input that sometimes includes smell. That's because certain rocks and minerals have a distinct odor. Sniffing a rock and breathing deeply and mindfully can help geologists detect, for example, sulfur (smells like rotten eggs), shale (smells like mud), and arsenic (smells like garlic). In fact, Japanese scientists are researching the smell of the moon—in this way they hope to identify the minerals that make up the moon's surface.

Discuss: A chef, a perfumer, and a tea connoisseur (expert) all live and work by their noses. Would a job that requires mindful smelling appeal to you? Why or why not?

Once a Day

Use mindful smelling as a way to enjoy your most rushed meal; take a moment to appreciate the smell of your food at breakfast or lunch before eating it.

Connecting to the Curriculum

Mindful smelling supports students' connection to their own learning process and to the content areas and literature.

Journal Writing

Encourage your students to reflect on what they've learned about mindful smelling and to record questions they may want to explore at another time. In addition, they may enjoy responding to these prompts:

- List three to five of your least-favorite place smells (e.g., "nervous-animal smells and dog breath at the vet's office").
- What are your favorite smells when you first wake up in the morning? Describe through scent how you typically start your day and what an ideal morning would smell like to you.
- Write the beginning of a story in which smell plays a central role. In the story's opening paragraph, set the scene by describing the scents that the main character experiences.
- Think of a special family gathering or holiday when there were many dishes of food. Draw a picture of the table and label the foods, giving descriptions of their scents.

SCIENCE

Flavorful Scents

What to Do

Give each student several different-flavored jelly beans. Direct them to plug their nose with thumb and forefinger, close their eyes, pick up a jelly bean, and begin chewing it. Have students try to name the flavor of the jelly bean. Then have them finish chewing and tasting the jelly bean with their eyes open and nose unplugged. Have students modify their prediction, if needed.

What to Say

What happened when you plugged your nose and tried to taste the jelly bean? What happened when you unplugged your nose? Our sense of smell allows us to taste flavors! Can you think of a time when it was difficult to taste food because your sense of smell was blocked? How would eating be different if you lost your sense of smell entirely? What could go wrong?

Why It's Important

This activity shows how two of our senses work in an interconnected way and provides a context for understanding the importance of our sense of smell to help keep us alive (enjoying food enough to eat it) and healthy (e.g., distinguishing edible food from spoiled food).

LANGUAGE ARTS

Nosy Interferences

What to Do

Have students track the way authors use scents to give us clues about a scene or situation. As you read aloud (or during students' independent reading), ask students to keep a T-chart on which they list pleasant and unpleasant scents an author describes along with the corresponding place or event. Use their lists to discuss inferences they can draw from these descriptions.

What to Say

Authors may describe unpleasant scents to give us a sense of discomfort or describe pleasant scents to help show us that a character is comfortable or happy. Let's keep a list of scent descriptions to help one another notice even more about what an author is trying to show us in his or her writing.

Why It's Important

Sensory details can often give powerful clues about the message of a story. Homing in on a detail, such as scent, can help students gather information in order to better analyze story elements.

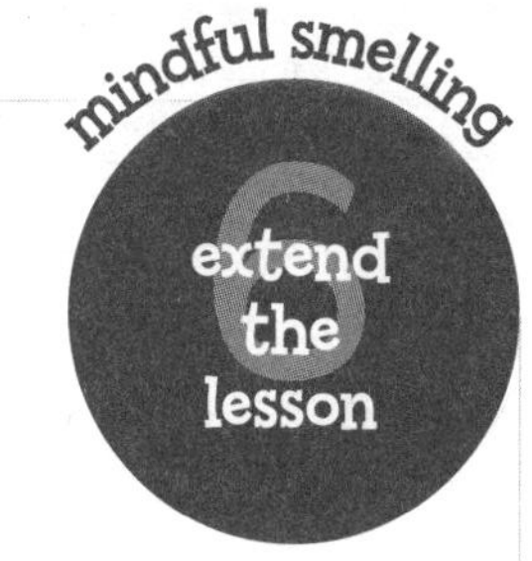

SOCIAL STUDIES

Scents of History

What to Do

As you study a specific time period and culture, ask students to collect sensory samples to represent foods or customs of a group. For example, a sensory sample from Colonial America might contain samples of herbs grown in a family garden for flavor or medicinal purposes. Encourage students to gather scent ideas about history from reference books and online texts. Remind students that until recent times, people seldom bathed!

What to Say

Getting to experience the same scents that people from another culture and time might have smelled, food they might have tasted, or even the clothes they might have worn can give us a window into their daily lives. As we study different groups, let's try to find details from their daily lives to better understand their history.

Why It's Important

History is filled with so much abstract information that providing sensory details such as the smell of herbs or the style of clothing can dramatically enhance students' sense of history. Experience-based information gives a concrete framework to which students can attach new learning.

SOCIAL-EMOTIONAL LEARNING

Be Scents-itive!

What to Do

Remind students that each of us has sensory preferences based on our experiences and sensitivities. Use the example of students' varied responses to the scent containers to remind them that we all have a unique way of experiencing the world through our senses.

What to Say

Some of you had a very positive association, or connection, with the scents we smelled, and others had negative associations with the very same scents. Can a few of you share your experience with one of the scents ? How might knowing that your classmates had very different reactions from yours affect the way you describe your surroundings?

Why It's Important

Making students aware of their different preferences and of people's unique ways of experiencing the world is a great reminder to be mindfully aware of expressing strong likes and dislikes and serves as an introduction to perspective taking.

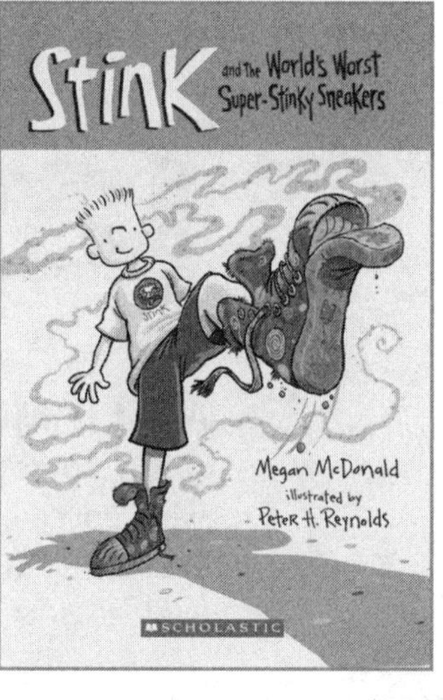

Literature Link

Stink and World's Worst Super-Stinky Sneakers

by Megan McDonald,
(2007) New York: Scholastic.

What's that awful smell? Stink Moody can tell you! Even his sister Judy is impressed by his talented nose.

In this laugh-out-loud book, Stink is sure his nose will make him famous one day. Determined, he devotes himself to studying the science of smelling. Encourage students to point out the ways in which Stink uses mindfulness to work towards his goal of wowing the judges at the stinky sneaker contest.

More Books to Share

Johnson, Angela. (2005). *A Sweet Smell of Roses.* New York: Simon & Schuster.

Hyde, Margaret. (2008). *Mo Smells Red: A Scentsational Journey.* Winnetka, CA: Mo's Nose LLC.

Kudlinski, Kathleen V. (1991). *Animal Tracks and Traces.* New York: Scholastic.

Mindful Tasting

What is Mindful Tasting?

To fully appreciate the food we eat—whether it's a complex treat, such as sweet grilled corn with hot chili and sour lime or a simple bowl of oatmeal—requires mindful tasting, or slowing down to savor our food and notice its flavor, texture, and temperature.

Why Practice Mindful Tasting?

Eating is something that is rarely done mindfully by young people. Mindful tasting can be a valuable task for demonstrating mindful awareness. The simple exercise of savoring and describing a morsel of food helps students understand the changes that can occur when an everyday act is performed slowly and with conscious attention to the experience.

Mindful tasting helps students identify discrete taste sensations, build descriptive skills, and approach food with a healthy outlook. It may also make them aware of the importance of healthful eating to their successful thinking and interacting at school. The exercise cues them to think carefully about what they're tasting and supports good digestion as they chew slowly and deliberately. With practice, students may be willing to try foods that are not part of their usual diet and make healthy food choices. Key social-emotional outcomes are building self-regulation skills and being accepting of new foods, which may lay the foundation for tolerance of cultural traditions outside of one's own.

What Can You Expect to Observe?

"When we repeat mindful tastings, students always share unexpected things about the food that they'd never noticed before and comment on how strong the flavor is. They are also more willing now to try new foods."

—Fourth-grade teacher

Linking to Brain Research

Relaxed and Alert: The Role of Neurotransmitters

Neurotransmitters are key to the dynamic and ever-changing ecosystem of our brain. These chemical messengers influence a wide range of feelings and behaviors and are affected by sensory input and general health. Stress—real or perceived—causes changes in levels of neurotransmitters, including these three:

- Dopamine plays a crucial role in motivation, pleasure, and addiction and influences paying attention, planning, and moving the body.
- Serotonin contributes to the regulation of appetite, sleep, aggression, mood, and pain.
- Norepinephrine is important for attentiveness, emotions, sleeping, dreaming, and learning.

Increases and/or decreases in the level of one or more of these neurotransmitters affect our mental state and the feelings and behaviors generated by it. Attentiveness, engagement, competence, and achievement are only possible when a learner's brain is in a receptive state, allowing for calm and mindful response. Mindful tasting, like mindful seeing and smelling, gives children an opportunity to be both relaxed and aware. The novelty of this activity, along with children's curiosity and engagement, helps to balance neurotransmitters and produce a relaxed, yet very alert, state of mind. Mindful activities help train the prefrontal cortex to pay attention, absorb details, and think clearly.

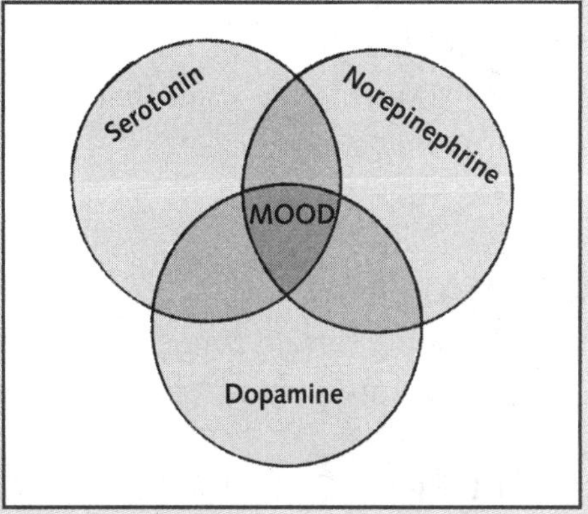

Levels and combinations of the neurotransmitters serotonin, norepinephrine, and dopamine influence our mental state.

Clarify for the Class

Use mindful tasting to compare real fruit juice and fruit-flavored drinks. Choose comparable flavors, such as grape juice and grape drink, and give each student a sample of both beverages in small paper cups. Ask students to take their time to savor each sample. Draw a Venn diagram to compare the tastes, textures, and smells of the beverages.

Discuss: Could you identify the real fruit juice? What tastes, textures, and smells were different? Draw a Venn diagram to compare the two.

Getting Ready

Examining the Morsel
One way to slow down the practice of mindful tasting is to apply the other senses, including sight and smell.

GOALS

- Students will focus their attention on savoring a morsel of food and describe their experience.
- Students will identify ways that mindful tasting can help them eat more healthily.

MATERIALS

- food morsels (one per student), such as raisins, chocolate chips, grapes, sliced baby carrots, mini pretzels, or strawberries

PREPARATION TIPS

- Be aware of any food allergies students may have and avoid high-risk foods such as nuts.
- Because this activity involves putting food in their mouths, have students wash their hands before the lesson.

CREATING THE OPTIMISTIC CLASSROOM

Brain-Inspired Instruction A surefire way to get descriptive vocabulary terms to stick is to create a visual reference chart. Work with students to create a list of terms that describe food. Bring in grocery circulars and have students cut out pictures of foods that fit each word (e.g., for *salty*, corn chips and a salt shaker). On a large sheet of butcher paper, write the descriptive word and have students paste the related pictures around it. The more visual cues they have, the better they will be able to access and use the terms. Some words to include are *sweet, spicy, salty, bland, crispy, sticky, chewy, crunchy, slimy, smooth, bitter, sour, chalky, juicy, dry, acidic, tender, tough, nutty, creamy, soft, hard, tart.*

Tasting: The Full Effect
Senses fully alert, students examine the flavor and texture of their morsel.

MINDUP Warm-Up

Mindful Tasting Practice

Talk about the job of our taste buds and that they detect sweet, sour, bitter, and salty flavors. Then guide students to draw on their memories to visualize a lemon in detail. Use prompts, as in the following script:

Imagine tasting a lemon. Start by picturing a bright yellow lemon. Now imagine the smell when you slice the lemon. Next, imagine bringing a slice of lemon to your lips. Bring the lemon slowly into your mouth and bite down on the pulpy inside. Let your mouth enjoy, or savor, the taste of the lemon.

After a discussion of their experiences with visualizing eating a lemon, guide students to understand that our minds and bodies are very connected. Even though there is no lemon in sight, our minds can bring the experience of tasting a lemon to our bodies.

Discuss: What did you notice in your body as you imagined the lemon? Could you taste the sourness of the lemon? Did you notice any physical reactions, such as your mouth watering and lips puckering? What foods might you let linger in your mouth to savor them?

Leading the Lesson

Tasty Clues

Engage

What to Do

Introduce the concept of mindful tasting and relate it to other mindful sensing activities.

- After air and water, food is the third most important thing our bodies need. But like breathing and drinking, we often eat without really paying attention to the details of how our food feels and tastes in our mouths.
- The mindful tasting activity we'll do helps train our brains to be mindfully aware of how we eat. What kinds of sensations do you think we'll focus on?
- When we practiced mindful smelling, our "specimens" were the canisters of scents. Today our "specimens" will be small pieces, or morsels, of food.

Remind students that their prefrontal cortex will be "on duty," working to notice every detail gathered by their RAS. Encourage the group to take a slow, deep breath to calm their amygdala and prepare to be mindful.

Why It's Important

Having several mindful sensing activities to relate to should give students a solid frame of reference and help them get ready to participate in this lesson. They may be able to predict that in a mindful tasting activity, they'll be focusing on the way a morsel of food feels in their mouth as well as the way it tastes (temperature, texture, flavor).

Explore

What to Do

Give students a morsel to hold in the palm of their hand. Have them mindfully look at their morsel, noticing shape, color, size, and any markings.

Then have students close their eyes and focus on smelling the morsel. Ask whether the morsel reminds them of anything and to think of words that describe this scent.

Finally, prompt students with cues that guide them to mindfully eat their morsel.

- Gently put the morsel in your mouth, but do not bite down yet! Try as hard as you can to focus on how the morsel feels in your mouth. Is your mouth watering? Can you taste anything?
- Use your tongue to move the morsel around in your mouth. Think about how it feels.
- Now, very slowly bite down and notice the taste and feel. Chew it slowly and swallow.

Point out to students that their senses of sight and smell can dramatically enhance their enjoyment of food.

Why It's Important

By now, most students can control their focus well enough to mindfully look at and smell the morsel before eating it. Drawing on three different sources of sensory data should reinforce focused awareness skills and also heighten the tasting experience.

From the Research

Classroom experiences that are enjoyable and relevant to students' lives, interests, and experiences correlate with superior learning and healthier lifestyles. (Ashby et al., 1999; Galvan et al., 2000; Iidaka et al., 2000; Kann et al., 2000)

Reflect

Invite students to discuss how eating a morsel in this activity was different from the way they typically eat food. Students may describe how they usually take a quick look at their food, chew it briefly, and swallow it without paying much attention. In this activity, however, they consciously looked at and smelled their food before they tasted it, then noticed the food's flavor and texture in their mouths.

Ask them how long they think it might take for the stomach to send a signal to the brain that it is full. When students have given their predictions, reveal the answer: 10 to 15 minutes! Have them consider how habitual unmindful eating could affect our health.

- What could happen if we're always in a rush to eat our food? How could unmindful eating be unhealthy?
- When are some times that you might use mindful tasting to slow down, enjoy your food, and eat healthily?

Mindful tasting can have a major impact on students' health when it's practiced regularly; not only does it have calming and focusing benefits, but it can assist with how well students digest their food and feel satisfied, which can prevent overeating. Further, the novelty of the tasting activity can make them more willing to try out new and healthy "morsels." This makes a great introduction to any unit on nutrition.

MINDUP In the Real World

Career Connection

Have professional taste buds, will report for work—that is, if you're a taste tester! Food scientists, who whip up all sorts of concoctions—from snack foods to beverages to condiments such as ketchup—conduct tests to comply with the standards and regulations that govern taste, texture, moisture, color, and nutrients as well as salt, fat, and sugar content. In order to meet quality controls, they rely on mindful tasters, who know how to use their tongues and taste buds to slowly, mindfully take in the full taste of every product. Taste testers might sample several dozen products and use a complicated scale to rate their choices.

Consider the work of a baker, cheese maker, or restaurateur; what would it be like to earn your keep by your tongue and taste buds?

Once a Day

Take mindful tasting to lunch! Instead of multitasking through your meal, take at least ten minutes to really taste (and digest) your food. You'll feel more satisfied, more able to focus, and more prepared to effectively manage the needs of your day.

Connecting to the Curriculum

Mindful tasting supports students' connection to their own learning process and to the content areas and literature.

Journal Writing

Encourage your students to reflect on what they've learned about mindful tasting and to record questions they may want to explore at another time. In addition, they may enjoy responding to these prompts:

- List several foods you enjoy. Use vivid language and illustrations to describe how each food looks, smells, and tastes.
- On a scale of 1 to 10, with 1 being very unmindful and 10 being very mindful, how would you rate each meal you have in a typical day? List all food, including snacks, mark each with its number rating, and say what you do to make eating that meal more or less mindful.
- If you were a chef, what kind of food what you like to cook? Is there a particular style or nationality of food you would make? Would you prefer to work at a bakery, café, deli, or fancy restaurant? Write a paragraph about yourself as a chef.
- Pretend that a sibling or friend sitting next to you at dinner refuses to try a new food. What would you say to convince him or her to be mindful in tasting it?

HEALTH

Tasty Reminders

What to Do

Invite students to create cafeteria posters to remind them and their peers about eating healthily. Let groups brainstorm their own topics or choose from topics you provide, such as tasting mindfully, using the food pyramid to make healthy food choices, and checking your portion size. Sources can include nonfiction books, articles, and online texts on healthy eating.

What to Say

We've learned that focusing our attention on tasting our food can help us enjoy our food more and even eat a little less. What other information about healthy eating could be helpful to learn about and to teach the rest of our school? Think about what information you could share through pictures and words that would make interesting reminders to hang in our cafeteria.

Why It's Important

Teaching about something is often the best way to learn it. Having students first gather information and tips to guide their peers to eat healthily and then find a way to make those tips compelling and memorable with pictures and words will reinforce what they've learned and give them a sense of expertise in this area, which also makes them more likely to follow and model their own advice.

LANGUAGE ARTS

How-to-Savor Paragraphs

What to Do

Have students write a "how-to" paragraph about mindful tasting. If necessary, set up a four-sentence writing frame with these transition words beginning each sentence: *first, next, then,* and *finally.* Have students mindfully focus on one food at lunch to write about.

What to Say

Restaurant reviewers visit a restaurant, taste special dishes mindfully, and recommend what to order and the best ways to eat it. Be a reviewer at our school cafeteria: choose one thing to taste mindfully, and take notes on how to look at it, hold or pick it up, feel and taste the food in your mouth, and chew it. You'll write about it in a how-to paragraph.

Why It's Important

Informative narrative writing is one of the best forms for students to practice summarizing and sequencing skills. Choosing a topic they know well makes the writing enjoyable and helps students apply mindful observations to a focused writing task.

SOCIAL STUDIES

Many Ways to Cook a Potato

What to Do

Some staples, such as wheat, corn, rice, and potatoes, span the cuisines of many cultures. Select one of these staples and have students research where it is produced and brainstorm all the foods they know that contain that staple. Then invite them to search for recipes containing that staple from a variety of cuisines. Work with a few families to organize a cross-cultural sampling day.

What to Say

How many different ways have you eaten a potato? Let's list as many as we can. Did you know that potatoes are grown as far away as China? Where else do you think they're grown? Together, we're going to find potato-growing countries around the world and favorite ways that their people prepare potatoes. Once we have a collection of recipes, we'll have a sampling day when we can use mindful tasting to try the same food in many different ways.

Why It's Important

Cross-cultural sampling is an exciting opportunity for students to try foods outside of their comfort zone and to be mindfully aware—and tolerant—of different ways of eating in the world. Tolerance develops further with each discovery and enjoyment of a food they did not expect to like.

SOCIAL-EMOTIONAL LEARNING

Mindful Eating at Home

What to Do

Students may want to bring mindful eating strategies into their daily lives but feel challenged by rushed timetables for breakfast, lunch, and dinner at home and at school. With students' help, draft a newsletter to families about the mindful tasting activities you've done and provide tips for doing mindful tasting at home,

What to Say

Some of you have mentioned that you'd like to try our mindful tasting experiences with your family and friends. We're going to write a letter describing our mindful tasting exercise, how it helps us to be healthy eaters, and how to set up a way to try it at home. Let's start taking notes together. Then we'll organize our ideas and have you work in groups to write the ideas and tips.

Why It's Important

This is a great way to recap students' work on building their focusing skills through mindful tasting. Parents may need to be reassured that mindful tasting practices encourage self-regulation and other healthy eating habits.

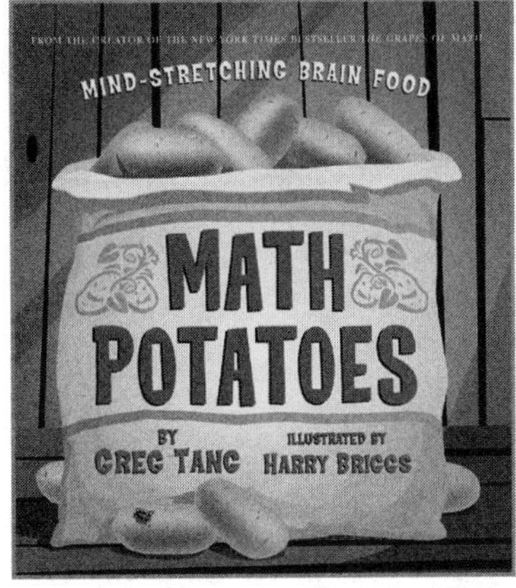

Literature Link

Math Potatoes: Mind-Stretching Brain Food

by Greg Tang
(2005). New York: Scholastic.

Exploring grouping strategies with food is a fun way to tie math in to your mindful tasting activities. Tang's book includes several food-themed rhyming couplets. Each poses an engaging problem designed to help you introduce sophisticated problem solving in addition and subtraction and to help kids find solutions to problems that really make sense.

More Books to Share

Cox, Judy. (2001). *Weird Stories from the Lonesome Café.* New York: Scholastic.

MacLeod, Elizabeth and Frieda Wishinsky. (2008). *Everything but the Kitchen Sink: Weird Stuff You Didn't Know About Food.* New York: Scholastic.

Paulsen, Gary. (1995). *The Tortilla Factory.* San Diego: Harcourt Brace.

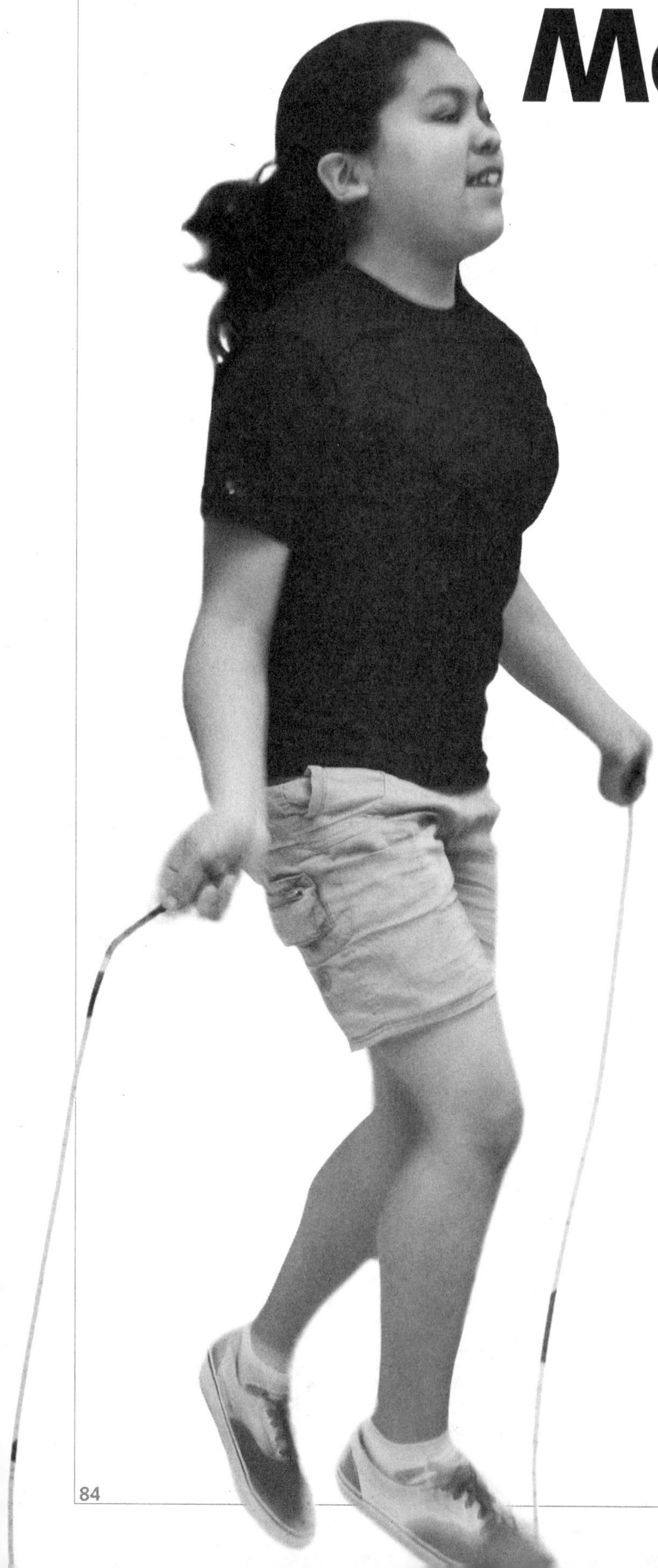

Mindful Movement I

What Is Mindful Movement?

How often are we conscious of putting weight on each part of the sole of our foot as we walk? Being alert to the sensations of the body, whether we are active or at rest, is a fundamental step in increasing mindful awareness.

Why Practice Mindful Movement?

Our body and brain are partners. We get burned and the nerve cells in our skin send a signal to our brain that registers pain. We get nervous and tense about an important test and our brain sends a signal to our body to sweat and cool down.

To move mindfully is to pay close attention to the sensations of our body when it is at rest and when it is active—the body gives us signals we can easily recognize to help us monitor physical and mental states such as exertion and stress.

In this lesson, students compare the signals their body sends after physical exertion and relaxation. They begin to learn simple self-regulation skills by controlling their breathing and heart rate. Developing an understanding of the brain-body relationship helps students become better able to identify the signals their body is sending and to manage their emotions and behaviors in response.

What Can You Expect to Observe?

"Students are fascinated by the way they can raise and lower their heart rate through movement and breathing. They are beginning to understand how much control they can have over their physical responses and their overall health by being in tune with their bodies."

—Third-grade teacher

Linking to Brain Research

Cortisol, the Stress Hormone

During a period of severe or persistent threat—perceived or real—the adrenal glands release extra cortisol, a hormone. Low levels of cortisol in the brain help us remain alert, and a sudden surge of the stress hormone is important in dealing with immediate danger. However, too much cortisol for too long can harm the brain and impair thinking, memory, and learning. High cortisol levels interfere with the function of neurotransmitters and can damage the hippocampus, which makes and stores memories. Excessive cortisol can make it hard to think and remember—"going blank" during a crisis may be an example of cortisol interference.

Brains in a constant state of alert due to physical, environmental, or emotional stress can have chronically elevated cortisol levels. During the crucial early years of brain development, high cortisol levels sustained over prolonged periods can cause significant damage and result in emotional dysfunction. Twenty-first-century life brings many stressors to children at an early age: lack of downtime, parental stresses, pressures to achieve, exposure to violence, over-stimulating or noisy environments, families dealing with substance abuse, unrealistic expectations, and poverty. As children learn to mindfully regulate their own breathing and heart rate, they learn to lessen their stress level and enable a healthy emotional balance.

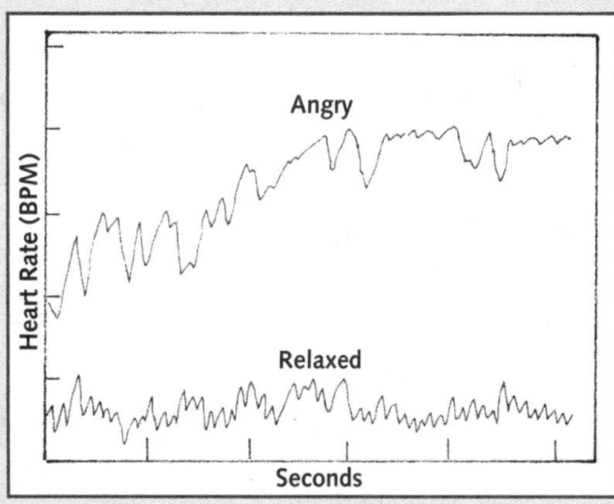

Our state of mind affects heart rate. The heart of someone who is angry can beat twice as fast as that of a relaxed person.

Clarify for the Class

Observe the connection between mind and body by having students measure their heart rate after active small-group work, when heart rates may be slightly elevated. (Need to know how to take a pulse? See page 87, Warm-Up, and page 90, Heart Rate Averages.) Explain that controlled breathing slows heart rate. To compare, measure heart rates again immediately after doing the core practices.

Discuss: Did the controlled breathing exercise slow heart rates? What emotions make your heart beat quickly? Is it easy or difficult to concentrate when your heart rate is fast?

Getting Ready

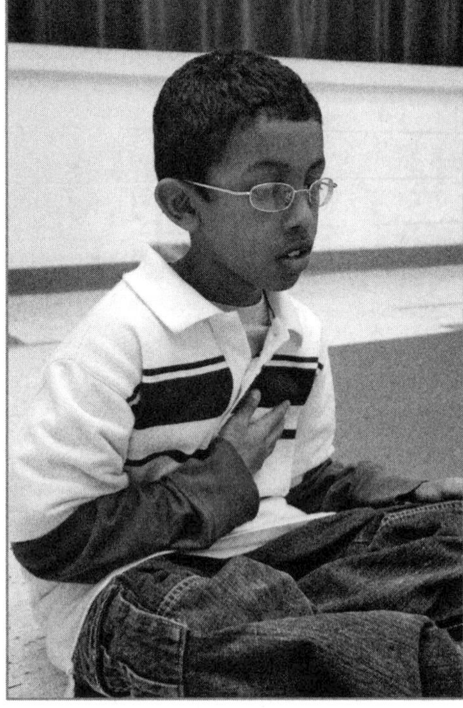

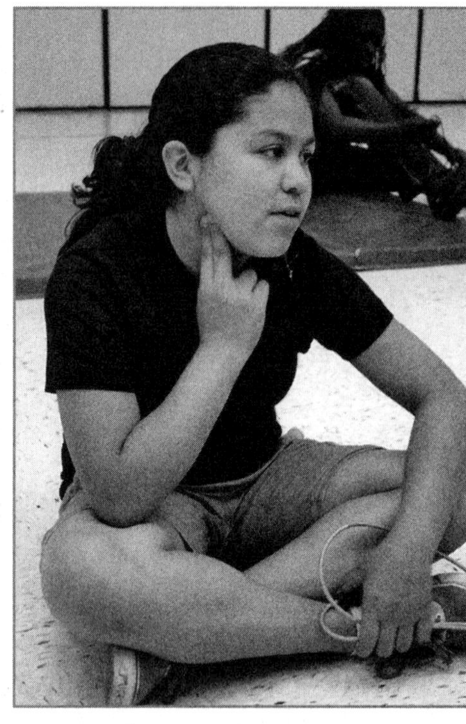

Detecting a Pulse
Students learn several ways to find their pulse.

GOALS

- Students will focus their attention on internal physical sensations, in both a relaxed and an active state.
- Students will monitor their own heart rate and exercise control over breathing and heart rate.

MATERIALS

- chart paper
- clock with second hand or stopwatch

PREPARATION TIPS

- Make space in the classroom for students to do simple exercises safely around their desks or find a clear area such as the gym or an outdoor court.
- For students with special physical needs, discuss appropriate adjustments for the active part of this lesson with the P.E. teacher, nurse, and parents as needed.

CREATING THE OPTIMISTIC CLASSROOM

Brain-Inspired Instruction When children are engaged in activities they enjoy, the amygdala relaxes, cortisol levels decrease, and positive neurotransmitters have time to rebuild. To allow the brain to return to an optimal state for learning, have students take a short "brain break," such as sharing a poem in two parts, listening to music, or enjoying a book read aloud to them, between higher-intensity activities.

Accelerate Your Heart Rate
Students get moving to boost their heart rate.

MINDUP Warm-Up

Taking a Pulse Practice

Have students rhythmically squeeze their hand into a fist to show how the heart, a muscle, pumps oxygenated blood throughout the body. Ask them to show what happens when we start exercising and the body needs more oxygen. Guide them to show you that their heart-fist has to pump harder and faster.

Tell students that to prepare for their mindful movement activity, they will learn to do what good athletes do: find and monitor their pulse without using stethoscope (you may want to have a picture for students who need a visual reference).

Demonstrate and have students practice finding their own heartbeat in any of these ways:

- Hold one hand palm up; press the index and middle finger of the other hand on your wrist just below your palm;
- Press the index and middle finger of one hand at the top of your neck, just under your jaw (about midway between your earlobe and chin):
- Press your index and middle finger firmly at the center of the base of the throat.

Discuss: When do you usually feel your heart working hard and thud-thudding during the day? What pulse point do you find easiest to use?

Leading the Lesson

Move and Relax

What to Do

Engage

Review finding a pulse from the warm-up activity. Explain that an elevated, or stronger and faster, pulse is one signal our body gives us when it's working hard. Introduce the goals of the lesson: to detect changes in pulse and other physical signals that show our body is working hard, and to change our movement or activity to help our body return to a normal, resting state when needed.

- How hard do you predict your heart is working right now as we're sitting and talking about it—not too hard, moderately hard, or very hard?
- How could we bring it to its slowest and gentlest and then to its strongest and fastest pulse?

Write down their ideas for slowing their pulse and elevating it. (Students will likely suggest breathing exercises or the Core Practices to slow their pulse and active movements, such as jumping jacks, to elevate it.)

Explore

Have students vote on the calming activity. Help them relax for several minutes, prompting them to sit or lie down comfortably and bring their attention to their breath.

- As you breathe deeply, allow your prefrontal cortex to focus on how relaxed your arms, legs, shoulders, and neck feels. Feel those slow, deep breaths fill up your lungs and escape.

On your cue, have students find their pulse and count silently for 15 seconds. As they share, note that the numbers are similar, but that everyone has a unique (and ever-changing) pulse.

Now have them vote on a high-energy exercise to boost their pulse. Let them exercise, encouraging them to move vigorously, for about 2 minutes. On your cue, have students find their pulse and count silently for 15 seconds. Ask them to discuss with a partner any other signals their body was sending as it worked hard. As they continue to cool down with mindful breathing, remind them to monitor their heart rate to see how it changes.

Why It's Important

Engage

Having students mimic their heartbeat with their hand is a helpful physical model that they will enjoy using to show the pulse they perceive through their fingertips.

Inviting students to generate ideas for the activity they'll do invests them in the exercise and the outcome. It puts them in the position of self-regulating their physical state.

Explore

Students enjoy discussing and comparing heart rates with peers and checking one another's pulse at the wrist, which helps reinforce the concept of the ever-present, ever-changing pulse. This is also a good time to have them use their heart-fist model to show how fast and hard their heart is beating during both the calming and the invigorating activities.

From the Research
Exercise ... optimizes your mind-set to improve alertness, attention, and motivation.
(Ratey, 2008)

Reflect

Invite students to discuss the way they created physical changes in their body through movement.

- You were able to drive your pulse to a fast rate and also slow it down. What other signals did you detect as you exercised more and your heart rate rose?

Students will likely answer that their skin got sweaty, their faces got flushed, and their whole body felt warmer. Guide students to understand that the brain signaled these changes to help the body cool down in order to perform better as it exercised. Review the changes they experienced as they slowed down.

- How can being mindful about the changes our body experiences help us understand what's going on?
- Are there other times when you're not exercising but your emotions are taking charge, that your body might be sending similar signals? What can you do to help yourself remain calm?

Make sure students understand that our brains and our bodies work together to keep us healthy and safe. By paying attention to body signals, we can better understand ourselves, and use those signals to help us make good choices about being healthy and calming ourselves in the face of stress.

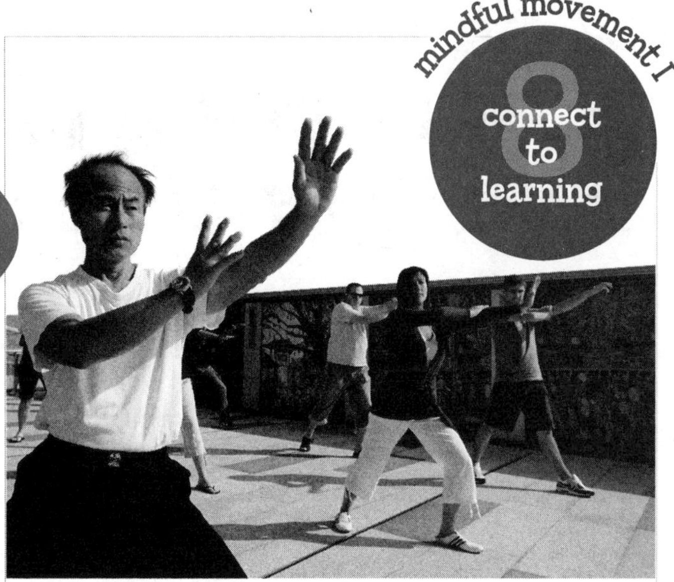

MINDUP In the Real World

Career Connection

A tai chi (tie-CHEE) instructor teaches the ancient art of "meditation in motion," which connects mind and body and promotes serenity through gentle movements. Originally developed in ancient China for self-defense, tai chi has evolved into a noncompetitive, self-paced system of postures or movements performed in a slow, mindful manner. Each posture flows into the next without pause; there are more than 100 possible movements and positions, all of them coordinated with breathing.

Discuss: Would you be interested in a job that requires mindful moving? Consider how the mindful movements of a school crossing guard, carpenter, or beekeeper are pivotal to their work.

Once a Day

Notice students' posture after they've been working in one place for awhile—how well they hold themselves upright reflects their degree of alertness. Take short breaks to allow them to move (e.g., shaking out or doing a few jumping jacks), refresh, and refocus as needed.

Connecting to the Curriculum

Mindful movement supports students' connection to their own learning process and to the content areas and literature.

Journal Writing

Encourage your students to reflect on what they've learned about mindful movement and to record questions they may want to explore at another time. In addition, they may enjoy responding to these prompts:

- Try the Move and Relax activity on your own, either during free time or at home. Describe and illustrate the exercise you chose. How hard was your heart working: lightly, moderately, or vigorously?

- Describe how your body feels when it is active. Describe your emotions also—during your favorite physical activities, exercising during P.E. class, or playing a favorite game or sport.

- Imagine yourself in your most relaxed state. What are you doing? In what position is your body? What is your breathing like? Write a letter from your relaxed self to your overexcited self, with suggestions for calming down.

- Write about a time when your body was giving you a clear signal and you responded. Maybe you were especially hungry or thirsty, anxious and nervous, or excited and eager. Draw a cartoon with thought bubbles and captions to show yourself getting the signal and afterwards, as you were returning to a calmer state.

MATH

Heart Rate Averages

What to Do

Show students how to calculate their heart rate using this formula: (beats in 10 seconds) x 6 = (your pulse in beats per minute). Ask the class to come up with a vigorous activity that requires constant movement, such as running a lap or jogging up and down flights of stairs. Show them how to get an average heart rate by adding a set of heart rates and dividing by the number in that set. Let small groups try their activity, calculate their average high rate, and share the averages as a class.

What to Say

The average heart rate of your group shows approximately where everyone's pulse is for this particular activity. That's helpful if you want to summarize your data with a single number rather than listing a whole set of numbers.

Why It's Important

Learning how to calculate a pulse gives students a practical application for math. Capitalize on their fascination with gathering data from their own efforts and comparing their data with that of their peers; finding averages is another useful application of key operations skills in addition and division.

PHYSICAL EDUCATION

Freeze and Thaw

What to Do

Have students move around an empty space (e.g., a hallway, the gym, or outside) and listen for your signal. When you call out "Freeze!" students tense up their entire body and freeze on the spot. When you call out "Thaw!" students relax and slowly melt to the ground, paying attention to how their bodies feel.

What to Say

In this game, when I say to freeze, tense up every muscle in your body—even your face and hands! When I say to thaw, imagine that you are melting, with every bone and muscle dissolving into a puddle on the ground. Notice how different the movements feel.

Why It's Important

Finding new ways for students to tune in to movement further develops mindful awareness about their bodies. Recognizing the feelings of tension and relaxation can help them identify when tension is building in their bodies and how relaxation feels (you might have them try a mini-melt on their desks before a test, for example).

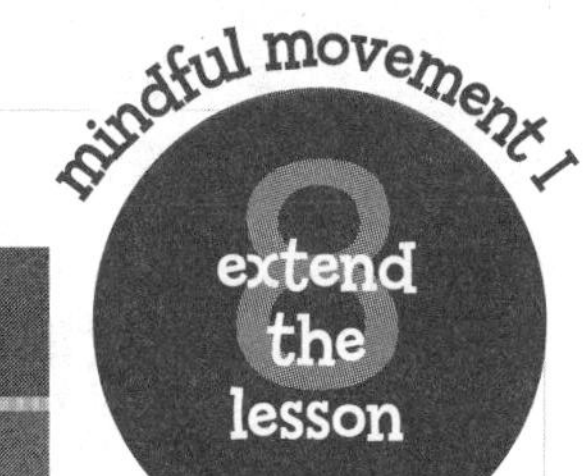

LANGUAGE ARTS

Mindful Movers

What to Do

Ask students to gather several photos of athletes caught in a moment of mindful movement, such as a basketball player aiming from the free-throw line. Have students explain to a partner how their pictures show mindful awareness. Then have students choose the photo they most enjoyed describing, paste it to a piece of construction paper, and write a caption vividly describing the mindful movement. Display these pieces on a wall or bulletin board labeled "Mindful Movers."

What to Say

As you describe the mindful movement to your partner, use details about the position and movement of the athletes' bodies and their facial expressions. Are they moving in a way that shows they are completely focused? Think of action words that describe what their arms, hands, legs, feet, and even face are doing.

Why It's Important

Studying how movement experts focus intensely to achieve their goals in sports provides students with a model of how our body can support our mind (and vice versa). In working to describe the movement, students will discover exciting nuances about the way the athletes are positioning themselves, as well as showing concentration in their expressions.

SOCIAL-EMOTIONAL LEARNING

Position Yourself to Learn

What to Do

Have students practice sitting upright, but not rigidly, with ears above shoulders, shoulders over hips, and feet flat on the floor or a block. Have them imagine that their head is a balloon, floating above their shoulders. Explain that sitting with good posture will get oxygen to their brains to help them think more powerfully.

What to Say

To get to the brain, blood travels through important arteries along the sides of the neck. When we slouch, we put a "kink" in those hoses, and our brain (especially the PFC) doesn't get its full dose of oxygen-rich blood. That makes it harder for us to be mindful and focused. Good posture is good for our thinking!

Why It's Important

Awareness-raising work with subtle movements can dramatically improve students' posture and ability to focus. Students literally put themselves in a position to learn! Visualization helps cue students to listen and participate mindfully.

Literature Link
Winter's Tail: How One Little Dolphin Learned to Swim Again

by Juliana, Isaella & Craig Hatkoff (2009). New York: Scholastic.

Winter, a young dolphin, was rescued after losing her tail in an accident at sea. This remarkable true story tells how a team of experts worked to develop a special prosthesis for Winter and to train her to use it. Link mindful movement to the descriptions of Winter's training and the ways in which the techniques used to help her have also been used to help people.

More Books to Share

Cohen, Arlene. (2007). *Stories on the Move: Integrating Literature and Movement with Children, from Infants to Age 14*. Santa Barbara, CA: Libraries Unlimited.

Spinelli, Jerry. (1995). *Do the Funky Pickle*. New York: Scholastic.

Simon, Seymour. (2006). *The Heart: Our Circulatory System*. New York: HarperCollins.

Mindful Movement II

What More Can We Learn About Mindful Movement?

Mindful movement begins with a developing awareness of our constantly changing physical sensations, as described in Lesson 8. We can build on this awareness by using movement challenges to help our brains focus and work more efficiently.

Why Revisit Mindful Movement?

In this second lesson on mindful movement, students continue to deepen their awareness of physical sensations they often overlook. From their Move and Relax activity in the last lesson, students learned how to exercise vigorously to accelerate their heart rate and use breathing to calm their heart; they discovered that they could both mindfully observe and help control their physical responses. With this understanding, students are ready to try a set of physical challenges that require focus and concentration in order to maintain their balance. Participating in the balancing activity helps students deepen their brain-body connection and build self-regulation skills as they work to control their physical and emotional responses in order to remain steady.

In addition, students work on strengthening their decision-making abilities in this lesson. Working on our physical balance is shown to have positive effects on our brain's health, reinforcing higher-order thinking skills and emotional control.

What Can You Expect to Observe?

"Students rise to the challenge of the exercises in the lesson—and then they start creating their own balancing exercises. You can see them really take control of their learning. They get excited about challenging themselves to improve their physical skills and they encourage one another to do the same."

—Fourth-grade teacher

Linking to Brain Research

Emotional Balance: Key to Efficient Executive Function

Executive function is mental management that takes the big picture into account. Executive function comprises many higher-order skills that depend upon the thinker's ability to reflect before reacting. Among these skills are evaluating information, organizing, focusing attention, prioritizing, planning, and problem solving. The control of executive function is guided by our prefrontal cortex, proportionally the largest of any primate. Executive function skills are affected by our emotional state in part because the neural networks for emotional response overlap with the neural networks for executive function. Thanks to the brain's neuroplasticity, both of these overlapping networks in the prefrontal cortex are strengthened when the brain is engaged in either an emotional response or an executive function.

Learners who can recognize and control their own emotional state become confident and successful, both socially and academically. Neuroscientist Adele Diamond notes that "activities that often get squeezed out of school curricula, such as the arts and physical exercise, are excellent for developing executive function skills [and] improving children's emotional state and social skills, and can be critical for academic success and for success later in life" (2009). Engaging in physical challenges, the arts, and mindful practices that enhance learning and reduce stress activate both emotional response and executive function networks simultaneously.

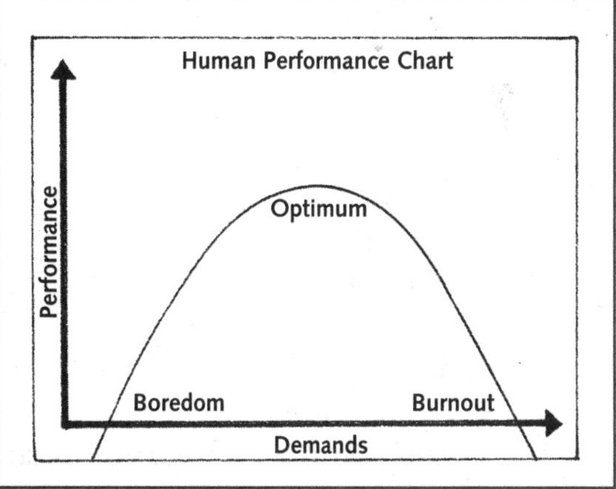

Some stress is necessary to normal functioning, but ever increasing amounts of stress produce diminishing returns on learning, achieving, socializing, and living.

Clarify for the Class

Mindful walking combines mindfulness with movement. Walk with good posture, paying attention to your moving body and focusing on your breathing. Feel the air move in through your nose and out through your mouth. Pay attention to each step—how each foot meets the ground, what your arms are doing, how your posture is. Bring stray thoughts back to your breathing and moving body.

Discuss: Do you pace when you think or worry? Why do you think moving around can sometimes help us process information?

Getting Ready

Challenge Your Balance! Students experiment with different balancing positions while keeping a beanbag steady on their head.

GOALS

- Students mindfully control their balance and describe the sensations they experience.
- Students will connect mindful balancing to being well balanced in life.

MATERIALS

- class set of small beanbags or any other object students can safely balance on their heads (e.g., soft plastic CD cases or notepads)

PREPARATION TIPS

- Make space in the classroom for students to do simple exercises safely around their desks or find a clear area such as the gym or an outdoor court.
- For students with special physical needs, discuss appropriate adjustments for the balancing activities with the P.E. teacher, nurse, and parents as needed.

CREATING THE OPTIMISTIC CLASSROOM

Brain-Inspired Instruction Taking brain breaks, described on page 86, can help balance high-intensity instruction with lower-intensity activities. Other practices that create a relaxed, brain-friendly classroom environment include

- limiting periods of sitting and listening
- encouraging peer-talk to cement learning
- offering choices of activities and materials
- using humor
- providing immediate positive feedback when possible

Angular Experiments
A group freezes in position, showing the angles they've made with their arms and legs.

MINDUP Warm-Up

Building Balance Practice

Give pairs of students four to six playing cards and challenge them to arrange the cards on a level "building" surface, such as a desk top or a hardcover book. Give students these criteria: each card must touch at least one other card and no cards may lie flat on the building surface. Encourage partners to work together on several different options. (They should find a way to lean cards together or structure them so that one card can lie on top of the rest.) Have partners circulate to observe one another's solutions.

Guide students to understand that their card "buildings" will stand when the cards are arranged in a stable structure, meaning each card has a position in the group that allows it to stay balanced on its edge. Introduce the terms *balance*, *steady*, and *stable*.

Discuss: When were your cards most likely to fall? What arrangements gave the cards the most stability? Which card groupings could balance with a card lying on top? What does this card building tell us about balancing weight?

Leading the Lesson

A Balancing Act

Engage

What to Do

Review the way students have been learning to observe the sensation signals their bodies send and to help their bodies rev up and calm down when needed. Relate balancing the card building in the warm-up to the next movement experience.

- Now that you know how to tune in to your body's signals and you can help control your body (for example, by breathing and relaxing), you're ready for a couple of physical challenges that require you to focus and balance your weight.
- To get us started, think about how you and your partner built a balanced card building. Are there times when you've felt balanced and steady? How about shaky and unbalanced?

Encourage students to share times when they've felt balanced and times when they've felt unbalanced. Make sure they can connect focusing and paying close attention to being able to be balanced and steady.

Why It's Important

Recalling the image of the balanced card building as well as their experience of controlling their body's physical states in the last lesson lays the foundation for making sure students are ready to give full attention and effort to the balancing they are about to do.

Explore

What to Do

Guide students through the first balancing exercise. Encourage them to stand in an open space and focus by taking a few deep breaths and feeling their feet on the ground. Have them lift one foot off the ground and suspend it. Cue them as needed to breathe deeply, pay close attention to the sensations in their feet and legs, and touch their floating foot down for a moment if they feel very unsteady. After 30 to 60 seconds, have students switch legs and try the challenge again. Have them reflect on their balancing work.

- What are you noticing about keeping yourself steady? Is it more challenging on one side than the other?
- How is your brain working with your body to stay focused and steady? Is your brain feeling calm or busy right now?

For the second exercise, have students balance a beanbag on their heads and either raise a knee as in the first activity or create a new one-legged balancing position.

Why It's Important

Starting with an easier challenge builds students' confidence. Allow students who find it very difficult to balance their weight to repeat and get comfortable with the first activity, assuring them that balancing, like any physical task, takes practice. Tell them when they have found a stable position, they can add to the challenge by balancing a beanbag on their head.

From the Research
Research shows that activities ... such as the arts and physical exercise, are excellent for developing executive function skills and can be critical for academic success and for success later in life. (Diamond, 2009)

Reflect

Invite students to discuss the increased challenge of the second activity and what they did to help themselves stay steady.

- Did this activity get difficult for you at any point? How did the beanbag add an extra challenge?
- What did your brain do when the balancing got more difficult? What part of your brain was working hard to guide your body and keep it steady?
- When could creating a balance challenge be a helpful focusing tool for you?

Guide the discussion to make sure you've covered the key points from both mindful balancing activities.

- When our bodies and brains work together, we can focus and think clearly.
- When we pay attention to the signals our body sends, our brain's ability to focus improves.
- Like all the other mindful activities, mindful movement and balancing help our prefrontal cortex practice focusing.

As students witness the power of their minds to help their body achieve a goal, they are likely to want to try new challenges and push their brain and body further. A great follow-up activity is Ready, Steady, Set Goal! on page 99, in which students help one another create balancing exercises and set goals for increasing the duration for which they can balance in the chosen position.

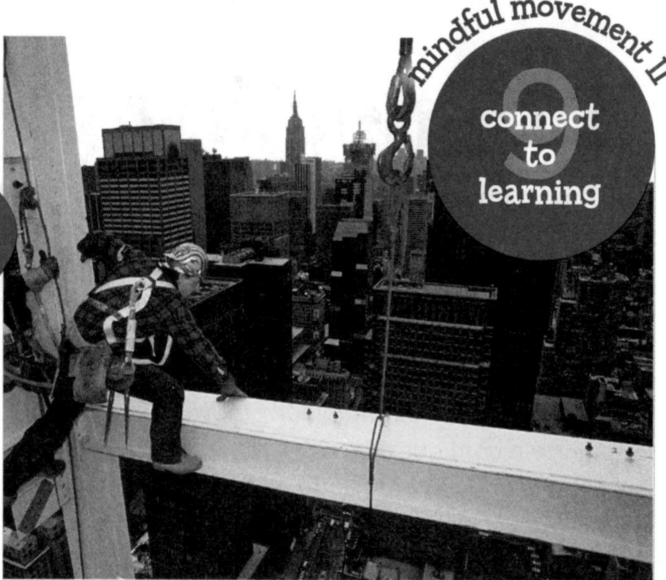

MINDUP In the Real World

Career Connection

Imagine walking on narrow beams of steel — more than 1,000 feet in the air. If you're a high-rise ironworker, mindful movement—combining graceful agility with a keen sense of balance—not only enables you to do your job, but also helps guarantee your survival. When you're 100 flights up overlooking a busy city street, one false step could mean a tumble to your death. While ironworkers take safety precautions such as ropes, harnesses, and safety nets, their best hope for survival is their own mindful movement—while being completely tuned in to all that's going on around them.

Discuss: What kind of job might require you to be very aware of how you are moving your body to do or make something? Consider the work of trapeze artists, drummers, jewelers, and potters.

Once a Day

Try a simple balancing action, such as standing on one foot, whenever you or your students are waiting (e.g., in line at the cafeteria, at dismissal). Balancing takes no preparation and keeps students focused and aware.

Connecting to the Curriculum

Mindful movement supports students' connection to their own learning process and to the content areas and literature.

Journal Writing

Encourage your students to reflect on what they've learned about mindful movement and to record questions they may want to explore at another time. In addition, they may enjoy responding to these prompts:

- Try the balancing activity at home. Invent three creative positions (you can use props) to give your body practice at balancing. For each one, make a sketch and write a caption, describing the degree of difficulty (easy, medium, or challenging), and tips for staying steady.

- Which of your favorite physical activities require you to focus and control your body? Choose one and list three ways you control parts of your body as you do this activity.

- Write about one job for which a worker needs to have good control of his or her movement. Explain how balancing and focusing help him or her do the job well.

- How is balancing time important? Think of the perfect "balanced" schedule for a Saturday or a school day. What would you be doing and for how long? Write your ideal schedule, listing times and events or activities during the day.

SCIENCE

Predator and Prey Moves

What to Do

Invite students to research animals with interesting predatory or defensive habits. Have individuals or pairs select an animal that interests them and learn about how that animal uses balance to attack or to defend itself and how other animals respond to this animal's movement. Encourage students to create a visual presentation with pictures and sketches that describe the habits of the animal.

What to Say

Think of how difficult it would be for a wild cat, such as a leopard, to hunt if one of its legs were injured. Animals must be able to balance and control their bodies in order to find food and survive. You're each going to get to know one animal very well by studying how it moves or balances mindfully. Get to know the habit of your animal well so you can share what you've learned with the rest of us.

Why It's Important

Animals make fascinating subjects for studying movement and reinforcing concepts of focus and balance that students have been working on. Emphasize that because animals rely on specific movements and habits for survival, they get regular practice. Those that survive tend to move in their natural way very well.

PHYSICAL EDUCATION

Mindful Moving in the Hall

What to Do

Take advantage of transition times, such as walking in the hallways and climbing stairs, to explore mindful movement. As you lead students through the halls and stairways, challenge them to pay close attention to the sensations they feel as they slow down and observe familiar activities we often take for granted.

What to Say

As you climb each stair, bring your attention to the soles of your feet. How does the feeling change as you step up and lift yourself to the next step? How does the floating leg feel? Which muscles are working to balance you? To pull your body up? Notice changes in your breathing and heart rates. How is climbing stairs mindfully different from our normal stair climbing?

Why It's Important

Activities like mindful walking help keep students focused on their immediate physical experiences and reduce the boredom of walking and waiting in line. Their observations during this activity help them see that sensations are ever-present, even in familiar experiences.

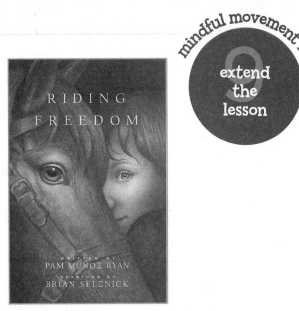

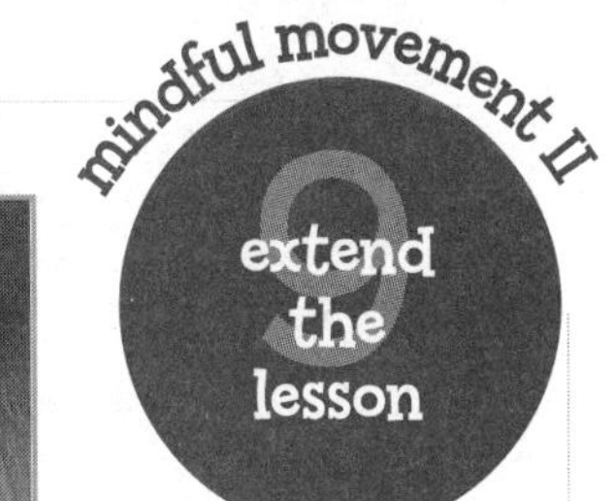

MATH

Body Geometry

What to Do

Encourage students to notice the types of angles they can make with their joints. Starting with their shoulders and elbows, have them make straight lines as well as acute, right, and obtuse angles. If space allows, encourage them to continue angle-making with other joints. For example, they may also hinge at their hips, knees, and ankles.

What to Say

Our joints are connecting spaces where our bones meet. Some joints, like our elbows and shoulders, give us lots of room to make different shapes. Can you find a way to make a straight line? How about using your elbow as the vertex and showing a right angle? Can you make that angle acute? Obtuse? How else can we show angles by moving the joints of our bodies?

Why It's Important

Students reinforce the neural pathways that help them identify angles by physically modeling angles and manipulating the shapes they make. Challenging students to make the same shape in several different ways is a motivating way to help them use critical-thinking skills.

SOCIAL-EMOTIONAL LEARNING

Ready, Steady, Set Goal!

What to Do

Have partners use a stopwatch, wristwatch, or wall clock to time one another's balancing during a set of three or more feats (e.g., standing on tiptoes, doing a handstand). Have them record their times and discuss a goal they would like to reach through practice (e.g., holding the handstand for five seconds longer). Each day for a week, provide several minutes for students to practice. Invite volunteers to share their improved times at the end of the week.

What to Say

Let's help our buddies focus and get their best time. Why is it important to practice to achieve goals? What if we set goals but never worked toward them?

Why It's Important

Setting a goal for a simple, concrete physical activity and ensuring that students practice to reach that goal, provides an excellent model for setting larger goals. Discuss modifying unrealistic goals; point out that making small gains through practice can help us see progress toward the goal.

Literature Link
Riding Freedom

by Pam Muñoz Ryan (1998). New York: Scholastic.

This exciting historical novel is based on the adventure-filled life of Charlotte (Charley) Parkhurst, the first woman to vote in the state of California. She lived her life on her own terms, during a time when women had little freedom. Connect Charley's love of riding and the demands of becoming a stagecoach driver with concepts of physical balance.

More Books to Share

Korman, Gordon. (2002). *Dive* (series). New York: Scholastic.

Sullivan, George (2005). *Built to Last*. New York: Scholastic.

Wong, Janet S. (1996). *Twist: Yoga Poems*. New York: Simon & Schuster.

It's All About Attitude

As students learn new ways to cultivate a positive mind-set, they prime their brain for learning and for building healthy relationships.

By looking at an event from different perspectives, students learn to mindfully consider viewpoints other than their own.

Students explore the meaning of optimism and pessimism and discover how these two attitudes affect our relationships and ability to learn.

This lesson demonstrates how recalling happy memories can help students regulate their emotions and maintain a positive mind-set.

The findings of researchers in the field of psychology seem logical: cultivating happiness in our lives has myriad benefits emotionally, socially, and physically—we relate to others better, we treat ourselves well, and we are more likely to adopt healthy habits and avoid destructive behaviors.

But can happiness really help us get smarter? Yes! Cognitive studies have shown that learning that is connected with a happy or positive emotional experience causes the information to get stored in our long-term memories, while learning that takes place in conditions that cause stress and anxiety is stored only in short-term memory; it is not available for long-term use (Pawlak et al., 2003; Shadmehr & Holocomb, 1997).

That's a research-based incentive to bring more laughter and joy into our lessons. Helping students develop skills in relating better to others and making happy memories of what they learn are key goals of the three lessons in this unit.

Perspective Taking

What Is Perspective Taking?

We live in a "small world" with as many different ways of seeing things as there are people. Perspective taking allows us to consider more than one way of understanding a behavior, event, or situation. This skill is particularly useful on a global scale as our ability to communicate and our need to share resources with other people and cultures expand.

Why Practice Perspective Taking?

On the most practical level, students who are able to accept that other classmates may behave or think differently than they do are much better equipped to tolerate and find ways to get along with peers. These students can talk out a problem and find a solution that is mutually agreeable.

Perspective taking, like the Core Practice and other mindful skills, simply takes practice to develop. As students routinely identify other perspectives, they learn to think with an "open mind"—to pause and consider other viewpoints mindfully.

This increasing ability to consider a situation in multiple ways has social benefits, such as reducing conflicts among students, facilitating group work, and cultivating an inclusive peer community. Perspective taking is an essential skill for problem solving in all subject areas, from understanding conflict in literature to finding strategies for problem solving in math and science.

What Can You Expect to Observe?

"Now that we use the language of perspective taking in all areas of the curriculum students see conflict, approached mindfully, as an opportunity to learn from one another and get along better."

—Fifth-grade teacher

Linking to Brain Research

Opening the Mind to the Prefrontal Cortex

Perspective taking is the ability to see situations and events from the viewpoint of another person. When we mindfully practice perspective taking, we become more skilled at accurately interpreting the behavior of those around us. Mentally standing in someone else's shoes requires reflection, which can forestall an unthinking reaction. Repeatedly viewing issues or events through different lenses builds and strengthens the neural networks that enable us to reason before we take action. Paying attention to a situation in a calm, focused, mindful manner is a physiological workout for the brain, actually stimulating blood flow to it. Calm perspective taking directs incoming information to the reflective, thinking prefrontal cortex instead of to the reflexive, reactive amygdala.

As students learn to consider alternate points of view, they can more effectively quell their own anxieties, exercise impulse control, and gauge their own behaviors and reactions in response to others. When differences of opinion are honored, and disagreement is respectful, students perceive the classroom as safe and risk-free. This unstressed state of mind allows their amygdala to "stand down" and puts the prefrontal cortex in control. A brain that operates primarily in the prefrontal cortex makes superior decisions, facilitating good choices for its owner.

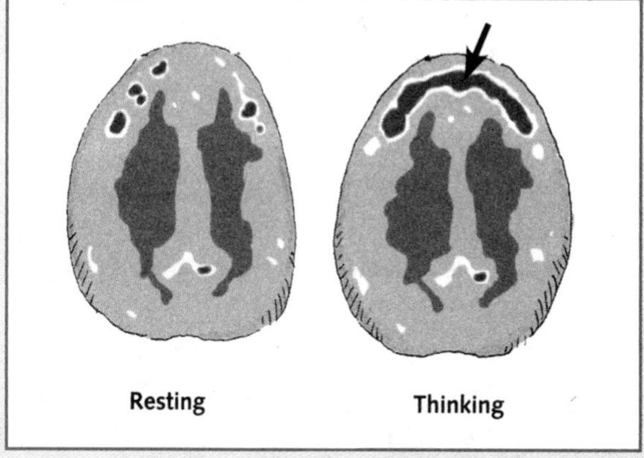

These scans show where blood is flowing in the brain. Notice the increased blood flow in the prefrontal cortex area (arrow) of the thinking brain.

Clarify for the Class

Model how neural pathways are built through repeated practices, such as perspective-taking, by creating a folded paper object. Explain that refolding an already creased paper is faster and easier than folding a new sheet, just like how repeatedly shuttling information along the same chain of connected neurons makes the pathway more efficient. Instruct students to fold a square sheet of paper into a fortune teller (often called a cootie catcher). Next ask them to unfold it until it's a flat sheet again, then refold it into a fortune teller.

Discuss: Was it easier to make the fortune teller the second time? Why? How is this like what happens in the brain when you learn to think before acting?

Getting Ready

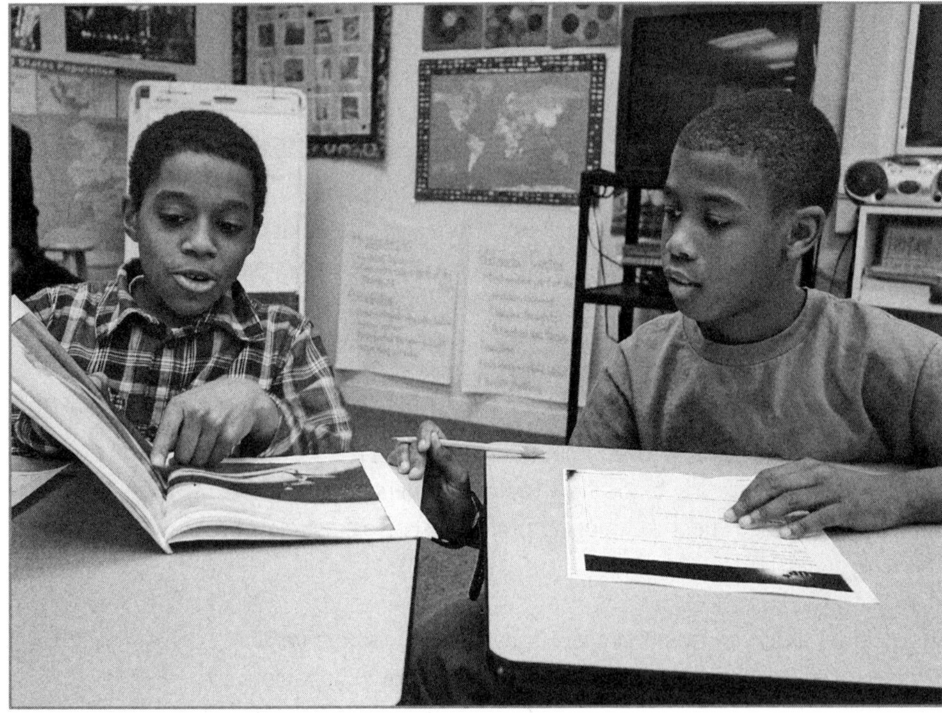

Getting Perspective on Characters
Stories with strong characters offer rich perspective-taking material.

GOALS

- Students identify different perspectives of characters in a story.
- Students apply open-minded perspective taking to social situations in their own lives.

MATERIALS

- picture book or short story featuring characters with different perspectives on the same event (Older students may enjoy "fractured" versions of fairy tales in which a traditional story is told from an alternative perspective, such as the bears in Goldilocks and the Three Bears or the wolf in The Three Little Pigs.)
- Character Perspectives activity sheet (p. 156)

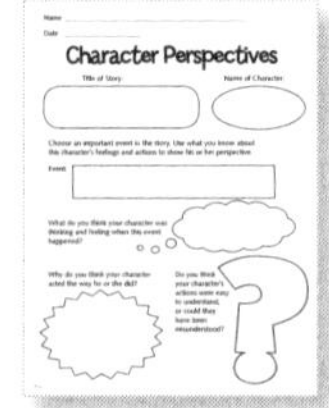

CREATING THE OPTIMISTIC CLASSROOM

Supporting English Language Learners Ask students to notice how their classmates react to what they say or do through facial expressions and body language ("How do you think he was feeling when he spun around after you said...?"). These observations especially help second-language learners build key language skills for describing emotions and emotional gestures. Equipped with apt descriptive skills, students are better prepared to reflect on why the behavior might have happened.

I See Where You're Coming From
Perspective taking helps students see the other side of an argument with a peer.

MINDUP Warm-Up

Perspective-Taking Practice

Generate a set of scenarios about choices your students might encounter that could have different outcomes based on the preferences, beliefs, and experiences of those involved. For example:

- Students get to choose the genre of the next read-aloud: (e.g., poetry or mystery)
- Teachers decide on whether the class science trip is to a nature preserve or a natural history museum
- Two friends plan to meet after school and either do a craft project or watch soccer practice

Describe the scenarios to the group, introducing the term *perspective.* Have students consider the personal backgrounds, interests, and experiences that might cause the different outcomes. Introduce or review the term *conflict* as they discuss what might happen when both parties want something different.

Discuss: What experiences or beliefs might have made one choice more likely than the other(s)? Think about what you might choose in these scenarios. What would happen if you always made choices with people who had similar perspectives? Let's use these scenarios to think about how people with different experiences and beliefs might handle conflicts mindfully or unmindfully?

Leading the Lesson

Character Versus Character

Engage

What to Do

Read aloud a short story or picture book (see Materials for suggestions). Have students listen closely for actions and words that describe the perspectives of the main characters. Help them connect their inferences to the perspective exploration in the warm-up activity.

- What did this character's actions and words tell you about how he [or she] was feeling? What experiences does the author suggest this character usually has?
- Remember that feelings, beliefs, and experiences help us understand a character's perspective, or way of looking at things and making decisions.

Discuss the fact that every character, like every person, has a unique perspective, which we can discover by reading and thinking mindfully about the clues the author is giving us. Have the class choose one character to study, display the Character Perspective activity sheet, and lead students through a character-perspective analysis. Record answers from volunteers so everyone has a record.

Why It's Important

Story characters make an engaging study for perspective. Because the characters are fictional, students are usually comfortable commenting on and learning from them. Help students avoid the use of judgment in this exercise, as judgments cut off mindful participation from everyone. Encourage students to approach the discussion with curiosity about the characters and why they do what they do.

Explore

What to Do

Invite students to explore events from the perspective of a different character. Hand out copies of the activity sheet to pairs or groups of three. Have each group choose another character in the story who experienced the same events as the first character.

- Think about another character in this story who also experiences the same event [or set of events]. Use the same questions to find out this other character's perspective.
- Which character are you more likely to agree with?
- Could there be another perspective?

If the different perspectives have created conflict in the story, ask students to come up with a way to see the situation from the perspective of the other character. Either have students discuss how the characters might talk together to understand one another or have them write out that dialogue and perform it as a group.

Why It's Important

Now that they're familiar with analyzing one character's perspective on a given event, they can use this perspective as a point of contrast to examine another character's perspective. Although the activity can be done independently, students benefit from group discussion in which they can clarify any confusion and narrow down their best ideas.

From the Research

Students experienced a greater level of understanding of concepts and ideas when they talked, explained, and argued about them with their group, instead of just passively listening to a lecture or reading a text. (Iidaka et al., 2000)

Reflect

Through a class discussion, lead students to conclude that there is more than one side to every story.

- When you try to understand something from someone else's point of view, you are 'taking a different perspective.' How is that like or unlike the mindful sensing activities we've been practicing?

Make sure students can connect that when they sensed mindfully, they had to pay attention to what their bodies were telling them. Now they are learning to pay attention to their own thoughts and feelings as well as those of other people in a curious, nonjudgmental way.

- How might a too-quick judgment about what someone says or does tell only part of the story? What happens when people are punished without having their perspective heard?

Key points that students are working toward understanding are:

- Different people may have different reactions to and different views or opinions about the same event.
- When we take the time to mindfully consider others' perspectives, we are less likely to make quick judgments and decisions, which can often be unfair to others.

perspective taking

10 connect to learning

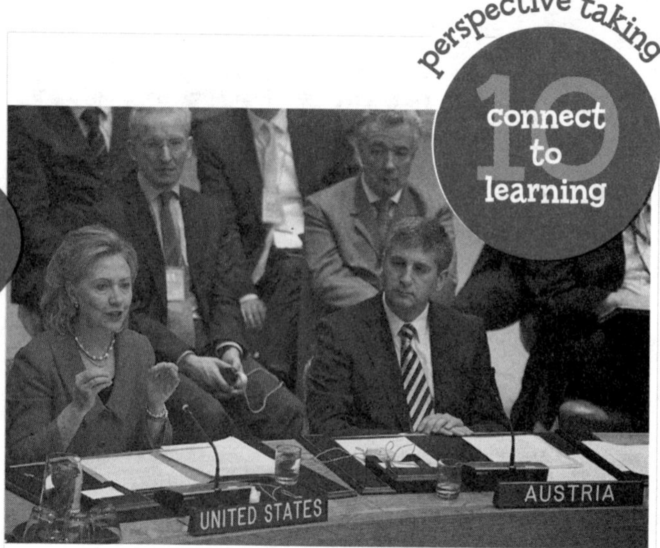

MINDUP In the Real World

Career Connection

Peace negotiators typically possess both an abundance of imagination and unique powers of persuasion that enable them to help those locked in conflict to transcend their own narrow views, take the perspective of the other, and bend toward a mutually acceptable solution. "Walk a mile in my shoes" is another way of saying "step outside of yourself and imagine what it feels like to be me."

Discuss: What might it be like to have a job that requires you to feel another's cares and concerns? What kind of jobs help people understand their feelings or thoughts better?

Once a Day

Each day, choose a different student to focus on; observe closely; listen in on his or her interactions; talk one-on-one. Your close attention can help you better understand how the student approaches his or her work and relationships—invaluable information for building community and differentiating instruction.

Connecting to the Curriculum

Perspective taking supports students' connection to their own learning process and to the content areas and literature.

Journal Writing

Encourage your students to reflect on what they've learned about perspective taking and to record questions they may want to explore at another time. In addition, they may enjoy responding to these prompts:

- Make two columns in your journal. At the top of one, write "My Thoughts." At the top of the other, write "Their Thoughts." Think of a recent disagreement in which you've taken part. Describe the thoughts for each side.
- Imagine yourself and friends having a picnic on a blanket in the park. There is a bird in a nearby tree, a dog lying beside you, and an ant at the edge of the blanket. Write a descriptive paragraph about the picnic scene from the perspective of one of those creatures. Add a sketch as well.
- Create a Venn diagram comparing yourself to a friend of yours. Include sports and activities that you like; foods you enjoy: music you listen to; and other things you share or don't.
- Choose a historical figure you have learned about. Write a journal entry from the perspective of that person.

LANGUAGE ARTS

Fractured Tale Skits

What to Do

Read aloud to your class several fractured fairy tales (such as Wendy Mass's Twice Upon a Time series and Jon Sciezka's *The True Story of the Three Little Pigs*) so students are able to identify changes the authors have made to the traditional personalities and perspectives of the characters. Encourage students to work in small groups to come up with skits that "twist" a fairy tale they know well. Have them map out the story, choose roles, and present it to the rest of the group.

What to Say

If you could rewrite a fairy tale, which would you choose? Think about the character who usually causes trouble (the antagonist—the wolf, troll, witch). How could that character see the event completely differently? What if the main character, the hero or protagonist—the pigs or the princess—didn't have very good intentions after all? How could you act out the story using the same events, but in a completely different way?

Why It's Important

Identifying character traits, motives, and perspectives is essential to dramatic and narrative texts. Using perspective taking to better understand the needs, concerns, and values of characters helps students apply the skill to relating to others, too.

SOCIAL STUDIES

The Other Side of the Story

What to Do

Brainstorm with students some current top news stories. Then have the class settle on a story that interests them and find articles and opinion pieces about it. Together read the pieces. Ask students to point out comments that show how the writer might feel about the topic (you may want to introduce the word *bias*).

What to Say

As we read these articles, think about how the writer is feeling about the events he or she is describing or commenting on. Is he or she writing a story that is favorable or unfavorable, pro or con? What facts did he or she focus on or leave out? Which article was least biased? Which do you agree with most?

Why It's Important

Understanding that writers have a bias and that every article is written from a certain perspective helps us see the bigger picture more clearly. This is a great rationale for the need to seek multiple sources of information when students want to learn about any topic in depth.

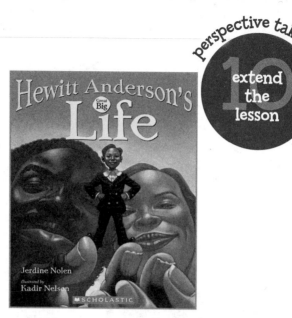

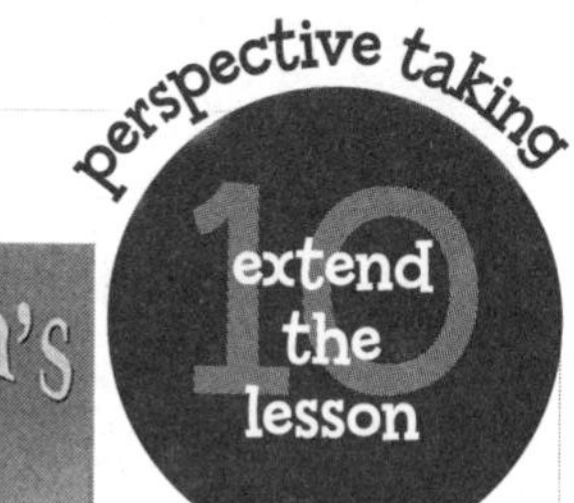

PHYSICAL EDUCATION

Making the Most of Recess

What to Do

Help students get more out of recess by helping them mindfully plan how to share space and materials and include everyone who wants to be involved. Have students work together to plan several activities, designate materials and space needed, and sign up for the activities. Ask them to take into account rotating schedules, if needed. Suggest that they serve as referees as well as players. Regroup after recess to discuss what worked and what didn't.

What to Say

Today, let's take a look at the big picture of recess—considering the perspectives of everyone in the class—and make a plan that works for everyone. First let's list the games we want to play. Then we'll look at how to share the materials and spaces. Last, we'll see what everyone wants to do and find ways to make sure everybody's included.

Why It's Important

Having students make plans for recess in order to prevent conflict and increase enjoyment is a mindful exercise. It can also be an effective way to forestall bullying by engaging aggressive students in a process that demands empathy and perspective taking. Planning in this way, by prioritizing sharing and inclusion, helps students adopt an open-minded approach to working with groups.

SOCIAL-EMOTIONAL LEARNING

Reading Expressions

What to Do

Have students collect pictures of faces displaying a range of emotions, such as discouragement, happiness, determination, sadness, surprise, and fear. Let each student choose one image, paste it to a piece of construction paper, and write in a speech bubble the words the person might say.

What to Say

Our feelings can sometimes cause us to react emotionally. As you look at your picture, think about how this person is feeling and what they might have just experienced. What words might this person be preparing to say? Write his or her words in a speech bubble.

Why It's Important

Reading faces is an important perspective-taking skill. It builds a foundation for empathy that your students will continue to develop in later lessons as they explore the feelings and needs of other people.

Literature Link
Hewitt Anderson's Great Big Life

by Jerdine Nolen
(2005). New York: Scholastic.

What would it be like to be the only average-sized boy in a world of giants? In this imaginative fantasy, being different has its challenges—but it also has its advantages. As you read this book with students, focus on how Hewitt's perspective on things differs from his parents' and how illustrator Kadir Nelson helps readers see things from Hewitt's point of view.

More Books to Share

Martin, Ann M. (2001). *A Dog's Life*. New York: Scholastic.

Hesse, Karen. (1998). *Just Juice*. New York: Scholastic.

Scieszka, Jon. (1991). *The True Story of The 3 Little Pigs*. New York: Scholastic.

Choosing Optimism

What Is Optimism?

Optimism is a way of seeing life hopefully and having an expectation of success and well-being. It correlates strongly with good health and effective coping strategies. Optimism is a learned trait and if practiced, can become a way of thinking.

Why Practice Optimism?

Choosing to view life optimistically can increase our brain capacity; it relaxes our amygdala, creates chemical balance in our brains, and allows our prefrontal cortex to take charge. In this frame of mind, students learn that they can make much better choices than if they take a negative or pessimistic approach, which effectively shuts down their higher-level thinking.

Practicing optimism also makes it easier to learn—optimistic thinkers prime their brains to be ready to focus and make more room for new information to be absorbed and new ideas to stretch their wings. Socially, practicing optimism allows students to strengthen their perspective-taking skills and accept viewpoints different from their own, as well as connect with other people. In this lesson, students explore the benefits of optimism and see how pessimism can negatively affect their ability to think and learn, make friends, and solve common problems. With a pessimistic attitude, a person can get bogged down and limit his or her ability to solve problems.

What Can You Expect to Observe?

"Learning that they can choose to think about situations and events in a positive, hopeful way helps make our classroom a friendly place where there's less self-doubt and worry and more healthy mental risk taking. Students help one another to see the brighter side of life events and that helps them put their own troubles in perspective."

—Fourth-grade teacher

Linking to Brain Research

Optimism: A Learned Skill for Success

The research is clear—attitude matters! Students who are generally optimistic enjoy better physical health, have more success at school, flourish in relationships, and are more equipped to handle stress in their lives. Brain research has confirmed that optimism is more a learned trait than a genetic one. We can train our brain to have an optimistic perspective, thanks to neuroplasticity. This brain process forms new branching-off dendrites and more neuron-to-neuron connections during repeated experiences and practice. When students regularly use self-talk for positive thinking and to work through everyday frustrations, neuroplasticity creates and strengthens nerve cell (neuron) connections in their brains.

Optimism is easily identified in brain scans. Levels of dopamine and other brain neurotransmitters rise, cortisol levels remain steady, and the amygdala is open and forwarding information to the prefrontal cortex. An optimistic state of mind enables mindful responses to stress and a downplaying of thoughts of failure, frustration, and hopelessness. Optimism breeds the expectation of success, which in turn makes it easier for the student to put forth the effort necessary to achieve that success.

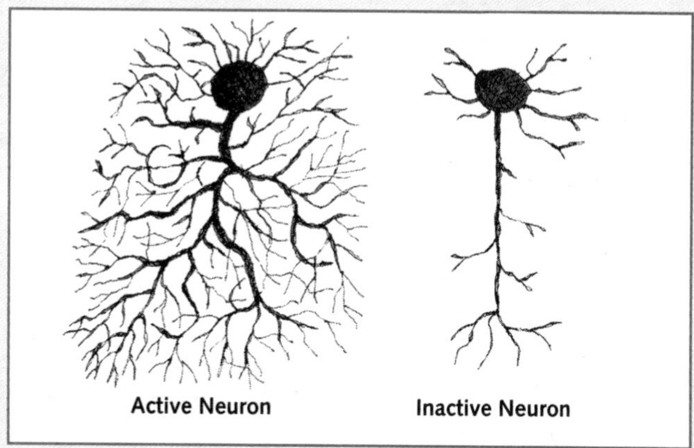

An active brain neuron, or nerve cell, forms many branching dendrites to make neural connections.

Clarify for the Class

Remind students that their brains, like their bodies, are trainable. Explain that we can train our brains to be optimistic, just as we can train our bodies to do specific tasks. By repeating thoughts and experiences, we become familiar with them. Over time, they come more easily and begin to happen automatically—practice makes permanent. Help students target times of the day when they may feel anxiety or experience negative thoughts.

Discuss: What sports or musical instruments do you play? What was most difficult to learn at first? How does practicing improve that skill? Think about training your brain to think optimistically. What times of the day might be toughest to think positively? What optimistic words can you use to coach yourself during these times?

Getting Ready

Different Approaches
A student acts out pessimistic and optimistic ways of approaching a problem.

GOALS

- Students will define two different mind-sets (optimistic and pessimistic) used to think about, react to, and approach a problem.
- Students will practice strategies that help them to develop and maintain optimism in their own lives.

MATERIALS

- chart paper
- clear glass or cup filled halfway with water
- (optional) Optimistic/Pessimistic Thoughts activity sheet (p. 157)

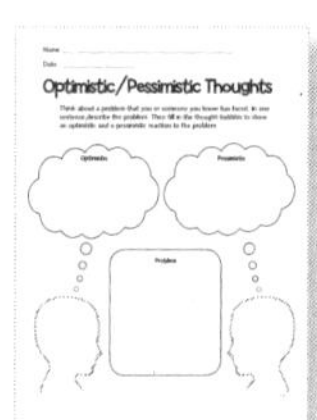

CREATING THE OPTIMISTIC CLASSROOM

Classroom Management "Teaching is the greatest act of optimism" writes poet Colleen Wilcox. Each day, make a point to model the type of thinking and positive self-talk you want your students to embrace. For example, you might

- acknowledge that current worries or sadness will pass.
- reaffirm that while we can't always control a problem, we can always control our reaction to it.
- encourage students with hopeful words, reminding them to make a fresh start.
- celebrate mistakes as opportunities to learn.

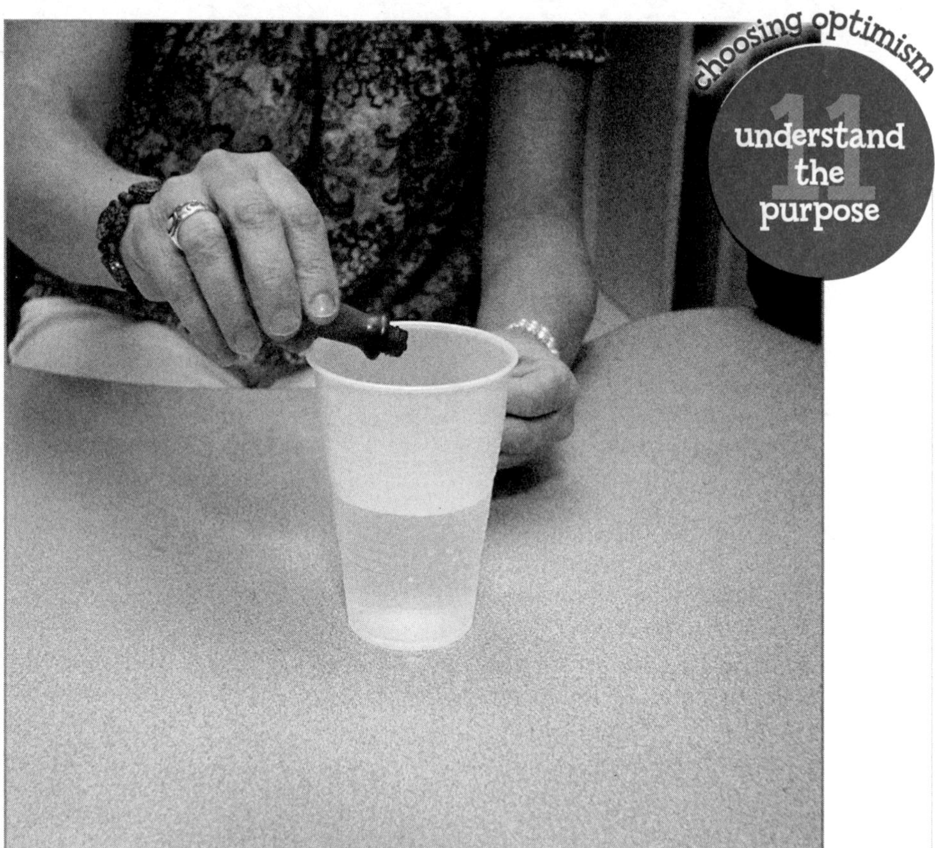

Is Your Glass Half Full?
Idiomatically speaking: A cup filled half-way with colored water is a visual cue for "glass half-full."

MINDUP Warm-Up

Word Splash-and-Sort Exercise

Create a word splash on the board, displaying words and phrases that could be categorized as "optimistic" or "pessimistic" without explicitly listing these terms. For optimistic, you might include *happy, hopeful, cheerful, thinking positively, and looking on the bright side*. For pessimistic, you might include: *hopeless, depressed, in the dumps, feeling blue*, and *worrywart*.

Give pairs of students a large sheet of paper and have them fold it in half. Have partners work together to sort the words and phrases from the splash into two groups, writing a list of terms on each side of the page. Have them give each list a label. After a few minutes, invite students to come to the board to sort the words, giving reasons for putting the different words into separate groups. Ask them to share their labels (e.g., *positive/negative, what we want in a friend/don't want in a friend,* etc.). Introduce the terms *optimistic* and *pessimistic* and have students write them as new headings on their sorting page.

Discuss: Most of the names you came up with for the two word groups describe thinking in a healthy, positive way or in an unhealthy, hopeless way. We call these perspectives *optimistic* and *pessimistic*. When have you thought in an optimistic way? In a pessimistic way?

Leading the Lesson

Seeing the Glass Half Full

Engage

What to Do

Ask students to reflect on the warm-up exercise as they look at a glass filled halfway with water.

- Would you describe this glass as half empty or half full?
- Why do you think people might see it one way or another?

Guide students to understand that optimistic (glass half full) thinkers usually believe that success will come with practice and focused work, and have hope in the face of problems. On the other hand, pessimistic (glass half empty) thinkers often feel discouraged and frustrated with themselves and others, and have little hope when faced with important problems.

Read these statements aloud (or create your own examples). Have students give a thumbs-up if they think the statement is optimistic and a thumbs-down if they think it is pessimistic.
"I've never done this, so it will be an adventure."
"I've never done this before. I don't want to. I might get scared."
"Our picnic is ruined! It's going to rain all day."
"So what if it's raining? We'll have our picnic inside!"

Why It's Important

This introduction helps students understand optimism and pessimism as perspectives people can adopt. Note that the terms *optimistic thinking* and *pessimistic thinking* are less judgment-oriented than the terms *optimist* and *pessimist*. From a brain perspective, we want students to recognize both types of thinking so they can experience optimism as a daily practice and not a hard-wired quality.

Explore

What to Do

Give students a scenario they can relate to and ask them to see it from an optimistic and a pessimistic perspective. For example, have students imagine that the principal of the school has just passed by with a frown on his or her face, and when you say "hello," he or she doesn't answer but hurries by.

- How might someone respond optimistically to that situation? Pessimistically?

Have students talk with a partner about how they would feel if they saw their own school principal in the same situation. You may want to have students write out their ideas in the thought bubbles on the Optimistic/Pessimistic Thoughts activity sheet.

- Which point of view do you think is more compatible with the job of your prefrontal cortex?

Why It's Important

Discuss optimism in the context of brain function. Explain that pessimistic thinking can set off the amygdala and shut down higher-order thinking. The PFC gets clearer information from a calm amygdala, and therefore works much better when a person believes problems can be solved. Behavioral scientists have linked optimistic thinking to happiness, good health, and better academic performance.

From the Research

Mindfulness has been found to be related to well-being, including optimism, positive affect, self-regulation, and lower rates of depression and anxiety.
(Brown & Ryan, 2003)

Reflect

Generate a class list of strategies students can use to adopt an optimistic perspective so their brain can stay healthy and work better.

- Considering other perspectives is one way to train your brain to think in a more open, positive way.
- What are some other ways to train your brain to think optimistically?
- How can you avoid a pessimistic way of thinking?

Record students' ideas on an "Our Best Ways to Stay Optimistic" class list that you can post in the room. Encourage students to keep a personal list as well. Ideas might include looking at another perspective on a problem, replacing a negative thought about something with a positive one, reminding ourselves that a worry is a feeling that can pass, doing a mindful breathing or sensing exercise, playing a game, singing a song, or sharing a joke.

This reflection should guide students to conclude that:

- Optimistic thinkers are happier, healthier, and more successful people.
- Optimistic thinking helps us to solve problems.
- We can choose to be optimistic and practice optimism so that it becomes a mind-set.

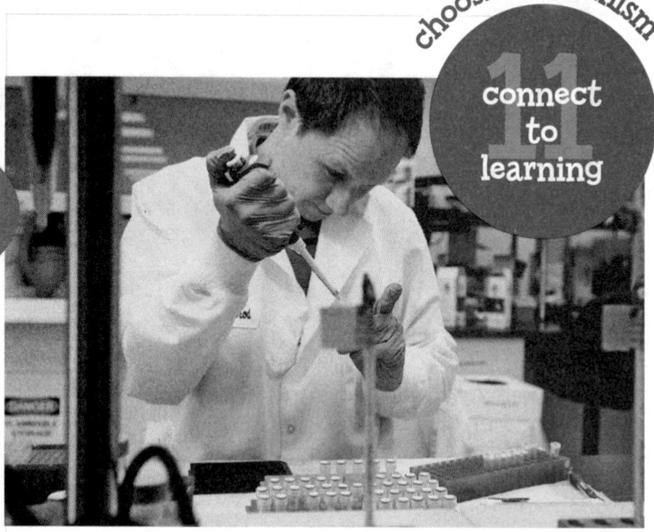

MINDUP In the Real World

Career Connection

Although it may seem incongruous, hope and optimism often motivate medical researchers. Effective researchers are optimistic that a solution exists and believe that with enough patience, perseverance, and diligence, they will find a cure that will save thousands of lives. Often against all odds—working long hours with limited funds—medical researchers press on through endless tests, hoping the next slide under the microscope will reveal the answer. What could be more optimistic than that?

Discuss: How might you rely on optimism in the face of unpredictable elements? What jobs might depend on the weather or chance?

Once a Day

Before they leave for the day, have students think of one thing they learned or enjoyed in class. Invite them to write it on an "optimistic exit" card and hand it to you on their way out. This helps you assess what they have accomplished and highlights for them how they've benefitted from learning.

Connecting to the Curriculum

Learning about optimism supports students' connection to their own learning process and to the content areas and literature.

Journal Writing

Encourage your students to reflect on what they've learned about choosing optimism and to record questions they may want to explore at another time. In addition, they may enjoy responding to these prompts:

- At the top of your journal page, write "A Rainy Day." Describe and illustrate three imaginative activities you could do to turn a dreary rainy day into an entertaining rainy day.
- Record three funny jokes or the lyrics to a humorous song that you can tell or sing to someone to lift their spirits.
- Think about how a character in a book you've read showed optimism. Write a paragraph from that character's point of view to describe his or her outlook on an experience.
- Picture two friends, real or fictional, who have different points of view. One shows optimistic thinking and the other pessimistic. Draw a scene that shows the three of you doing something together, and add voice bubbles for what each of you might say.

ART

Optimistic Collage

What to Do

Have students look through magazines and cut out images that reflect optimistic thoughts, feelings, and actions. Encourage them to look for photos and drawings that show positive situations, such as people with optimistic expressions engaged in work or play. Also have them collect uplifting words. Ask students to arrange their images and words in a collage that reflects optimism.

What to Say

What pictures and words show a feeling of hopefulness? Happiness? Working hard to solve a problem? When you've found your positive words and pictures, arrange them in several different ways to make a picture that really shows what optimism looks like. As you look at one another's collages, you may want to ask the artist what made certain images seem optimistic to him or her.

Why It's Important

Creating a visual representation of optimism helps students show their ideas in a format you and their peers can learn from and ask about. (Do the pictures represent only images and expressions of exceptionally happy people? Can students also make room for visual representations of peace, harmony, and hope?) Including pictures of optimistic situations will help students see optimism not only as thoughts and words, but as action in real-life settings.

SOCIAL STUDIES

Uplifting News

What to Do

Discuss that news stories are often pessimistic and leave us feeling that we can't change things. Give students the opportunity to find and report on a school or community event in which they see positive change taking place. Reports can be shared as in-class oral presentations or posted in a class newsletter or website.

What to Say

As we read, watch, or listen to the news, is it mostly optimistic or pessimistic? Why do you think pessimistic views are more common? Let's look for events around us in which people are being helpful or successful at something positive. Why might it be useful for us to focus on optimistic news in addition to feature news?

Why It's Important

Assigning students to seek out positive news is a way to help them practice optimism. Seeking out and sharing good news primes the brain for learning, and it provides real-life examples of positive everyday actions that can help students generate ideas for personal and community actions of their own. (See Unit 4)

LANGUAGE ARTS

Upbeat Lyrics

What to Do

Select popular classic songs students may enjoy singing, such as "What a Wonderful World," "Here Comes the Sun," and "Lean on Me." Display the lyrics, which can be found online, and invite students to read and sing along. Ask students to identify the optimistic message of each song and idiomatic expressions and figurative language that make the message memorable.

What to Say

I'm going to play a song that you might describe as "optimistic." Mindfully listen to the song the first time and then read along with the lyrics the second time I play it. What feeling does the music alone convey? What instruments or sounds gave it that feeling? How do the lyrics reinforce that feeling? Do you notice any poetic language or vivid descriptions? Any figurative language—similies, metaphors, or idioms? What's most effective?

Why It's Important

Learning optimistic songs by singing to lyrics is a great way to build both reading fluency as well as classroom community. Like poetry, song lyrics offer an opportunity to focus in on expressive and descriptive language, helping you target reading and writing goals.

SOCIAL-EMOTIONAL LEARNING

Put a Positive Spin on It

What to Do

Have each student create a three-column chart with the headings "Situation," "Pessimistic Response," and "Optimistic Response." Have them think of an experience they've responded to pessimistically and fill in the first two columns. Then ask students to trade papers with a classmate and generate an optimistic response to the situation they receive. Have partners share their optimistic alternatives.

What to Say

Think of a time when you felt frustrated about a situation and responded pessimistically. Fill in the first two columns on your chart. What made you feel pessimistic? Trade papers, and write an optimistic response to your partner's situation. How could your classmate's suggestion help you the next time you face a similar situation?

Why It's Important

Students are usually eager to read the suggestions of a classmate regarding a situation they had a problem with. Also, suggesting alternative ways of looking at someone else's situation is useful practice for managing negative responses in one's own life.

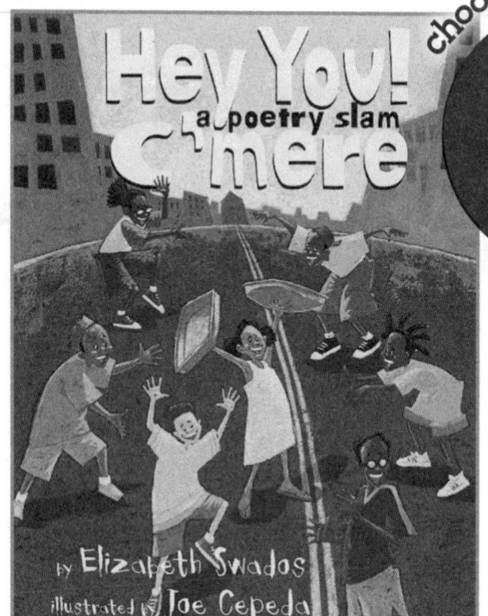

Literature Link

Hey, You! C'mere: A Poetry Slam

by Elizabeth Swados
(2002). New York: Scholastic.

Students will enjoy reading aloud these 17 slangy, jangly poems from the voices of kids getting together on a hot summer day to make their own game with rhythm and rhyme.

Connect this book to the idea of creating our own fun and playing games with others as strategies for building optimism. Encourage students to think of ways they can entertain themselves and enjoy the company of friends—perhaps even challenge the class to their own poetry slam!

More Books to Share

Krull, Kathleen (2000). *Harvesting Hope*. New York: Scholastic.

Musgrove, Marianne. (2008). *The Worry Tree*. New York: Henry Holt.

Robinson, Sharon. (2006): *Safe at Home*. New York: Scholastic.

Appreciating Happy Experiences

What Does It Mean to Appreciate Happy Experiences?

We can make ourselves laugh over the memory of a hilarious situation shared with friends or flood ourselves with a feeling of warmth by recalling the hug of a beloved grandparent. To remember a happy experience fully and mindfully is to appreciate it and reap physical, emotional, and cognitive benefits.

Why Appreciate Happy Experiences?

Remembering a happy memory releases in our brain the same "feel-good" chemicals that flooded it at the time of the actual experience. We can practice mindfully recalling favorite memories as a strategy to achieve a variety of goals, including

- cultivating optimism
- alleviating negativity (e.g., boredom, worry)
- priming our brain for learning new material
- generating ideas from past experiences
- boosting our physical health

Students can learn to savor happy memories to help overcome specific negative feelings, such as sadness or insecurity. You can also integrate the concept into your teaching by creating learning experiences that are engaging and involve positive interactions and laughter, when possible. Those memories will be easy for students to recall and use as background support for classroom experiences.

What Can You Expect to Observe?

"Appreciating happy memories is one of the most concrete tools we've used to build optimism in our classroom. Students have learned to re-create mini-movies in their minds to help lift their spirits when they're stressed out or feeling down and to remember important learning experiences linked to an exciting or novel discovery."

—Third-grade teacher

Linking to Brain Research

Happy Memories Support a Can-Do Attitude

Recall from lessons 6 and 7 the critical role of the neurotransmitter most associated with pleasure, attention, reward, motivation, and perseverance—dopamine. Higher levels of dopamine in our brain result in feelings of hope, tolerance, motivation, and a can-do attitude—optimism. Dopamine release is triggered when we engage in pleasurable experiences such as play-filled activities, laughing, physical exercise, acts of kindness, and positive social interactions.

Brain scans show that dopamine is released not only when we engage directly in pleasurable experiences, but also when we reflect on and remember these salient moments. In fact, remembering a positive experience can trigger dopamine release as powerfully as the real thing. By repeatedly referencing past successes, we build confidence and are more able to rebuff the "I can't" voice in our head. Happy memories can become a tool to prime the brain for new social, academic, and physical challenges.

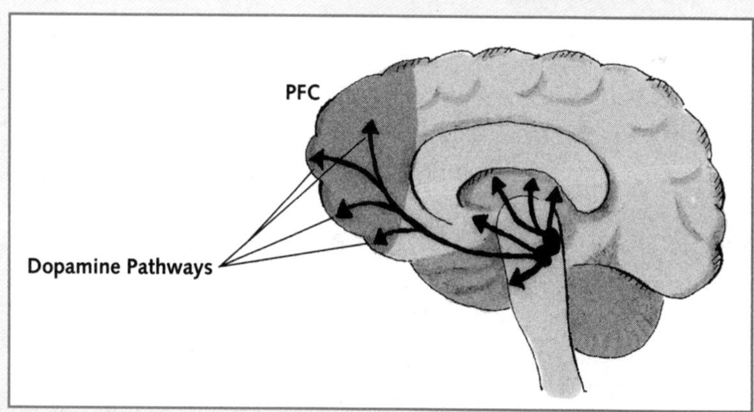

A major pathway of dopamine leads to the prefrontal cortex.

Clarify for the Class

Remembering a positive experience can trigger dopamine and help fight off hopeless thoughts. Learning to recall past successes related to a present challenge is a powerful weapon against the panic and hopelessness of "I can't." Try the following exercise with students: On a small piece of paper, have each student write something he or she would like to achieve, but feels is unattainable (e.g., "I can't get all A's or run a mile."). Then have them write on the back of the card a related thing that they *have* accomplished (e.g., "I got one A on my last report card" or "I can run farther now than I could a few months ago.").

Discuss: How did you feel when you wrote the "I can't..." side of the card? Do you feel differently after remembering what you had accomplished? How?

Getting Ready

Making a Mini-Movie
Students visualize their memory as a mini-movie to help recall vivid details.

GOALS

- Students visualize and describe their thoughts, feelings, and physical sensations during a pleasurable experience.
- Students use recalling a pleasurable experience as a way to build optimism.

MATERIALS

- chart paper

CREATING THE OPTIMISTIC CLASSROOM

Brain-Inspired Instruction Each lesson you teach is an opportunity to create a pleasurable learning experience—not only as you teach it, but also as children reflect on it and appreciate it. Surefire dopamine boosters that enhance lessons include

- music and purposeful movement
- novel sensory activities
- positive and supportive peer interaction
- personal emotional connections
- activity choices and opportunities to learn collaboratively

Lighten Up!
Students share a happy memory, deepening their relationship and priming their brain to learn.

MINDUP Warm-Up

Memory-Sharing Practice

Share a happy memory about the class that makes you smile as you tell it aloud. For example, you might tell students about a special moment you remember on the first day of school as you were just getting to know them.

Invite students to turn to a partner and share a favorite class memory from this year. Then have the group come up with a list of memories that involve the class. Record their ideas on chart paper. As you review the list of memories, have them raise their hands to their chin if the memory makes them smile a little, to the top of their head if it makes them smile widely, and above their heads if it fills them with happiness or laughter.

Discuss: Think about the memories that made you raise your hands high. What kinds of situations produce really happy memories? Why do you think some memories are stronger than others? Does recalling a memory change the way you feel? What is one of the main places in our brains where memories are stored?

Leading the Lesson

Happy Memory Mini-Movies

Engage

What to Do

Review the warm-up activity and relate remembering happy times to practicing optimism.

- One way to train our brains to think more optimistically is to take time to enjoy happy memories we've had.
- We're going to learn to remember very mindfully—to savor a happy memory the way we've savored a morsel of food in our mindful tasting activities.

Give an example of how to draw out and appreciate a memory by fully narrating aloud the class memory you selected or choosing a different one. Make sure the memory visibly makes you feel happy.

- I'm going to show you how I can see my memory fully and enjoy every bit of it by closing my eyes and creating a mini-movie in my mind. Listen to my voice and watch my expression as I recall how the memory went and the little details that made it so special.

Why It's Important

Taking time to model how to recall a memory will help students understand that they must slow down and notice the details that make the memory more complete and special. These may include the people involved, their expressions, their funny or meaningful actions, the roles of weather and other setting factors, and so on. It's a good idea to practice telling your memory aloud before you present it to students.

Explore

What to Do

Invite students to choose a memory from the class memory list or choose another that made them especially happy, such as a memorable field trip or exciting news about a family member.

Review how savoring their happy memory will be like making a mini-movie in their minds. Encourage them to close their eyes or look into their hands. You might begin and end the visualization with a sounding of the instrument you use for the Core Practice. Offer cues to help students fully visualize their happy experience.

- Bring all your attention to your happy experience.
- Start the mini-movie in your mind.
- See the people involved, notice the things that make you happy. Notice your thoughts and how your body is feeling.
- Picture the way your happy memory ends, and focus on how it makes you feel.

Encourage students to create simple story boards of the memory they recalled. In this way they can narrate the memory for classmates, with visual support.

Why It's Important

Providing plenty of structure and quiet space for students to recall their memories will allow their amygdala to relax and their prefrontal cortex to receive and process all the input it's gathering.

From the Research

Learning connected with positive emotional significance leads to the new information being stored in long-term memory. (Pawlak, et al., 2003)

Reflect

Guide students to share their experience making the mental mini-movies.

- As you savored your memory, how did your brain feel? How did your body feel?
- What do you think was happening in your brain and body during the memory? How is that similar to or different from the mindful movement activity we did?

Help students understand that their brains can help change how they feel physically and emotionally—recalling happy memories is one way to do that.

Point out that while nobody is happy all the time, we can use happy memories as a tool to feel better, enjoy special times with friends and family, and build optimistic thinking skills. Ask students to be very aware of happy moments that arise over the next few days. Remind them to "make the movie in their mind" to savor and revisit the happy feelings. Be sure to emphasize to students that feeling sad or discouraged is natural and is not always an obstacle. In fact, feeling "blue" often leads to reflectiveness and to productive thinking.

The experience of being flooded by warm emotions from a memory they chose provides students with proof that they can control their thoughts and feelings, even if they can't always control what happens around them. It also shows how quickly feelings can change—that students can improve their mood by a simple mindful practice that takes about a minute to complete.

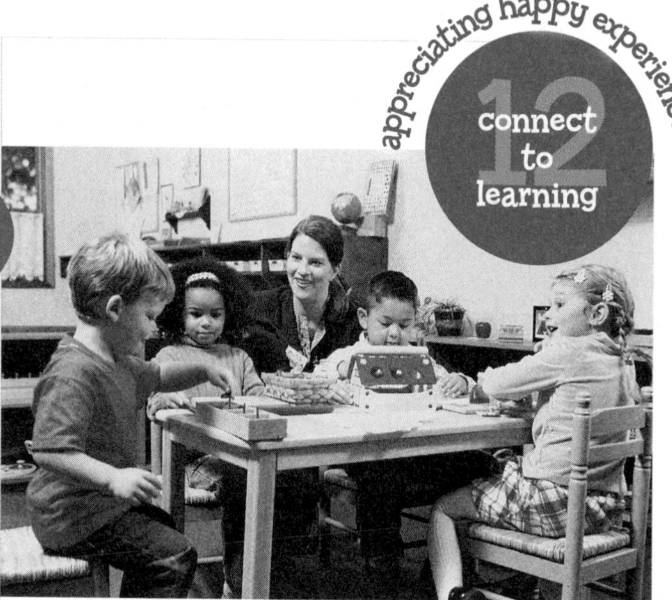

MINDUP In the Real World

Career Connection

Pleasure may begin with our ability to notice and relish details—appreciation for the hands that made a tasty soup, enjoyment of a shared song, and deep satisfaction of a handmade gift. One of the joys of being around young children is their natural ability to appreciate the smallest details of an experience. A prekindergarten teacher will often witness with a sense of wonder and delight—splashing in a rain puddle, watching a butterfly or playing with shadows on a wall as she or he sees the world through the eyes of young children. Spending time with young children allows us to pay attention to the small events that are ours to appreciate too.

Discuss: Think of people who do their jobs mindfully, with an effort to create happy moments to savor. Recall people you notice regularly enjoying themselves—who are they and what are their jobs?

Once a Day

As you teach, think of ways to create happy memories, whether you incorporate humor, a song, a game, or some other kind of positive group interaction. These memories become a platform on which to build new instruction.

Connecting to the Curriculum

Appreciating happy experiences supports students' connection to their own learning process and to the content areas and literature.

Journal Writing

Encourage your students to reflect on what they've learned about appreciating happy experiences and to record questions they may want to explore at another time. In addition, they may enjoy responding to these prompts:

- Sketch a favorite scene from the "mini-movie" you created in your mind during the lesson. Use thought and speech bubbles to show what people were thinking and feeling.
- Recall a time when something you did or said gave another person a happy moment. Describe how you created a pleasant memory for someone else.
- Draw two columns. At the top of one write your name. At the top of the other write the name of an adult you care about. In each column, write/draw four events, activities, or experiences that you think would produce happy memories for that person.
- On the top half of your journal page, tell about a time when you felt sad. On the bottom half, write about a happy memory that you could revisit next time you feel sad. Add illustrations if you like.

LANGUAGE ARTS

A Character's Memorable Day

What to Do

Have small groups discuss what makes one character in a book you've shared (or one they're reading together) feel quite content. Have students use information from the book and inferences about the character's preferences to create two schedules: one for a typical day (the character's usual schedule) and an unforgettably good day. Have groups compare schedules and discuss what similarities they reveal.

What to Say

Think back through the book to find clues about what your character does each day. Now that you have an actual schedule, consider this character's favorite experiences, sensations, wishes, happy memories, and dreams. What friends, food, and events would his or her ideal day include? Would he or she have an exciting, packed schedule or a leisurely one? How different are these schedules?

Why It's Important

This activity requires two key comprehension skills: reading for details (collecting information about a character's daily life) and making inferences (using thoughts, actions, and dialogue) to better understand a character. The schedules provide a concrete way to contrast the actual and ideal experiences of a character and provide insight into character motivation and perspective.

SOCIAL STUDIES

Historical Memories

What to Do

Dozens of online sites, such as "American Memory" from the Library of Congress, provide letters, maps, photographs, paintings, advertisements, and firsthand accounts of specific times and events. Integrate primary sources—fragments of our historical memory—whenever possible in any social studies lesson.

What to Say

As you look at sketches, photographs, and maps and read the letters, diaries, poems, or songs of people from the time we're studying, ask yourself, "Who might have created this artifact and why?" "What perspective does this image or these words show?" "How does it help us build historical memory about this time?"

Why It's Important

Primary sources help students see that history is made of multiple perspectives—the more sources we have, the bigger the picture we have of our history. Lead students to see the similarity between primary sources and memories—both are colored by the beliefs, life experiences, and culture of the person who created them.

MATH

Class Favorites Data

What to Do
Ask students to collect data about their classmates' favorite activities to get a perspective on class preferences. Help students generate activity categories (e.g., recess games, board games, subject-area activities, after-school activities, or sports), make a list of four or five activities for the category they've chosen, then take tallies of their classmates' favorites. Have students present their findings on a bar graph and share the graph with the class.

What to Say
Once you've taken the tally, talk to a friend about your findings—did anything surprise you that you'll be able to show in your bar graph? Was there a certain activity that was more popular than you expected or vice versa? What did you learn about our class from the data?

Why It's Important
Using real-life information that interests students is the best way to build any kind of skill; classroom data collection invites them to investigate topics of interest. As students analyze the data, let them share what they're discovering. In addition, help them see purposeful ways their data collection could be used (e.g., to plan recess activities, research topics, field trips, or class speakers).

SOCIAL-EMOTIONAL LEARNING

Class Memory Album

What to Do
Share an example of a scrapbook, showing students how people frame happy memories with artifacts such as photos, sketches, ticket stubs, and so on. Set up a station in class to collect items related to class events. Have a small group create an album page for each event.

What to Say
An album is a wonderful tool for savoring memories. For each special event, we can add artifacts we've collected. This scrapbook is a record of happy memories. Which artifacts really capture a feeling? What are some memories we'll want to savor this month? What artifacts would best capture them?

Why It's Important
A class memory album helps students form bonds based on shared experiences and provides a class history of examples of effort, teamwork, cooperation, and other social skills.

Literature Link
Thirty Days Has September: Cool Ways to Remember Stuff

by Chris Stevens
(2010). New York: Scholastic.

Full of illustrations, rhymes, phrases, acronyms, rules, and popular sayings, this book offers strategies to help kids remember important information. Let students browse the book and present their favorite tips and strategies to the class.

Connect this book with study skills, the role of the hippocampus in storing memories, and with reviewing happy events to save them in our memories.

More Books to Share

Corman, Carolyn. (2010). *The Memory Bank*. New York: Scholastic.

Korman, Gordon (2009) *Radio Fifth Grade*. New York: Scholastic.

Rylant, Cynthia. (1993). *When I Was Young in the Mountains*. New York: Dutton.

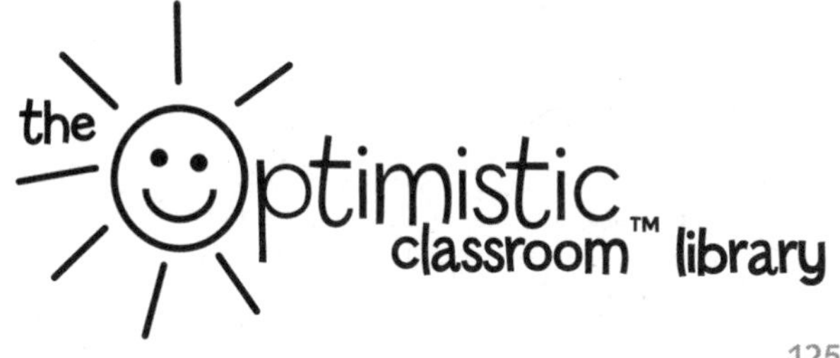

Taking Action Mindfully

Learning to express gratitude and perform acts of kindness helps students build the awareness, cognitive skills, compassion, and confidence to contribute in a meaningful way to the classroom and the world.

Students gain an appreciation for special people and things in their lives and discover the social, emotional, and cognitive benefits of showing gratitude.

As students perform small acts of kindness for friends, classmates, teachers, and family, they learn how these positive actions can increase their optimism and brain power.

Students collaboratively plan and perform a group act of kindness and reflect on the way combined efforts can make an important difference in the world and connect them to their peers and the larger community.

unit IV

"When you give yourself, you receive more than you give." The lessons in this unit give credence to Saint-Exupéry's famous quote. Certainly, there are obvious benefits for the recipients of kind actions students will do in these lessons—from helping lift a classmate's spirits to raising funds for victims of a natural disaster on the other side of the world. Yet participating mindfully in positive social actions can affect students' social, emotional, and cognitive growth in transformational ways.

By expressing gratitude and performing acts of kindness, students develop a stronger understanding of the feelings of other people and a concern for the well-being of others. Research shows that actions that engender feelings of empathy and compassion have a number of positive benefits, such as boosting the production of the feel-good neurotransmitter dopamine, increasing the likelihood that students will continue to act on their social concerns, and improving their capacity to take care of themselves.

Expressing Gratitude

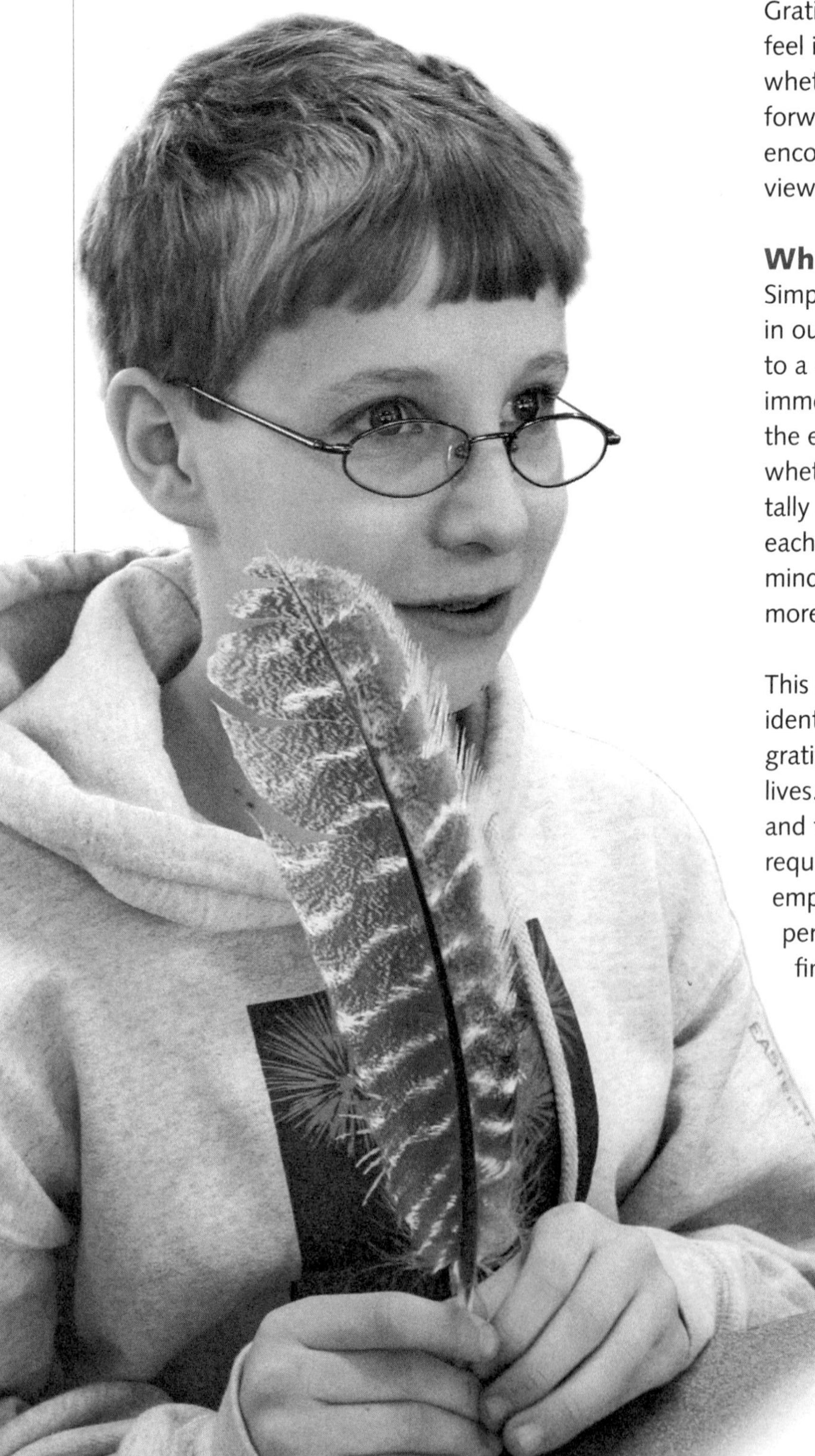

What Is Gratitude?

Gratitude is a feeling of thankfulness and joy we feel in response to something we've received, whether the gift is tangible, such as a book we look forward to reading, or intangible, such as a smile of encouragement from a loved one or a breathtaking view of a landscape.

Why Practice Expressing Gratitude?

Simply focusing for a minute on the experiences in our lives we're grateful for shifts our thinking to a calmer, more content perspective, which can immediately uplift and comfort us. When we make the expression of gratitude a regular practice—whether we make a daily written list or a mental tally of things we're grateful for as we start or end each day—we train our brain to shift to a positive mind-set more efficiently and maintain a healthier, more optimistic perspective.

This lesson gives students the opportunity to identify and share with peers expressions of gratitude for people, events, and things in their lives. This sharing forges stronger connections and trust among peers. The mindful listening required in the lesson also cultivates students' empathy, laying the foundation for planning and performing acts of kindness over the course of the final two lessons.

What Can You Expect to Observe?

"Expressing gratitude in a weekly class gathering is something students really look forward to. They now actively look for important things in their lives—big and small—that make them glad to be alive. The feeling is contagious. Our circle generates many smiles and resonates with their shared joy."

—Third-grade teacher

Linking to Brain Research

The Many Gifts of Gratitude

Gratitude has powerful physiological effects on the brain—and body. Researchers have found that when we think about someone or something we truly appreciate, our bodies calm themselves. The feelings that come with gratitude trigger the calming branch of the autonomic nervous system, the parasympathetic system. The sympathetic system is the "fight, flight, or freeze" responder during emergencies, stress, and intense activity. The counteracting parasympathetic system is all about "rest and digest." It slows the heartbeat, shunts blood from the muscles to the organs, and contracts the pupils of the eyes. Feeling appreciative also produces a more even heart rhythm, which may reduce the risk of heart attacks and relieve hypertension.

Feeling thankful and appreciative also affects levels of brain neurotransmitters, including releasing dopamine toward the prefrontal cortex where reasoning and logic occur. Dopamine not only fosters contentment, it is also the main player in the brain's reward and motivation system. Experiments have shown that those who keep gratitude journals or lists feel more optimistic and make more progress toward their goals. And young people who do daily self-guided exercises in gratitude have higher levels of alertness, enthusiasm, determination, attentiveness, and energy (Emmons & McCullough). Students who practice grateful thinking not only have a more positive attitude toward school, their brains are more ready to learn.

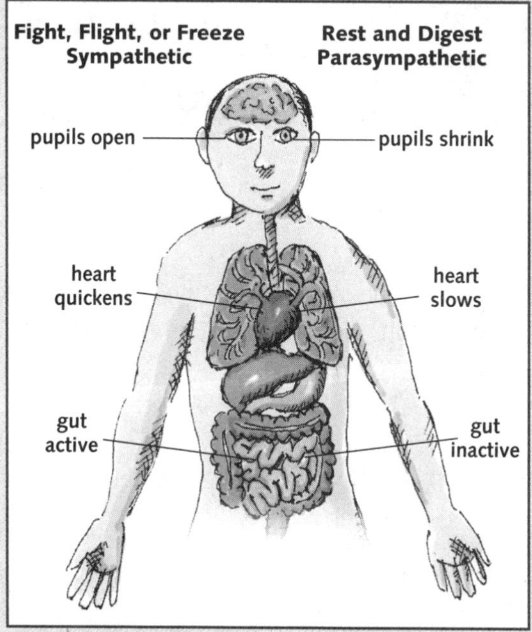

The autonomic nervous system has two parts: sympathetic and parasympathetic.

Clarify for the Class

Tell students that the autonomic nervous system automatically controls many functions of our bodies, such as digestion, blood circulation, and breathing. In times of stress the "fight, flight, or freeze" side of this system is in control. During sleep, rest, and relaxation the calm side of the system takes over. Ask students to describe how they feel when stressed and when calm. Ask students to think about a number of situations (an upcoming test, receiving a compliment, remembering a kind act, speaking in front of the class, etc.) ask them to say which system it likely engages—the calm or stressed one?

Discuss: What thoughts of thankfulness and appreciation help calm you?

Getting Ready

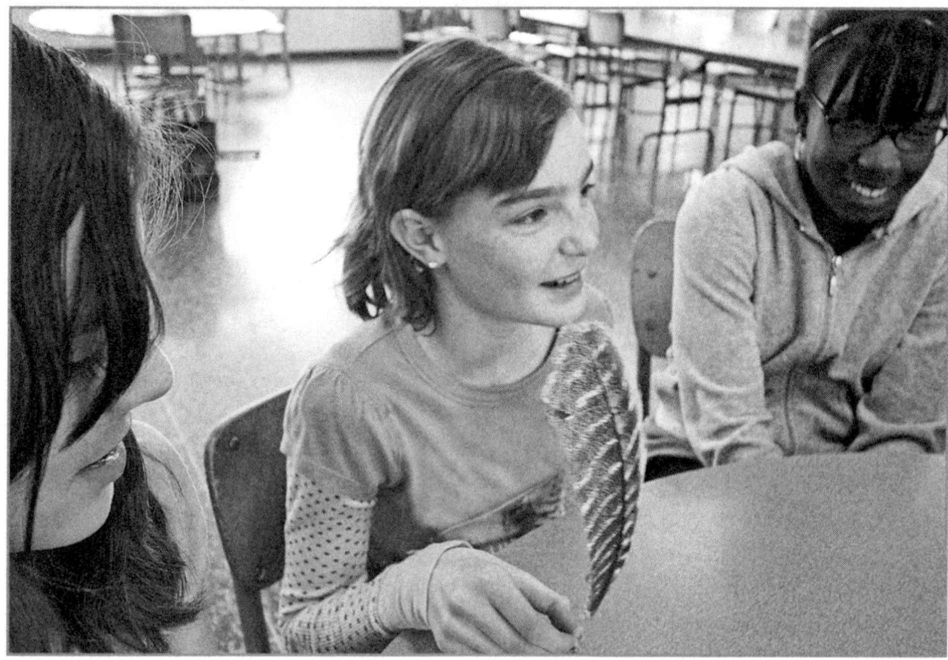

Passing the Feather
Students hold the space for one another to share what they are thankful for.

GOALS

- Students learn the meaning of gratitude and the importance of expressing gratitude.
- Students identify things in their life for which they are grateful.

MATERIALS

- chart paper
- small stone, crystal, feather, or other special object students can hold during the sharing activity

CREATING THE OPTIMISTIC CLASSROOM

Supporting English Language Learners Help students with limited English language skills participate in the sharing part of the lesson in alternative ways:

- allowing students to sketch the thing(s) for which they are grateful and write a short caption with your help or the help of a peer. Let them show the image and read or choose someone to read the caption.
- giving students a frame for participating in the circle, such as "I am grateful for ________." Students can add why they are grateful or simply share the one word or idea.

expressing gratitude

13 understand the purpose

A Place to Express Myself
A student creates the cover of a journal for recording personal expressions of gratitude.

MINDUP Warm-Up

"Thank You" Practice

As you engage in Core Practice at the start of class, ask students to recall one or two times recently when they said "thank you." Have a few volunteers share what they were thankful for and the person they thanked. As students share, ask the class to think about the types of things their classmates are thankful for. On chart paper, write down any categories students suggest, such as polite gestures (e.g., saving a seat), kind acts and words (sharing a lunch with someone who forgot his or hers), giving a gift or something needed (giving a birthday gift), spending time or giving attention (playing a game with someone), and so on.

On scratch paper have students list five things they've said thank you for recently. Assign a color to each category on the class list. Then have students highlight or underline each event or item they've listed according to the color category in which they think it belongs. Have students compare the patterns they're finding.

Introduce the word *gratitude* and discuss that being grateful means to feel thankful without necessarily actually saying "thank you" to anyone.

Discuss: Are there things you are grateful for that you can't buy in a store? Look at the colors of the items on your list. What are you most likely to say thank you for? Are there things you might be thankful for that you don't usually say thank you for?

Leading the Lesson

Gratitude Circle

Engage

What to Do

Review from the warm-up activity that gratitude is a feeling and a way of thinking that expresses our thanks. Provide an example by sharing things you are grateful for, such as being in good health, teaching in a classroom where you learn new things every day, and enjoying time with your family.

Have students gather their chairs or sit on the floor in a circle as you introduce the activity.

- Your "thank-you" lists from our warm-up show that you, too, have many things in your life that you are thankful for.
- Today we'll each share one of those things in a special group meeting—a gratitude circle.

Make sure students understand that in this circle, they'll offer gratitude only for things that cannot be purchased from a store.

- Do you feel grateful for certain people who are part of your life? special activities you do or games or sports you play? fascinating or beautiful things in nature?

Why It's Important

It may be easiest for students to remember tangible things. Help students understand that you want them to focus on things that don't necessarily cost money but that bring happiness and can be cherished. That will empower students to recognize wonderful life experiences not linked to ownership and wealth, as well as the satisfaction derived from generous actions.

Explore

What to Do

Explain that the group will pass around the gratitude stone (or other special object).

- When you receive the stone, you may name one thing you are grateful for, then pass the stone to the next person.
- Please give the speaker your full attention and listen mindfully, without commenting on what that person says. Our goal is to make everyone feel comfortable about sharing.
- If you choose not to share out loud, hold the stone in your hand, think your thought of gratitude, and pass it along.

Congratulate students for sharing and listening mindfully. Ask them to share how it felt to say and hear the many expressions of gratitude.

For the next few days, have them keep a journal in which they will make a daily list of things that they are grateful for. You may have them keep a separate Gratitude Journal or use their MindUP Journal.

Why It's Important

Providing two different modes for students to express thoughts of gratitude (group circle and journal) offers them a chance to appreciate the thoughts of classmates and to present their own ideas safely. Establishing a "no comments" (positive or negative) rule for the sharing will increase students' sense of security in sharing something personal, as will the option to express the thought silently. (See the box on page 130 for ELL support.)

From the Research

. . . by experiencing gratitude, a person is motivated to carry out prosocial behavior, energized to sustain moral behaviors, and is inhibited from committing destructive interpersonal behaviors. (McCullough et al., 2001)

Reflect

After a few days of keeping notes, invite students to discuss their experience with the gratitude practices.

- How did you feel when you wrote about the things you were grateful for?
- What did you notice about your mood? What did you notice about your thinking?
- How was sharing in the circle different from writing on your own? How could both kinds of sharing be useful in different ways?

Build on students' responses to help them recognize the positive effects that gratitude practices can have, such as improving our mood, helping us think more clearly, connecting us with the people and things we're grateful for, connecting us with others who are expressing gratitude, and giving us a sense of well-being or happiness.

Plan with students how they can make gratitude journal writing and gratitude circle sharing a daily or weekly practice to add to their tool kit.

Cognitive research suggests that when people focus on the things they are grateful for, their happiness increases. Making a habit of expressing gratitude helps us be mindful about our lives and the bigger picture, leading to greater appreciation for other people and the larger world. Give students a say in helping you design a plan to make gratitude practices a helpful tool to integrate into the school day.

MINDUP In the Real World

Career Connection

Feeling grateful enables people in any circumstance to relax and experience a sense of peace and happiness. That's especially important when the type of task a person is doing is stressful, such as working late to meet a deadline, or tiring, such as spending many hours standing or sitting. One way to generate feelings of gratitude and find ways to do the work at hand even better is to seek feedback from coworkers and supervisors. When we receive genuine, constructive criticism from people whose goal is to help us do our job better, we discover new ways to do tasks or solve problems—and that is something to be grateful for!

Discuss: Give an example of a way you've helped a classmate build a skill, such as reading or learning multiplication tables. Now think of when a teacher or classmates have helped you do something better. How can getting feedback make you feel grateful?

Once a Day

Seek feedback from students on the way you explain a concept, lead a routine, or implement a strategy. Consider how the perceptions and ideas of others can plant the seeds of growth.

Connecting to the Curriculum

Expressing gratitude supports students' connection to their own learning process and to the content areas and literature.

Journal Writing

Encourage your students to reflect on what they've learned about expressing gratitude and to record questions they may want to explore at another time. In addition, they may enjoy responding to these prompts:

- Make a "Top 10" list of things, events, and people in your life that you feel grateful for.
- Think about an exciting skill you recently learned from a family member, friend, or teacher, such as juggling or baking cookies. Write a short note expressing your gratitude for the teaching.
- Imagine that you are a plant, animal, or any other natural thing. From that perspective, write about what you are grateful for.
- Compose an acrostic poem about someone you are grateful to have in your life. Write this person's name vertically on your journal page. Use each letter of his or her name to begin a word or phrase that describes the characteristics or actions you admire.

SCIENCE

Food Gratitude

What to Do

Provide each student with a paper cup, soil to fill the cup, and several seeds of a plant that sprouts quickly and is edible and nutritious, such as basil, parsley, mint, or bean sprouts. Assign students to monitor their seedlings, noting each day on a class calendar whether there was sunshine, when the seeds were watered, and the number of seeds that have germinated. You might keep a couple of "control" samples in a dark cabinet for comparison.

What to Say

Thanksgiving is traditionally a time to show gratitude for the year's harvest—any farmer knows it takes lot of work to generate enough food for everyone to eat. In addition, certain conditions in nature need to be present for a plant to grow—can you name some? Let's see what it takes to make just a few seeds sprout and develop into a plant we can enjoy and use for food.

Why It's Important

Students will appreciate that vegetables and fruits require time and energy to grow and in turn give us the energy we need to grow. Remind them that the beginning of every food chain is a green plant, and that the growth and development of our brains and our bodies derive from the energy contained in green plants.

SOCIAL STUDIES

Gratitude Long Ago

What to Do

Discuss a historical topic you have studied in class, such as the life of Native Americans or of settlers in Colonial New England. On the board, chart details students recall about daily life, such as the types of dwellings the people lived in, their family structure, and the way they spent their time. Have students write a gratitude diary entry from the perspective of a child who lived at the time.

What to Say

What are some of the things a person your age from this period in history might be grateful for that are different from the things you are grateful for? What are the things that might be the same, no matter what period or place in the world?

Why It's Important

This activity can help students identify time- and culture-specific experiences of someone their age from a historical period they are studying. It can also help students realize that some important things (family, friends, good weather, health, and so on) top gratitude lists in almost any period.

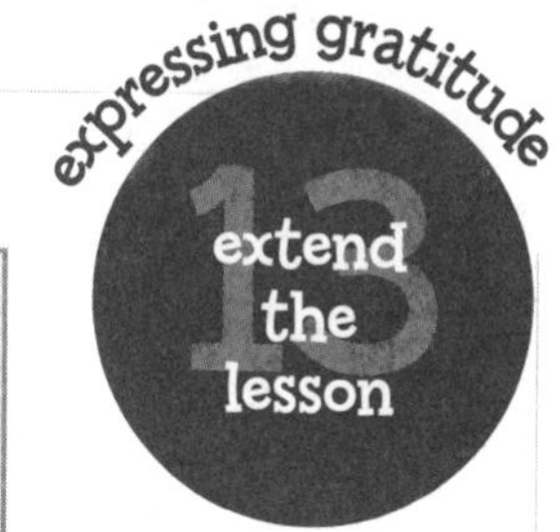

HEALTH

Nature's Gifts

What to Do

Have students generate a list of the natural elements we depend upon for survival, such as water, air, soil, and sunshine. Organize students into groups that will explore how one of these elements supports human life. Let students come up with a visual display showing the many ways humans benefit from this element. They might use sketches, images found online, or magazine photos to enhance their work. Have groups share their presentations.

What to Say

Scientists tell us that human bodies are 60 to 70 percent water. How does that help you understand our need for water every day? Can you imagine life without water? What other natural elements do we depend on for survival? As your group collects images and information on the element you're investigating, think about how to show what you're learning in a memorable way.

Why It's Important

This activity helps students recognize how essential to our health and survival the natural world is. That understanding gives students a sense of connection to nature, provides perspective on what students regard as important, and helps them expand their gratitude list.

SOCIAL-EMOTIONAL LEARNING

Gratitude Stones

What to Do

Collect smooth, small stones so that there is one for each student. From their journals or circle sharing, have students choose one key experience, thing, or person for which they are grateful. Have them write a short reminder on their stone in fine-point permanent marker. Place the marked stones in a basket and set them in a special spot. Invite students, whenever they need a boost, to hold their stone and spend a moment being grateful.

What to Say

Our gratitude stones are reminders of the things that make us happy to be alive. By coming to the basket, holding your stone, breathing deeply, and reflecting mindfully, you have a soothing way to remind yourself of the things you value and love in life.

Why It's Important

Giving students tools to practice gratitude increases the likelihood they'll engage in the practice on their own. That cultivates mindful thinking and encourages students to self-regulate and take good emotional care of themselves.

Literature Link
My Rotten Redheaded Older Brother

by Patricia Polacco
(2007). New York: Scholastic.

Whether picking blackberries or playing games, Richie always manages to outdo his sister Patricia. When their grandmother teaches her to wish on a falling star, Patricia knows just what to ask for. The next day her wish comes true—sort of. She remains on the carnival carousel longer than Richie. Guess who becomes her hero, however, when she gets dizzy and tumbles? Connect this book to a discussion of the people and things that students have on their own gratitude lists.

More Books to Share

Sepulveda, Luis. (2001). *The Story of a Seagull and the Cat Who Taught Her to Fly.* New York: Scholastic.

Mazer, Norma Fox. (2007). *Ten Ways to Make My Sister Disappear.* New York: Scholastic.

McKissack, Patricia. (1997). *Run Away Home.* New York: Scholastic.

Performing Acts of Kindness

What Are Acts of Kindness?

Good deeds…gestures of generosity…paying it forward. These expressions describe mindful action intended to help another living thing. Participating in such an action constitutes an act of kindness. Acts of kindness can be big or small, spontaneous or well planned.

Why Perform Acts of Kindness?

Think back to a time when someone helped you out unexpectedly or gave you a compliment. Memories like this have intense staying power (in fact, they may be part of a larger happy memory) and often remind us that we can act in the same way to help, encourage, or comfort someone else. Socially, acts of kindness cultivate shared happiness, build relationships, and give people a sense of connectedness to a group, community, or place—they are an excellent way to build a classroom community full of good will and optimism.

In this lesson, students plan several acts of kindness, which not only benefit the larger community but also help develop the neural networks that build students' sense of compassion and empathy. The more people practice acts of kindness, the more likely they are to recognize and act on situations in which others are in need.

What Can You Expect to Observe?

"Doing acts of kindness puts a sparkle in the eyes of my students—we've made doing acts of kindness a weekly challenge. I find students are not only more friendly toward one another, they are more aware of the needs of those around them."

—Fourth-grade teacher

Linking to Brain Research

Our Brains Are Built for Compassion and Empathy

Being concerned about the welfare of others and understanding the feelings of those around us are basic skills for emotional intelligence. Compassion and empathy can be developed through mindfully practicing acts of kindness. As children develop compassion and empathy, they learn to recognize that their words and actions have an impact on others. This feeling of interconnectedness helps them reflect on their responses to the words and actions of others and better monitor and control their emotional responses. Practicing compassion and empathy builds the social and emotional competence that children need in order to be resilient and confident.

Brain research studies confirm the power of practicing kindness. Brain scans reveal that neural pathways involved in detecting emotions are dramatically strengthened in people with extensive, focused experiences in practicing compassion. Other studies have shown that our brains are rewarded for altruism with a release of dopamine during acts of kindness. We are hard-wired to feel good about doing good.

Scientists are discovering that compassion is an emotion as evolutionarily ancient as fear or anger. Brain scans of subjects feeling compassion while watching videos of strangers in despair and grief show activity not only in the higher brain's cortex but also in the hypothalamus and brain stem.

Clarify for the Class

Explain that the way our brain works encourages us to feel compassion, understand how others feel, and do kind acts. When we do selfless things for others, our brain releases the feel-good neurotransmitter dopamine.

Discuss: What are some examples of selfless acts? Have you ever felt better after being kind to someone? Describe how you felt before and how you felt after. What do you think was going on in your brain?

Getting Ready

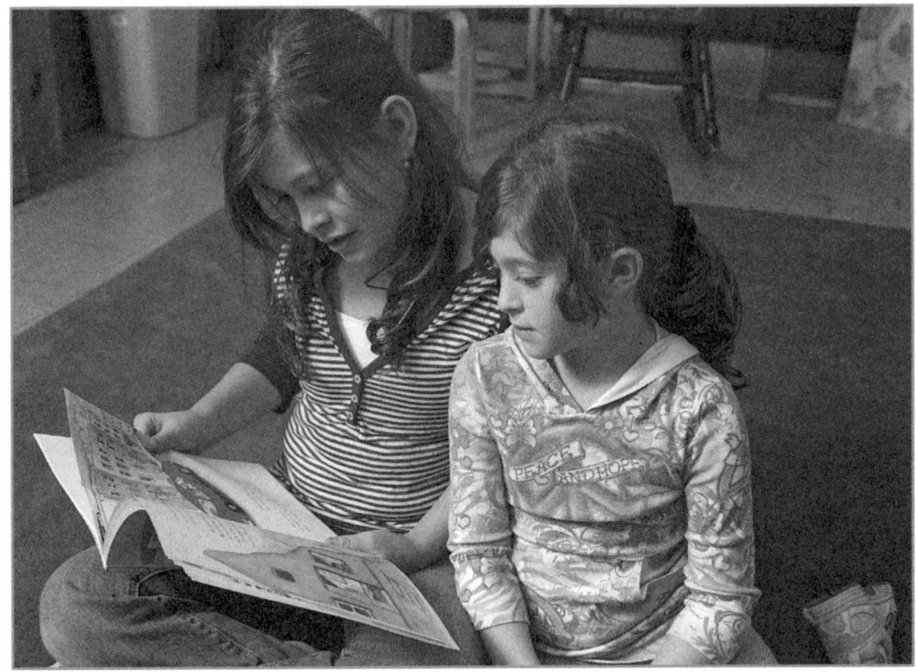

Gift of Literacy
Older students can serve as reading buddies to younger peers.

GOALS

- Students find three opportunities to show kindness and perform three acts of kindness.
- Students explore the benefits—for themselves and for others—of being kind.

MATERIALS

- chart paper
- index cards

CREATING THE OPTIMISTIC CLASSROOM

Classroom Management Through mindful speech and actions, you and your students can develop a culture of social responsibility. The time and attention you invest in leading a socially responsible classroom pay big dividends. Students who are socially responsible trust their classmates, are more able to solve interpersonal problems, and have better school (and life) success than their less socially competent peers.

A job list that includes rotating roles for everyone in the class (or a list of acts of kindness that students can sign up to accomplish periodically) are two ways to expand students' sense of responsibility.

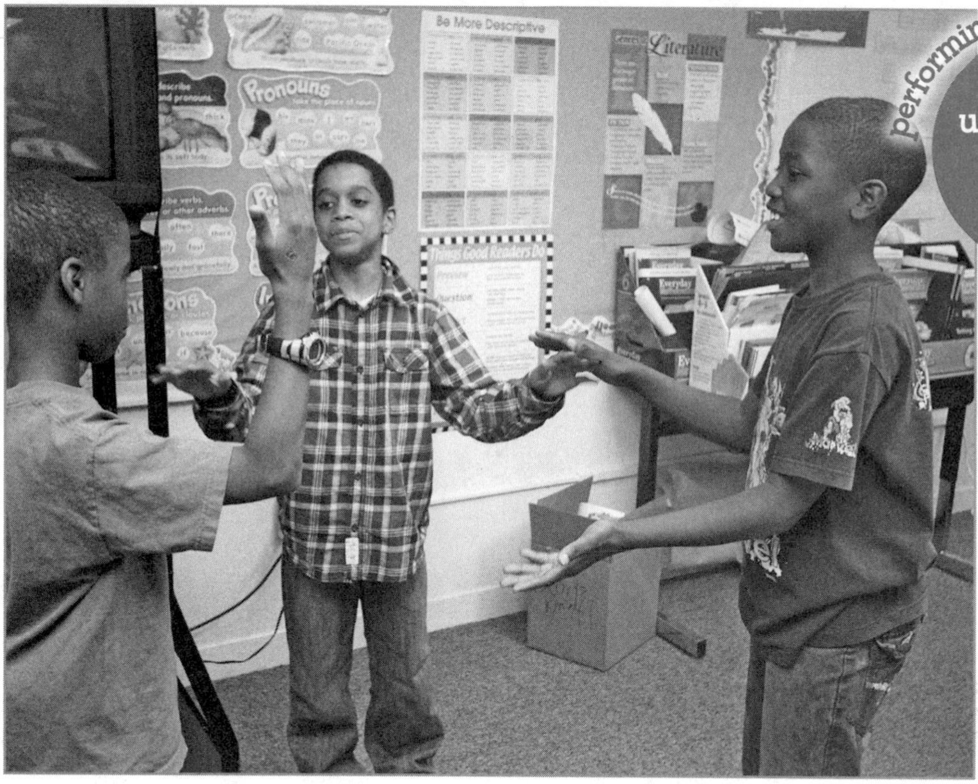

Fun-Filled Greeting
Classmates devise a special three-way greeting.

MINDUP Warm-Up

Kindness Practice

Challenge the class to generate gratitude and optimism with a round of compliments for the entire group. (Give an example of a compliment that focuses on someone's positive effort or behavior and avoids judging physical appearances.)

Have students write their name on an index card and put it in a container. Shake up the collected slips and tell students that they are going to pick the name of a classmate and keep it a secret. Have them watch the peer whose name they selected for the rest of the period or day. Before gathering again, have students write a compliment on the back of the card. Students may read aloud to the group the compliment they wrote out or silently exchange compliments and savor the one written about them. Encourage students to watch the expression of the person receiving the compliment and to notice how they feel as both giver and recipient.

Discuss: How does doing a kind act like giving a compliment look and sound? Think of other acts of kindness you have seen at school. What did you see and hear that signaled to you that someone was being kind?

Leading the Lesson

Three Acts of Kindness

Engage

What to Do

Review the warm-up exercise to focus students' attention on what kindness means and the ways in which it is already part of their life experience.

- Based on our compliments challenge, how much time would you say it takes to be kind? Describe what you observed.
- Does it cost anything to be kind?
- Do you need special expertise to be kind?
- Who or what in our world deserves our kindness?
- How do you feel after you've done something kind?
- Do you have to see the effect of a kind act to feel good about it?

Have students talk in pairs to come up with a definition of kindness. Work with the class to synthesize a definition, such as "Kindness is a mindful choice to treat someone or something in a friendly, caring way."

Why It's Important

This discussion helps students understand that acting on kindness is a choice they can make easily and often and that kindness can take many forms. It is helpful to share examples that expand students' understanding of kindness from a single type of action, such as paying a compliment, to a range of acts that involve caring for people and other living things.

Explore

What to Do

Connect kindness to gratitude, optimism, and perspective taking.

- When you feel optimistic, are you more or less likely to act kindly?
- Could doing a kind act cause you to feel grateful? Could being grateful cause you to do a kind act?
- Was there a time when seeing the way someone else felt (seeing their perspective) helped you perform an act of kindness that really helped that person?

Announce that for the next day, the challenge is to test out their answers by performing at least three acts of kindness. Have students brainstorm a list of kind actions they might perform. Encourage them to come up with specific actions, such as saying hello to a new student, assisting a peer with a challenging assignment, inviting someone who looks left out to join their group, and recognizing a classmate's hard work. Have them check off on their list or note the acts they performed.

Why It's Important

Making connections among the concepts students have been learning and practicing may help them see how this positive, brain-building work all fits together. Older students may be able to grasp the role of perspective taking in acting kindly more easily than younger students; you may want younger students to review with you the ideas on their list and commit to three specific ones.

From the Research

Children who are socially responsible, trust their classmates, and solve interpersonal problems in adaptive ways earn higher marks than those who do not.
(Wentzel, 1991)

Reflect

After a day's time, gather students together to reflect on their experiences performing the three acts of kindness. Have them select their most memorable act of kindness, make a sketch of the event, and describe it to a peer.

Then ask volunteers to share. Help students make connections by having them revisit the questions you asked before their brainstorming.

- Did anyone experience an optimistic feeling before or after their act of kindness?
- What role did gratitude play in your act of kindness?
- Before you performed your act, did you use perspective taking to understand what might help someone?

Help students understand the importance of being kind and the positive impact of kindness on the brain.

This reflection should guide students to conclude that:

- Helpful actions improve our mood and make us feel connected to other people in our lives.
- Kindness is linked to optimism and gratitude—these practices reinforce one another.
- Acts of kindness boost our brain power and help us see the bigger picture.

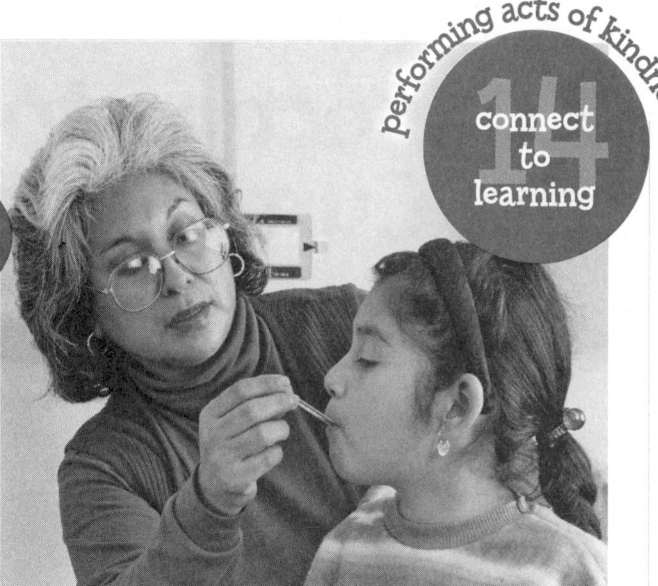

MINDUP In the Real World

Career Connection

Those who bring sunshine to the lives of others cannot keep it from themselves, wrote J.M. Barrie, the author of *Peter Pan*. It is one of life's mysteries that a gift that costs nothing rewards the giver with both happiness and health—that gift, of course, is kindness. Performing acts of kindness has been shown to boost the positive energy of all involved, both the one who gives *and* the one who receives. The Center for Compassion and Altruism Research and Education at the Stanford University School of Medicine aims to conduct scientific research on the neural underpinnings of kindness, altruism, and compassion: What happens to your brain when its focus is on kindness?

Discuss: Describe how helping someone made you feel more peaceful and happy. The nursing profession provides many opportunities for acts of kindness. Can you think of other jobs that might be similar?

Once a Day

Reach out professionally and personally to colleagues. Share a creative teaching tip, remember a birthday, and build a more supportive and cohesive work environment.

Connecting to the Curriculum

Performing acts of kindness supports students' observation of their own learning process and awareness in content areas and in literature.

Journal Writing

Encourage your students to reflect on what they've learned about doing kind actions and to record questions they may want to explore at another time. In addition, they may enjoy responding to these prompts:

- Replay the "movie in your mind" of yourself performing one of the acts of kindness that you did for this MindUP lesson. Describe what you did, and give details about how the recipient responded.
- Make a comic strip that involves you and a friend or family member. Write a kind comment you say, followed by the other person's reaction. Include the other person's name in your speech bubbles.
- Reflect on a time when someone was especially kind to you. Use descriptive writing to paint a picture of the kindness you felt, including details about who was kind to you, what the kind words or actions were, and how you felt when you received that kindness.
- Imagine that a new student is expected to join our class tomorrow. Write a plan for what you would do and say to show kindness to that student.

SCIENCE

Ripple Effect of Kindness

What to Do

Demonstrate how to release a drop of water into the very center of the bowl of water, and watch the ripples move outward, making a progressively wider circle. Provide small groups with a bowl, pan, or tub of water. Have students experiment dropping in water with an eye-dropper and bigger "droppers" such as a nasal aspirator or a turkey baster to observe the differences in the ripple effect. Compare the drop of water to one act of kindness and discuss how an act of kindness can be seen as possessing a quality of resonance similar to the ripple effect, as it affects the actions of others who receive kindness.

What to Say

Imagine that the droplet is one act of kindness. What do you observe when the water is dropped into the bowl? How might we compare that rippling to a person's actions? Can you see that an act of kindness can have a similar ripple effect on others? How would you describe your observations of the rippling action?

Why It's Important

This visual representation will stay with students. You can use it to remind them that their kind act, no matter how small, makes a difference.

MATH

Kindness Decision Tree

What to Do

Use a word problem to illustrate how kindness can multiply, such as "If you perform two acts of kindness on Sunday, and each of the people who received kindness performs two acts of kindness on Monday, and so on, how many acts of kindness will have been performed by the end of Saturday?" Have students draw a tree diagram to solve the problem and then design their own problem.

What to Say

How does this problem show the way the original acts "multiply" into many more acts of kindness? How can we show this in a drawing? What about this tree structure makes this a helpful model for this type of problem?

Why It's Important

Creating a visual branching model is another way to show the concept of one act inspiring many others.

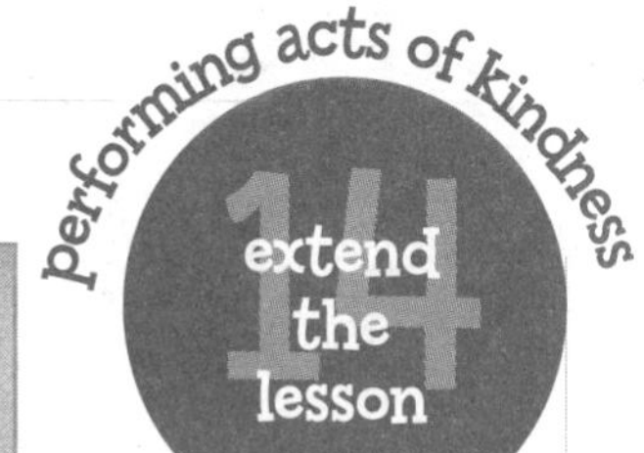

SOCIAL STUDIES

Kindness in History

What to Do

Whenever possible, connect historical people to their famous acts of kindness: Mother Teresa and her charity to the poor; Clara Barton's care of wounded soldiers; Abraham Lincoln's work to emancipate people from slavery, and so on. Help students see the relationship between the kindness of those people and their success in leadership and other endeavors.

What to Say

As we learn about important historical people and look for role models in today's world, let's ask what role kindness may have played in the positive work they are remembered for. How can kindness be a means to success in life?

Why It's Important

Asking students to evaluate the positive actions and choices that famous people are remembered for helps them connect concepts of kindness, perspective taking, and optimism into their understanding of social responsibility.

SOCIAL-EMOTIONAL LEARNING

Class Narratives

What to Do

Have each student write a personal narrative about a special act of kindness he or she has performed. Bind the narratives into a book. Have students illustrate their kind act on a small square of paper and create a collage for the covers. Have students give a reading and then store the book in the classroom library to be read independently.

What to Say

In your narrative, try to give readers a clear picture of your kind act by telling what made you decide to do the action, whether the act of kindness was easy or challenging to perform, and how your action made you and the people who benefited from your action feel.

Why It's Important

A class book reveals the priorities and mind-set of the group. Using students' experiences as the topic provides a meaningful context for writing personal narratives, aligned with writing standards.

Literature Link
Any Small Goodness

by Tony Johnston
(2001). New York: Scholastic.

When Arturo and his family move from Mexico to Los Angeles, they discover that the acts of kindness help them forge new relationships and begin to feel at home in this new place. Discuss how family and community action can lead to socially responsible acts of kindness that make for safer and happier lives.

More Books to Share

Moore, Eve. (1989). *Johnny Appleseed*. New York: Scholastic.

Freedman, Russel. (2002). *Confucius: The Golden Rule*. New York: Scholastic.

Naylor, Phyllis Reynolds. (2000). *Shiloh*. New York: Atheneum.

Taking Mindful Action in the World

What Are Mindful Actions?

Whether they involve one or many individuals, mindful actions are purposefully planned activities that create a healthier, happier world and set a precedent for other people to follow. You might say that mindful actions take acts of kindness to the world beyond the classroom.

Why Go Beyond the Classroom?

At this point in their MindUp learning journey, students have a range of optimism-building strategies to call on. They are beginning to feel confident in their ability to monitor and nurture themselves and to be receptive to the perspectives and needs of others. They are ready to expand their kindness practice to create a bigger "ripple effect" in their world.

In this culminating lesson, students work together to select, plan, and execute a group act of kindness for the school, community, or the world. Through actions like this, students are able to see themselves as part of a larger context—they glimpse the big picture of the world around them, and link their own peace of mind to a more generalized sense of peace. Their role as active participants in building that community fosters a sense of comfort, belonging, and optimism and increases their desire to make thoughtful, ethical decisions both independently and with others.

What Can You Expect to Observe?

"This is the best kind of group work. Students make a commitment to a cause they all believe in, design a plan of action, and execute it together. They want their plan to succeed, to make a difference. It makes us a cohesive community."

—Fifth-grade teacher

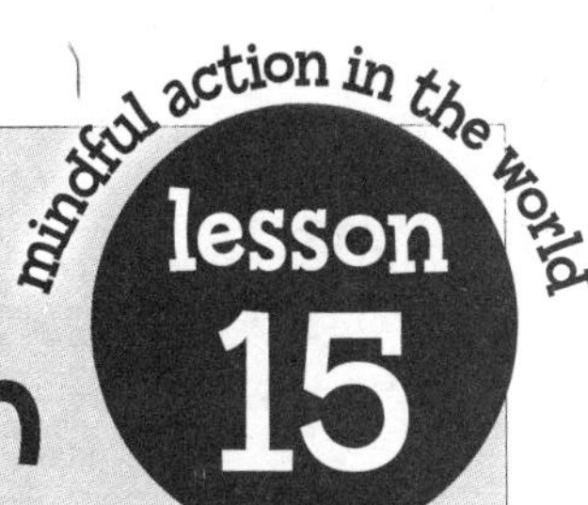

Linking to Brain Research

Mirror Neurons: Kindness Is Contagious!

Research on mirror neurons is helping us understand the power of social interactions and connections. Mirror neurons are a kind of brain nerve cell that allows the brain to imitate the actions of others, and also to feel the emotions experienced by others. Our pain receptors flinch (as does our body) when we see someone stub a toe. Our amygdala relaxes when we see a mother gently rocking her baby. The neural pathways associated with specific emotions such as pain, joy, and fear are activated when we see a face expressing that emotion.

When a group works together in a positive way—specifically, through altruism—feelings of kindness, levels of dopamine, and opportunities for activating the neural pathways of pleasure and reward multiply. This makes kindness "contagious." Recent studies show that individuals who belong to social groups that focus on kindness and altruism have higher levels of dopamine, and more empathy and compassion. As we engage in acts of kindness, and are emotionally rewarded for it, our need to be kind becomes a deciding factor in our choice of words and actions.

Mirror neurons in certain regions of the brain activate in an identical manner both during an emotional experience and when seeing someone else have that emotional experience.

Clarify for the Class

Have students gather some dramatic emotional images from newspapers, magazines, or online news sources (ballplayers in jubilation at winning a game, natural disasters, firefighters rescuing people, happy reunions, etc.). Explain that special nerve cells called mirror neurons help our brains experience empathy—an understanding of the feelings of others. Invite students to share what they think the people in the images are feeling.

Discuss: Did any of the images make you feel the way the people in the pictures do? What do you think was going on in your brain when you felt that way?

Getting Ready

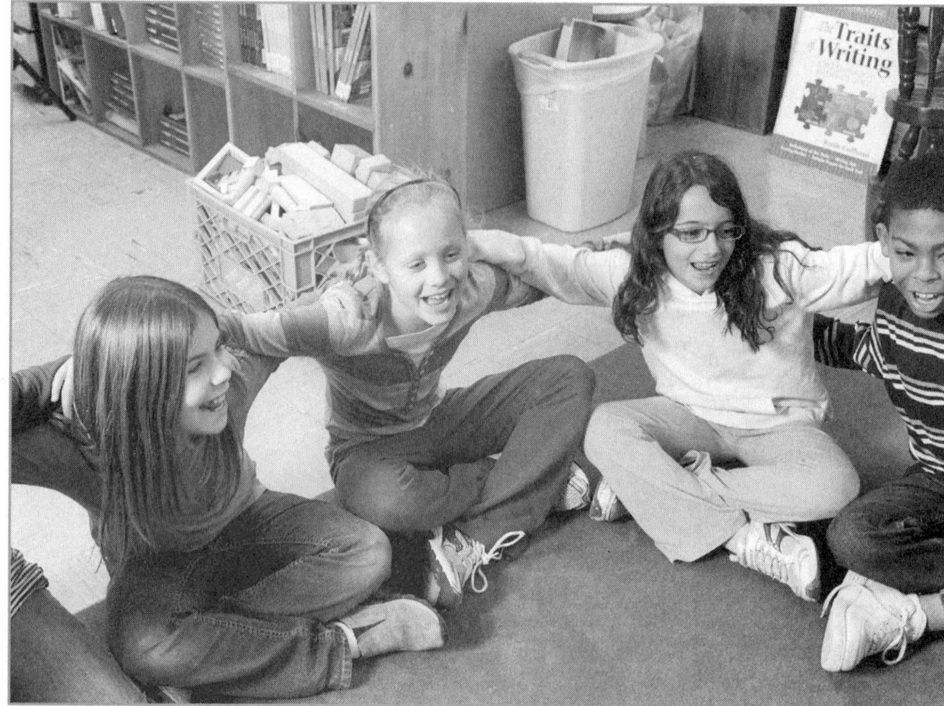

All Together Now!
Students lend their individual voices to create a powerful group sound.

GOALS

- Students work cooperatively to plan and perform an act of kindness for the school or the larger community.
- Students reflect on their feelings as they make a positive difference through acts of kindness.

MATERIALS

- chart paper
- Mindful Action Planner (p. 158)

Mindful Action Planner

CREATING THE OPTIMISTIC CLASSROOM

Brain-Inspired Instruction Neuroscience validates what teachers know instinctively: kindness begets kindness. Set the kindness cycle in motion by:

- offering sincere and specific compliments to students and colleagues regularly.
- welcoming students every day with a smile and a greeting that addresses each by name.
- doing a check-in with students about important events in their lives.
- being available to discuss concerns students need to share with you one-on-one.
- acknowledging the kindnesses you see among students.

Above all, strive to model the kindness that you expect to see in your students.

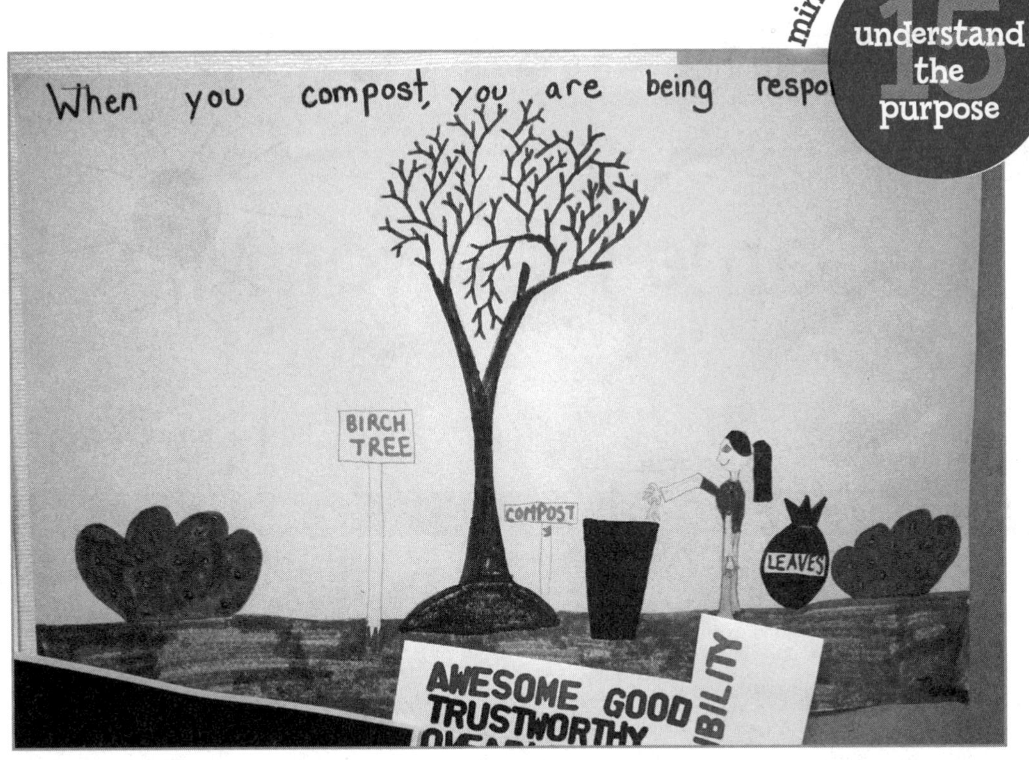

Spreading the Word
This poster, created by fifth graders, promotes a community conservation-awareness program.

MINDUP Warm-Up

Expanding Our Sound Practice

Gather students in a circle and have them use a mindful awareness exercise to get focused, if needed. Tell students they're going to use mindful listening to be aware of the changing sounds they hear. Invite one volunteer to begin clapping (you might also try snapping or humming). One at a time, have each student join in until the whole group is making the same sound together. Then have students stop making the sound one by one until it is silent again.

Discuss with students how one person clapping creates a unique sound in the silence. When more hands join in, the power of the sound grows, becoming more noticeable, more powerful. Relate this to the concept of taking group action; kind action becomes increasingly strong the more people join in.

Discuss: Imagine that each person clapping is a single act of kindness. What happens as others join in?

Leading the Lesson

A Game Plan for Mindful Action

What to Do

Engage

Invite students to reflect on the way the class expanded their sound in the Warm-Up. Relate the exercise to the power of unified group action in this lesson.

Ask students to brainstorm some mindful acts of kindness that would make a difference for a lot of people—a class at your school, a group in the community, or a group in need far away.

- You are all now noticing more ways you can help out through acts of kindness. Let's think of how we can make a powerful impact for another group or cause in our school, our neighborhood, or even across the world.
- What are some problems nearby or far away that you've heard about lately? What actions might help?

Make a class list of concerns and actions. Guide students toward projects you will be able to help them manage, such as collecting clothing for flood victims or cleaning up a neighborhood park. Narrow the list and have the class take a vote to choose one.

Explore

Involve students in planning for the group's chosen act of kindness.

Inviting student input, make a general to-do list or fill in the Mindful Action Planner activity sheet. Then have students sign up for tasks such as

- making a detailed event schedule
- writing invitations or announcements
- listing and finding materials needed
- communicating with people who may be willing and able to help

Alternatively, you may want to tackle each task together as a class.

Show students on a calendar how to work backward from the tentative date of the event to set due dates. Allot time for students to work together to complete the tasks. Revisit the to-do list and any other checklists or reminders students have developed as you prepare for the mindful action event.

Why It's Important

Engage

Brainstorming helps students become invested in the group action. Adjust the amount of information and guidance you provide, based on student responses. To provide extra support, gather students' general ideas (e.g., hunger, natural disasters), then browse charitable organizations online by category to find several in which students may be interested.

Explore

Planning uses important executive functioning skills that call on the prefrontal cortex—predicting, evaluating, backward planning, delegating, and so on. To keep students engaged and focused, assign different tasks over the course of several days in short, focused periods. Consider marking a calendar with key dates for completing or reviewing tasks. Color coding may also be helpful.

From the Research
A comprehensive mission for schools is to educate students to be knowledgeable, responsible, socially skilled, healthy, caring, and contributing citizens. (Greenberg, et al., 2003)

Reflect

After the event (or after the entire class has had a chance to participate, if the action is spread over days or weeks), invite students to share their experiences and thoughts about the group's act of kindness.

- How did you feel while we worked together to be kind?
- What did you notice about the way your classmates worked together?
- Have any of your thoughts and feelings changed since we completed our mindful action? What were they?
- Would you like to do more group acts of kindness in the future? Why?

Ask students to connect their experiences to what they've learned about their brains.

- How could taking mindful action with a group be a healthy workout for your brain? How could your own peace of mind affect the peace of mind of your community?

By working as a group, students realize that they can accomplish great things and build community. They also get the "big picture" of the world around them—and see how they fit into it.

Students should be able to explain that when we are mindfully helping others, our amygdala calms down and our mirror neurons help us experience the joy we bring to others.

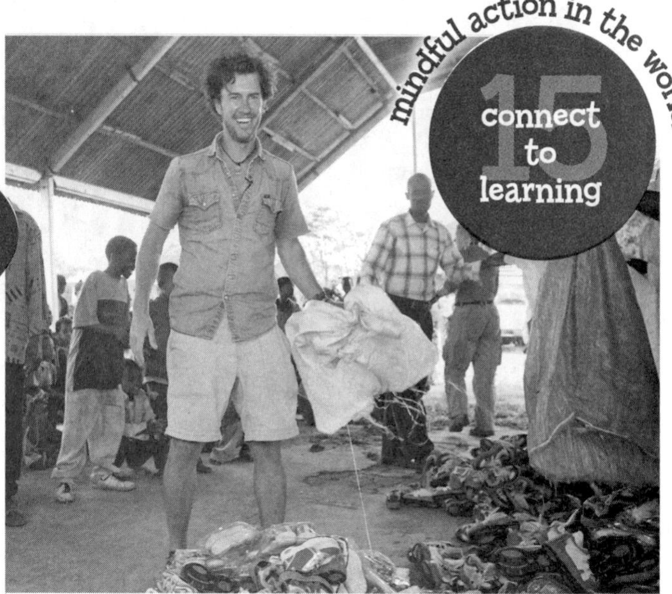

MINDUP In the Real World

Career Connection

One for one—that's not only the philosophy behind TOMS shoes, founded by Blake Mycoskie, but also the business model. For every pair of shoes this innovative company sells, it donates a new pair to a child in need. So when you buy a pair of TOMS shoes, you're not just buying for yourself, you're also putting shoes on the feet of a child without. Why shoes? Because in developing countries many diseases are soil-transmitted—they penetrate the skin through bare feet. Also, shoes protect feet from cuts and sores and enable children to go to school.

Discuss: If you could run a company or service that used the "one for one" model, what would you make, create, or grow? Consider items that might address the needs of people, not just their desires.

Once a Day

Consider how teaching can be a "one for one" service. How can you create situations in which your teaching is absorbed by students and then passed along to others in the school (e.g., buddy teaching with younger students)?

Connecting to the Curriculum

Taking mindful action supports students' connection to their own learning process and to the content areas and literature.

Journal Writing

Encourage your students to reflect on what they've learned about taking mindful action and to record questions they may want to explore at another time. In addition, they may enjoy responding to these prompts:

- Make a three-column chart. Describe our group act of kindness, including how you felt before, during, and after the event.
- Draw a diagram that shows the cause-and-effect relationship our group act of kindness has created.
- Write a persuasive letter to a friend, convincing him or her to join you in a group act of kindness. Include at least three strong arguments, based on what happened to you, your classmates, or others as a result of our group act of kindness.
- Imagine that you will be the leader of a group doing an act of kindness for the earth. What part of the world will your act focus on? Describe your plan for environmental kindness.

LANGUAGE ARTS

Kindness Mottoes

What to Do

Invite students to develop a kindness motto for your class community that can be put on the class newsletter or website or any e-mail that is sent to parents and members of the community. Explain the motto will be a short expression or phrase that captures the spirit or purpose of the group. Provide some models by searching online for "top charities" and presenting effective mottoes of the top-ranked organizations.

What to Say

As we brainstorm ideas for our motto, keep in mind that we're trying to find a few words that will help people understand that we've made kindness and service a part of our mind-set. That's what we'll call our "main idea." Let's take a look at the mottoes of some well-known organizations that do acts of kindness and see which ones you think use just the right words to send a message about what they stand for.

Why It's Important

Developing a motto is a meaningful way to evaluate and use persuasive language and a unique way to discuss a main idea. The motto project both develops and represents the class's sense of unity and purpose.

MATH

It All Adds Up

What to Do

Work with students to decide how to measure the results of their mindful-action project and to create a chart or graph to show their goal and progress toward it (use increments added daily or weekly). For example, students can use bar graphs to show the types and numbers of books and toys collected. Also, you might use the data to create word problems.

What to Say

What categories can we use to organize the materials we've collected? How can we represent a daily or weekly total with a bar graph—how would we set that up? What kind of graph might help us compare two weeks' totals? What questions can you ask about the graph to help you draw conclusions about your findings?

Why It's Important

Representing student work in a graphic format provides useful data on their efforts and may motivate them to try a different strategy or work harder. The graphs also offer a handy source for student-generated math problems.

TECHNOLOGY

Public Announcements

What to Do

Have students prepare the script for a short public service announcement about the mindful-action project, to be read during school announcements. Alternatively, have small groups create digital slide shows with their own captions (and a voice-over, if possible). These could be posted on the class website or shown at school and community-involvement functions.

What to Say

Public service announcements are often made by groups to raise public awareness of a problem in a community. We're going to make sure your script provides an informative message about the problem we decided to work on, what we are doing to help, how our work has been going, and what others can do to chip in.

Why It's Important

Students present their work in a short, engaging format that is both informative and persuasive. This helps students understand that they can be both a source of information and a role model for others. Tie in fluency practice by having students rehearse their scripts aloud.

SOCIAL-EMOTIONAL LEARNING

Great Projects in the News

What to Do

Regularly share with students news about global philanthropic projects (e.g., Pennies for Peace, Heifer International) that will spark their interest and invite their participation. Have students discuss the causes and effects of the issues these organizations target.

What to Say

How does this group describe the problem they're addressing? What is their perspective on it? What parts of the world are affected? How is this group helping? Which suggested actions seem like something you or our class could do?

Why It's Important

A frequent check into the work of organizations dedicated to mindful actions will help keep in focus many of the MindUP skills (e.g., mindful awareness, perspective taking, choosing optimism). This international focus will expand their understanding of the larger world and remind them that people are involved in mindful actions every day, to make our world a better place.

Literature Link
March On!: The Day My Brother Martin Changed the World

by Christine King Farris (2008). New York: Scholastic.

Told from the perspective of Dr. King's older sister, this book describes the 1963 March on Washington that culminated in the "I Have a Dream" speech. This short, down-to-earth book offers a great way to discuss the range of emotions Dr. King and civil rights advocates experienced as well as the actions they took. Have students determine the type of problems Dr. King faced, the mindful decisions he made, and how he involved others in the cause. Connect to causes that have captured students' interest.

More Books to Share

Amsel, Sheri. (2009). *365 Ways to Live Green for Kids: Saving the Environment at Home, School, or at Play–Every Day!* Avon, MA: Adams Media.

Engel, Trudie (1998) *We'll Never Forget You, Roberto Clemente,* New York: Scholastic.

Raven, Margot Theis. (2002). *Mercedes and the Chocolate Pilot.* Chelsea, MI: Sleeping Bear Press.

Name ______________________________

Date ______________

Brain Power!

Label each part of the brain and tell how it helps you.

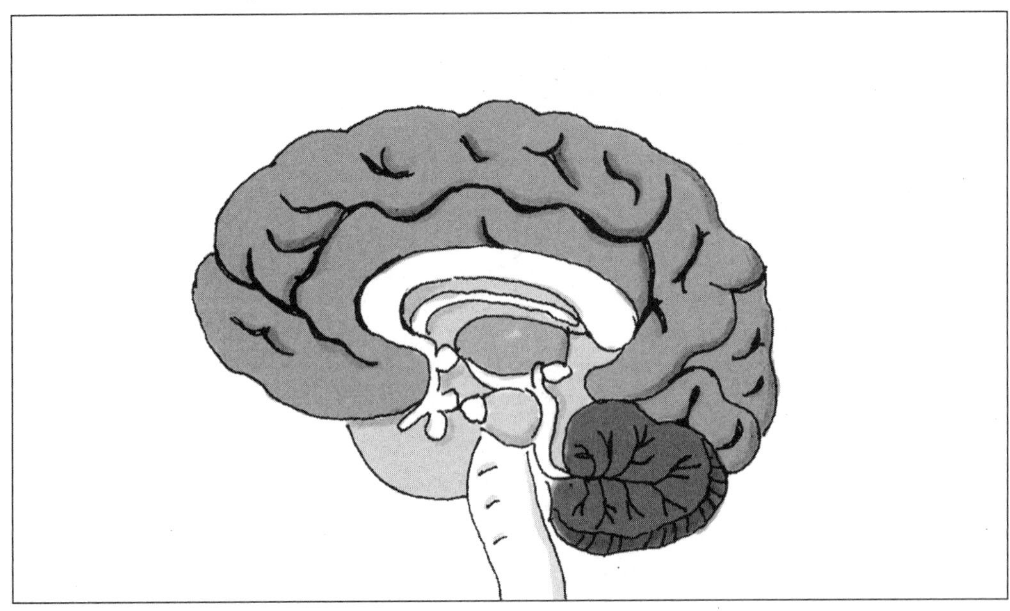

prefrontal cortex **hippocampus** **amygdala**

The ______________________________ helps me ______________

____

____.

The ______________________________ helps me ______________

____

____.

The ______________________________ helps me ______________

____

____.

Name ____________________

Date ____________

Mindful or Unmindful?

Mindful	Unmindful
Paying such close attention to what someone is saying that you can repeat or explain it to someone else	Deciding not to speak to someone because he or she has not spoken to you
Practicing a new skill during a sports practice or music lesson until you feel your body improving	Choosing a style of shirt you don't like just because your friend says you should wear it
Listening to a friend's favorite new song all the way through before making a judgment about it	Trying to do too many things at the same time
Being willing to try a new food that you've never tasted before, even though it looks different from anything you've eaten	Rejecting a new food because it is unfamiliar to you
Helping someone in need, someone with physical challenges, or someone whose needs are different from your own	Daydreaming or "tuning out" what is happening around you without really noticing and hearing what is going on
Listening attentively when someone is speaking and not reacting until the person has finished	Intentionally ignoring a classmate who seems eager to join your game or group

Name ________________________________

Date ________________

Mystery Sounds/Scents

Listen to the mystery sound or smell the mystery scent. List some sensory details you notice and jot down any thing or person the sound or scent reminds you of. Now make a guess. Were you right? Fill in the name of the actual sound or scent when it is revealed.

Details I Notice	What It Reminds Me of	My Guess	Actual Sound or Scent
1.			
2.			
3.			
4.			
5.			

Name ____

Date ____________________

Sensory Web

In the middle of the web, write the name of the object or specimen you're observing. Fill in as many sensory details as you notice to describe it.

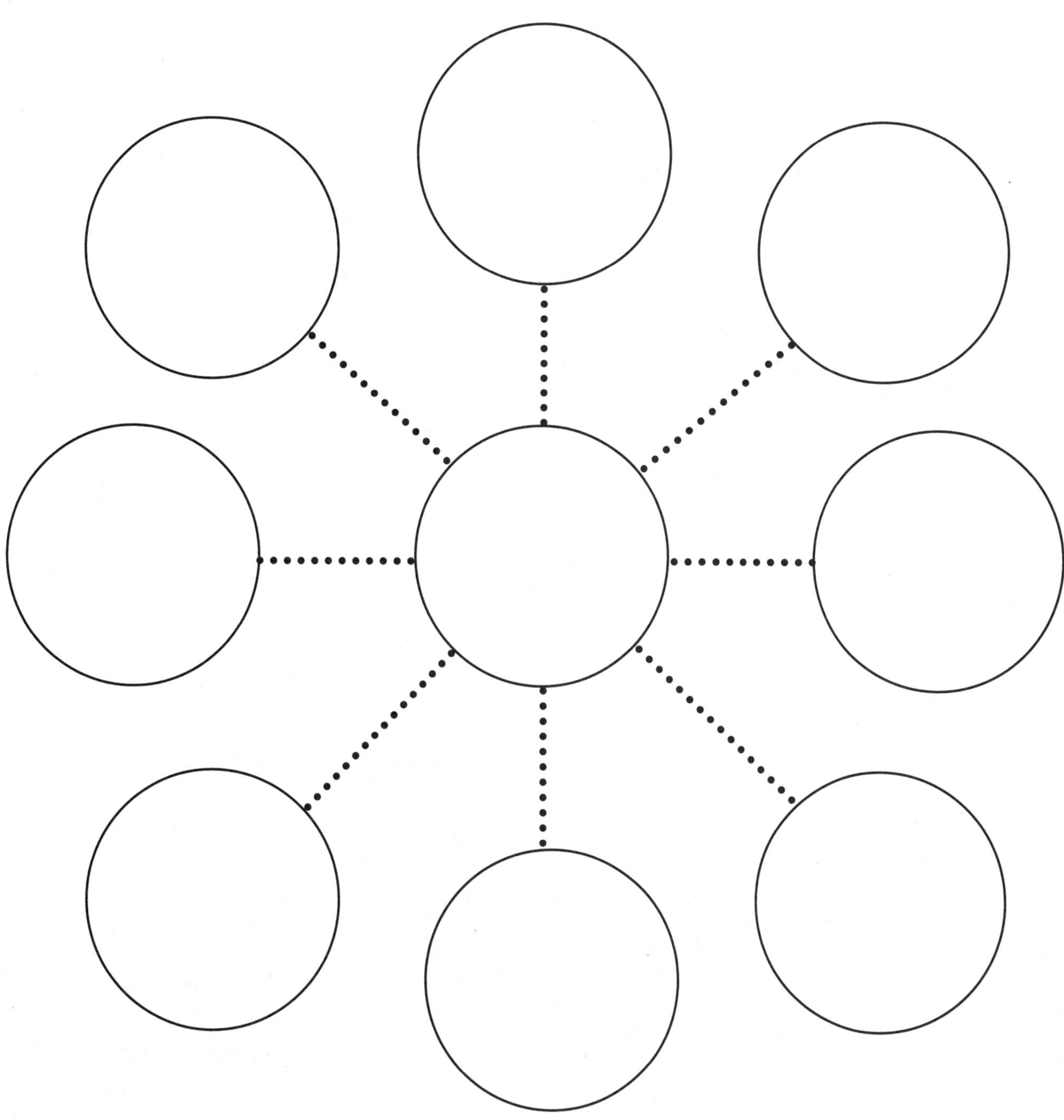

Name ______________________________

Date ______________

Character Perspectives

Title of Story:

Name of Character:

Choose an important event in the story. Use what you know about this character's feelings and actions to show his or her perspective.

Event:

What do you think your character was thinking and feeling when this event happened?

Why do you think your character acted the way he or she did?

Do you think your character's actions were easy to understand, or could they have been misunderstood?

Name ______________________________

Date ______________

Optimistic/Pessimistic Thoughts

Think about a problem that you or someone you know has faced. In one sentence,describe the problem. Then fill in the thought bubbles to show an optimistic and a pessimistic reaction to the problem.

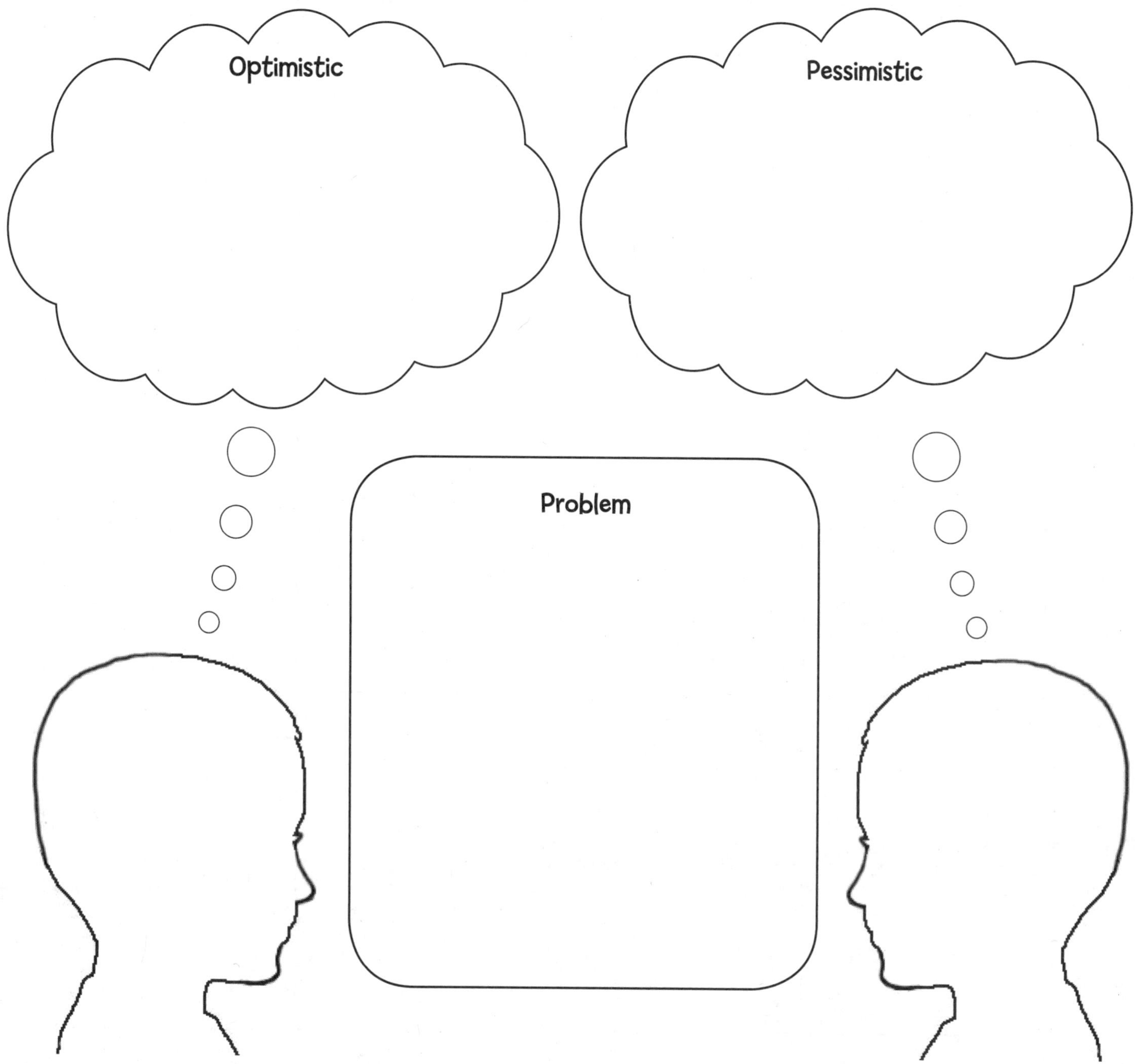

Name ______________________________

Date ______________

Mindful Action Planner

Event ______________________ Event Date ______________________

Task	Materials We Need	Date to Finish	Who's in Charge
☐	☐	☐	☐
☐	☐	☐	☐
☐	☐	☐	☐
☐	☐	☐	☐
☐	☐	☐	☐
☐	☐	☐	☐

Glossary

adrenal glands
organs located on the kidneys, responsible for releasing stress hormones such as cortisol and adrenaline (epinephrine)

amygdala
an almond-shaped structure which is a part of the limbic system that encodes emotional messages for long-term storage in the brain.

brain stem
a brain part, comprising midbrain, pons, and medulla oblongata, which receives sensory input and monitors vital functions such as heartbeat, body temperature, and digestion. The RAS is located in the brain stem.

Core Practice
deep belly breathing that relies on mindful, focused attention; it is recommended that the core practice be done three times each day for a few minutes—depending on the age of the student.

cortisol (hydrocortisone)
a hormone produced by the adrenal gland in response to stress or to a low level of blood glucocorticoids, the primary functions of which are to increase blood sugar, suppress the immune system, and aid in fat, protein and carbohydrate metabolism

dopamine
a neurotransmitter that produces feelings of pleasure when released by the brain reward system; has multiple functions depending on where in the brain it acts.

endorphin
a neurotransmitter with properties similar to opiates that are important for pain reduction and the creation of pleasant and euphoric feelings

epinephrine (adrenalin)
a hormone secreted by the adrenal glands

executive function
mental management that includes higher-order skills dependent upon the thinker's ability to reflect before reacting: evaluating information, organizing, focusing attention, prioritizing, planning, and problem solving

fight, flight, or freeze response
neurophysiological mechanism of the sympathetic nervous system in response to real or perceived threat

glutamate
the most common excitatory neurotransmitter in the brain

hippocampus
a brain structure that compares new learning to past learning and encodes information from working memory to long-term storage.

hypothalamus
a brain structure at the base of the limbic area that regulates body functions in response to internal and external stimuli, controls the pituitary

limbic system
the collection of cortical and subcortical structures, including amygdala and hippocampus, situated at the base of the cerebrum that control emotions, motivations, and other behaviors, and are important for memory functions.

mindful attention
focused awareness; purposeful, nonjudgmental attentiveness

mindfulness
state of being in touch with and aware of the present moment in a nonjudgmental way. Mindfulness is an approach used by mental health professionals as a kind of therapy that helps people suffering from difficulties such as anxiety and depression.

mirror neuron
a neuron that responds when one performs a certain action or when one observes the same action performed by another. Thus, the neuron "mirrors" the behavior of the other, as though the observer were performing the action

neural pathway
usually, a series of nerve bundles that connect relatively distant areas of the brain or nervous system

neuron
a nerve cell, which is a cell specialized for excitability and conductivity, composed of an axon, a soma, and dendrites. (All neurons have one soma and one axon; some neurons have many dendrites and others have none.)

neuroplasticity
the brain's lifelong ability to reorganize neural networks as a result of new or repeated experiences

neuroscience
an interdisciplinary science focused on the brain and nervous system and closely associated other disciplines such as psychology, mathematics, physics, philosophy, and medicine

neurotransmitter
one of many chemicals that transmit signals across a synaptic gap from one neuron to another.

norepinephrine
a neurotransmitter and a hormone that is part of the fight, flight, or freeze response. In the brain, norepinephrine acts as a neurotransmitter—usually excitatory, sometimes inhibitory—to regulate normal brain processes.

positive psychology
scientific study of the strengths and virtues that enable individuals and communities to thrive. (Understanding positive emotions entails the study of contentment with the past, happiness in the present, and hope for the future. Understanding positive individual traits consists of the study of the strengths and virtues, such as the capacity for love and work, courage, compassion, resilience, creativity, curiosity, integrity, self-knowledge, moderation, self-control, and wisdom. Understanding positive institutions entails the study of the strengths that foster better communities, such as justice, responsibility, civility, parenting, nurturance, work ethic, leadership, teamwork, purpose, and tolerance.)

prefrontal cortex
a part of the brain that dominates the frontal lobe, implicated in executive function, planning complex cognitive behavior, personality expression, decision-making and moderating correct social behavior and considered to be orchestration of thoughts and actions in accordance with internal goals.

reticular activating system (RAS)
a dense formation of neurons and fibers in the brain stem that controls major body functions and mediates various levels of brain response

social-emotional learning (SEL)
the process of developing the fundamental life skills needed to effectively and ethically handle ourselves, our relationships, and our work

synapse
the microscopic gap between the axon of one neuron and the dendrite of another, which serves to connect neurons. Synapses connect them functionally, not physically, enabling neurons to communicate by passing signals between them.

thalamus
receives and integrates all incoming sensory information, except smell, and directs it to other areas of the cortex for additional processing.

unmindfulness
lack of awareness; uncontrolled actions, emotions, or thoughts

Resource List

Allyn, P., Margolies, J. & McNalley, K. (2010). *The Great Eight: Management strategies for the reading and writing classroom.* New York: Scholastic.

Alston, L. (2007). *Why we teach: Learning, laughter, love, and the power to transform lives.* New York: Scholastic.

Ashby, C. R., Thanos, P. K., Katana, J. M., Michaelides, E. L., Gardner, C. A. & Heidbreder, N. D. (1999). The selective dopamine antagonist. *Pharmacology, Biochemistry and Behavior.*

Brown, K. W. & Ryan, R. M. (2003). The benefits of being present: Mindfulness and its role in psychological well-being. *Journal of Personality and Social Psychology*, 84(4), 822–848.

Caprara, G. V., Barbanelli, C., Pastorelli, C., Bandura, A. & Zimbardo, P. G. (2000). Prosocial foundations of children's academic achievement. *Psychological Science, 11*: 302–306.

Collaborative for Academic, Social, and Emotional Learning (CASEL). (2010). Retrieved from: **http://www.casel.org/basics/skills.php**.

Diamond, A. (2009). *SoundSeen: In the room with Adele Diamond.* NPR. November 19, 2009. Retrieved from: **http://being.publicradio.org/programs/2009/learning-doing-being**.

Durlak, J. A., Weissberg, R. P., Dymnicki, A. B., Taylor, R. D. & Schellinger, K. B. (2011). Enhancing students' social and emotional development promotes success in school: Results of a meta-analysis. *Child Development.*

Galvan, A., Hare, T., Parra, C., Penn, J., Voss, H., Glover, G. & Casey, B. (2006). Earlier development of the accumbens relative to orbitofrontal cortex might underlie risk-taking behavior in adolescents. *Journal of Neuroscience.* 26(25), 6885-6892.

Greenberg, M.T., Weissberg, R.P., Utne O'Brien, M., Zins, J.E., Fredericks, L., Resnik, H. & Elias, M.J. (2003). Enhancing school-based prevention and youth development through coordinated social, emotional, and academic learning. *American Psychologist, 58*, 466-474.

Greenland, S. K. (2010). *The Mindful Child: How to Help Your Kid Manage Stress and Become Happier, Kinder, and More Compassionate.* New York: Simon & Schuster, Inc.

Goleman, D. (2008). Emotional intelligence. Retrieved from: **http://danielgoleman.info/topics/emotional-intelligence**.

Iidaka, T., Anderson N., Kapur, S., Cabeza R. & Craik, F. (2000). The effect of divided attention on encoding and retrieval in episodic memory revealed by positron emission tomography. *Journal of Cognitive Neuroscience*, 12(2). 267–280.

Jensen, E. (2009). *Teaching with poverty in mind: What being poor does to kids' brains and what schools can do about it.* Alexandria, VA: ASCD.

Jensen, E. (2003). *Tools for engagement.* Thousand Oaks, CA.: Corwin Press.

Kann, L., Kinchen, S. A. Williams, B. I., Ross, J. G., Lowry, R., Grunbaum, J. A. & Kolbe, L. J. (2000). Youth risk behavior surveillance in United States, 1999. Centers for Disease Control MMWR Surveillance Summaries, 49(SS-5), 1–96.

Kato, N. & McEwen, B. (2003). Neuromechanisms of emotions and memory. *Neuroendocrinology*, 11, 03. 54–58.

Lutz, A., Dunne, J. D., & Davidson, R. J. (2007). Meditation and the neuroscience of consciousness: An introduction. In Zelazo, P., Moscovitch, M., & Thompson, E. (Eds.), *The Cambridge Handbook of Consciousness* (499–554). Cambridge, UK: Cambridge University Press.

McCullough, M. E., Kilpatrick, S. D., Emmons, R. A. & Larson, D. B. (2001). Is gratitude a moral affect? *Psychological Bulletin*, 127, 249–266.

Pascual-Leone, A. Amedi, A., Fregni, F. & Merabet, L. B. (2005). The plastic human brain cortext. *Annual Review of Neuroscience*, 28, 377-401.

Pawlak, R., Magarinos, A. M., Melchor, J., McEwen, B. & Strickland, S. (February 2003). Tissue plasminogen activator in the amygdala is critical for stress-induced anxiety-like behavior. *Nature Neuroscience*, 168–174.

Payton, J. Weissberg, R.P., Dulak, J.A., Dymnicki, A.B. Taylor, R.D., Schellinger, K.B. & Pachan, M. (2008). The positive impact of social and emotional learning for kindergarten to eighth-grade students. Findings from three scientific reviews. Chicago, IL: Collaborative for Academic, Social, and Emotional Learning. Retrieved from: **www.casel.org** or **www.lpfch.org/sel**.

Posner, M. I. & Patoine, B. (2009). How Arts Training Improves Attention and Cognition. The Dana Foundation. Available: **http://www.dana.org/news/cerebrum/detail.aspx?id=23206**.

Ratey, J. J. (2008). *Spark: The revolutionary new science of exercise and the brain.* New York: Little, Brown & Co.

Revising the rules of perception, retrieved from **http://news.vanderbilt.edu/2010/07/binocularvisio**, posted 7/29/10.

Schonert-Reichl, K. A., & Lawlor, M. S. (2010). The effects of a mindfulness-based education program on pre- and early adolescents' well-being and social and emotional competence. *Mindfulness, 1*, 137–151.

Schonert-Reichl, Kimberly A. (2008). Effectiveness of the Mindfulness Education (ME) Program: Research Summary, 2005-2008. Retrieved from: **http://www.thehawnfoundation.org/.../2007/.../summary-of-the-effectiveness-of-the-me-program_april2009ksrfinal1.pdf**.

Shadmehr, R. & Holcomb, H. (1997). Neural correlates of motor memory consolidation. *Science 277*: 821.

Tatum, A. (2009). *Reading for their life: Rebuilding the textual lineages of African-American adolescent males.* Portsmouth, NH: Heinemann

Wentzel, K. R. (1991). Social competence at school: Relation between social responsibility and academic achievement. *Review of Educational Research*, 61(1), 1–24.

Willis, J. (2006). *Research-based Strategies to Ignite Student Learning: Insights from a Neurologist and Classroom Teacher.* Danvers, MA: Association for Supervision and Curriculum Development.

Willis, J. (2008). *How Your Child Learns Best: Brain-Friendly Strategies You Can Use to Ignite Your Child's Learning and Increase School Success.* Naperville, IL: Sourcebooks.